Praise for *l*

"There are a select number of b
ers of my role in the ministry tu wnich God has called me. I will be
adding *My Burden Is Light* to that group. The Covid-19 pandemic has
forced us to reexamine how effectively we carry out Christ's mission
as preachers. However, more than a primer on preaching, these pages
offer countless and vivid examples of how God is with us, Christ is in
us, and the Spirit is all around us. To quote Craig Satterlee himself,
imagining Jesus in the pulpit, in the pew, leaving the building, and
elsewhere, 'assists me in setting and resetting my expectations of both
myself as a preacher and others as they respond to my preaching.'"

–Rev. Abraham D. Allende, Bishop Emeritus,
ELCA Northeastern Ohio Synod

"Bishop Satterlee captures well the current challenge in preaching and
provides clear, pastoral wisdom for preachers. His words are simple,
playful at times, and a needed resource for preachers in any stage of
their preaching life. With humility and grace, Satterlee gives practical suggestions for keeping Jesus at the center of our proclamation.
Reading this book is balm for a weary preacher's soul."

–Bishop Tracie L. Bartholomew, ELCA New Jersey Synod

"Bishop Satterlee engages the preacher to spend time in the church
building with Jesus so that the proclamation of the Gospel becomes
real and alive as the Good News moves out into the community and
neighborhood. Incarnational theology lived and practiced. Preach
Jesus!"

–Bishop Suzanne Darcy Dillahunt, ELCA Southern Ohio Synod

"In this wilderness time of division in spirit and isolation in body, to preach
Jesus is the Church's only hope and its most important duty. In words
both passionate and profound, Bishop Craig Satterlee calls us back to our
vocation as preachers of the gospel, 'showing forth Christ' at every turn,

and setting an example each of us will feel as a challenge and an aspiration. I cannot imagine a more faithful or trustworthy guide to help us re-center ourselves on Jesus."

–Rev. Dr. R. Guy Erwin, President,
United Lutheran Seminary

"The most important questions in preaching, as in life, are often the most basic ones. Drawing from his experience as preacher, professor of homiletics, and liturgical scholar, as well as ELCA bishop, Craig Satterlee issues a series of profound challenges to Christian preachers as well as to those who gather to hear their words: What is the good news? How is it both 'good' and 'news'? What does it mean to proclaim Jesus as Savior in a way that hearers experience the power of the Spirit at work in their lives and world and are drawn to live the gospel more faithfully? Do those who are called to preach truly believe the words they announce? Is it possible for those who hunger for a word of hope to 'taste grace' in hearing the good news proclaimed? This book is a valuable resource not only for preachers and teachers of homiletics, but for all who are concerned about the quality of Christian preaching today."

–Dr. Mary Catherine Hilkert, O.P., Professor of Theology,
University of Notre Dame

"Jesus in the room when we preach—that's the aim of this book, and it works. Like the best preaching, *My Burden Is Light* empowers rather than exhorts, built on the premise that a relationship with Jesus is the most important ingredient in preaching. This book more than any other helped shape my preaching for this time and context. It gave me, as a parish pastor, support to stay committed to the central message of the church's proclamation: Jesus Christ crucified and risen."

–Rev. Betsy Jansen Kamphuis, St. Paul Lutheran Church,
Greenville, Michigan

"Blessed with vivid insight and holy imagination, Bishop Satterlee closes the distance between physical space and metaphorical space in his appeal to locate Jesus in our preaching. Jesus fills these pages. Buy this book to improve your preaching. Read this book to meet Jesus."
—Rev. Kurt Kusserow, Bishop, ELCA Southwestern Pennsylvania Synod

"The author brings his experience as a seminary professor and Lutheran bishop to this foundational primer for beginning preachers. His theological depth and insights into the call to preach also make this a useful volume for seasoned preachers, who wish to rediscover the joy of this calling. Readers will have ample reasons to look afresh at this ministerial art and will be surprised, as I was, to discover where Jesus is to be found."
—Rev. Patricia Lull, Bishop, ELCA Saint Paul Area Synod

"Preaching Jesus is to embody the message of grace, power, and joy. It is equally powerful when the preacher and the assembly receive this as equal gift. Craig Satterlee poignantly points to the centrality of this gift in Jesus, a gift to all preachers who seek to have their burdens lifted and their souls refreshed."
—Rev. Kevin L. Strickland, Bishop, ELCA Southeastern Synod

"Craig Satterlee understands the personal and pastoral realities of preaching in a pandemic world. He brings the depth of Christian tradition into conversation with today's challenges, including the searching question: 'Have we lost our confidence and ability to proclaim Jesus as Savior?' Each sentence is informed by the clear-eyed, honest insight of a lifetime's experience as pastor, preacher, professor, and bishop. For those who too often preach on the run, or those just beginning their preaching ministry, it is a blessing to dwell awhile with this eloquent teacher."
—Rev. Dr. Melinda J. Wagner, First Emmanuel Lutheran Church, Portland, Oregon

My
Burden
Is
Light

MY BURDEN IS LIGHT

MAKING ROOM FOR JESUS IN PREACHING

Craig Alan Satterlee

FORTRESS PRESS
MINNEAPOLIS

MY BURDEN IS LIGHT
Making Room for Jesus in Preaching

Chapter 1 originated as Craig Alan Satterlee, "Where Is Jesus When You
Preach?" 2019 John S. Marten Lecture in Homiletics, University of Notre
Dame, October 27, 2019.

Cover design: John M. Lucas

Print ISBN: 978-1-5064-6581-4
eBook ISBN: 978-1-5064-6582-1

In Memoriam

John Allyn Melloh, SM

Contents

Preface

I returned to Notre Dame to teach preaching for a semester after the six-year hiatus that resulted from the North/West Lower Michigan Synod ELCA calling me from my classroom to the office of bishop. This opportunity allowed me to do as Ronald Heifetz metaphorically directs and step off the dance floor and go up to the balcony.[1] Heifetz writes, "The only way you can gain both a clearer view of reality and some perspective on the bigger picture is by distancing yourself from the fray." So I spent much of fall 2019 staring out my office window and contemplating the church's future, which brought me to the question of what preaching is and ought to be.

One October afternoon, the golden trees adorning the Golden Dome reminded me this was the twenty-fifth autumn since my family and I stepped on campus, and I began my journey as a teacher of preaching. From my vantage point in that balcony, I realized spending a quarter century asking what preaching is and ought to be had not answered my real question. Rather, it served to dress up my real question in academic garb and make it polite.

My real question is this: *While the church declares Jesus the heart of its proclamation, do we make room for Jesus in preaching?* Too often we usher Jesus to the back of the pulpit, invite Jesus to make a cameo appearance, or even excuse Jesus from the sermon altogether. As a preaching professor and bishop, I learned how hard it is to insist preachers give Jesus a prominent place in their sermons. I also learned how offended preachers get if I come out and ask if they make room for Jesus in their preaching, either because they thought they had or because they know they should and had not. As a preacher, I know how offended I get when I ask this question of myself. No wonder I dressed my question up in academic garb and found roundabout ways to ask it. Throughout my twenty-five-year inquiry, I gave each version of the question a name. I find revisiting the previous versions of the question helpful as each one brings forth a different aspect of how we ultimately make room for Jesus in our preaching.

The Notre Dame Question is, *What is the good news?* More than any other, this question is the North Star of my preaching and teaching. Studying and teaching preaching in Notre Dame's John S. Marten Program in Homiletics gave voice to my conviction, shared by so many other teachers of preaching, that every homily is and ought to be a declaration of good news. I am gratified when former students tell me that every time they sit down to prepare a sermon, the question *What is the good news?* echoes in their head in my voice and will not let them go.

What is the good news? The message must be *good,* and it must be *news.* It is not exhortation, explanation, entertainment, or anything else. The good news is for the gathered assembly, for the people sitting in front of you, making it particular and concrete. The good news is active and depends upon God, not upon us, and not upon circumstance. For me, the good news is the life, death, and resurrection of Jesus. Whether preparing to preach myself or teaching others to preach, I am guided by 1 Corinthians 1:22–24: "For Jews demand signs and Greeks desire wisdom, but we proclaim Christ crucified, a stumbling block to Jews and foolishness to Gentiles, but to those who are the called, both Jews and Greeks, Christ the power of God and the wisdom of God." To preach good news is to make room for Jesus. My greatest reward as a teacher is students discovering the power, wisdom, and joy of proclaiming Christ.

The Chicago Question *What do you mean by the gospel?* is named for my years teaching in the racial, cultural, ecumenical, and interfaith diversity of the Lutheran School of Theology at Chicago and the ACTS Doctor of Ministry in Preaching Program. In answer to this question, some preaching students and preachers express longing for the in-breaking of God's reign in this world. They share their lament over the state of society and the church; their heartbreak over the plight of so many around the planet and even of the planet itself; their desire that those entrusted to our care grow in faith, knowledge, and the fear of the Lord; their feelings of tension between gathering and comforting the flock and wanting to seize the prophet's mantle and beat them with it—"My rod and my staff shall convert thee."

And the gospel? Well, I frequently heard the gospel proclaimed as a call to do and to be this or that. The gospel was proclaimed as instruction, exhortation, and the admonition "to do justice and love kindness and to walk humbly with God."[2] And Jesus, I am dismayed to hear, is proclaimed as teacher, role model, cheerleader, prophet, community organizer, and even life coach. Proclaiming Christ crucified becomes rare as preachers appear unable or unwilling to "name Grace."[3] Whether the church places the burden of addressing everything of significance on preachers or preachers place this burden on themselves, addressing everything in preaching leaves less and less room for Jesus.

These days, I find the gospel in John 12:32. Jesus said, "And I, when I am lifted up from the earth, will draw all people to myself." Preaching the good news of Jesus as Savior relieves the preacher of the burden of acquiring expertise in everything and convincing anyone to do anything. Instead, together, preacher and congregation can live into the new life Jesus brings and participate in his own work of reconciling the world to all God intends.

The Wabash Question *Did you taste the gospel?* is named for the Wabash Center for Teaching and Learning, which awarded me a grant, so I could rediscover what it is like for students to learn by learning to be a barista. I learned that, when you pull a shot of espresso and someone drinks it, you cannot persuade them it is good. Their taste buds determine that for them. This is likewise true of preaching. People decide for themselves whether they hear good news, experience grace, or encounter Jesus.

As my preaching students and I reviewed their sermons, I started asking them, "Did you taste the gospel?" We learned that, while the preacher might have said the words "justified by grace through faith" or "Christ has died. Christ is risen. Christ will come again," people sometimes experience or taste guilt, shame, obligation, bitterness, or condescension. We also learned that, when people both hear the gospel as the good news of Jesus and experience or taste grace, there is nothing better.

Since becoming a bishop, I now ask what I call the **Bishop's Question**: *Where is Jesus when you preach?* I find the company of preachers I care for and oversee are not overly interested in feedback from their bishop who used to teach preaching. So this question changes the focus from sermon evaluation to the preacher's relationship with Jesus, which I now consider the most important ingredient in preaching. Imaginatively contemplating where Jesus is when we preach provides a powerful way for preachers to consider their relationship with Jesus and, when necessary, take Jesus's yoke upon them and learn from him. For when preachers are yoked to Jesus, we make room for Jesus in our preaching.

Not long after I completed my semester at Notre Dame, the world was visited by the Covid-19 virus, which launched a global pandemic and ushered in months of stay-at-home orders and social distancing. I soon found myself plagued with the **Pandemic Question**: *Have we lost our confidence and ability to proclaim Jesus as Savior?*

People in certain quarters of my denomination swiftly responded to the suspension of in-person worship by vigorously debating the efficacy of virtual Communion, the propriety of authorizing someone in every household to preside at Holy Communion, and the wisdom of leaving consecrated bread and wine outside the church building, so people could drive by and pick it up. I was surprised this debate began so quickly and became as heated as it did because my Christian tradition holds that Christ is truly present in the word in the same way Christ is truly present in the sacraments. As recently as thirty years ago and throughout much of its history, my denomination was content to celebrate the Lord's Supper less frequently than every Sunday. Today, many congregations continue to expect baptized children to wait years before receiving Holy Communion for the first time.

As I tried to understand the urgency to resolve this issue, some wise and perceptive laypeople recalled that when the Lord's Supper was celebrated once a month, the pastor had to preach about Jesus as Savior on the other three Sundays or the gospel would not be proclaimed. These parishioners wondered whether an unanticipated consequence of the more frequent celebration of Holy Communion is that we unintentionally came to rely on the Eucharist to proclaim Jesus in a way that communicates grace and the gospel to such a degree that the sermon could be devoted to other purposes: instruction, social commentary, moral exhortation, congregational and denominational promotion. In the process, preachers lost our confidence and ability to preach about Jesus as Savior. These listeners speculated preachers' incapacity to preach about Jesus contributed to the urgency for virtual Communion because pastors were afraid of leaving people bereft of the gospel.

Do we make room for Jesus in preaching? Or have we lost our capacity to preach about Jesus as Savior? Even this possibility causes me, as a homiletics professor, great heartache; as a bishop, great concern; and as a preacher, significant pause. I recognize validity to this question that we dare not dismiss because our need for preaching about Jesus is urgent.

As the Covid-19 pandemic continues, we feel this urgency. Our nation has lost millions of lives and jobs to the coronavirus, and the world remains uncertain. We've endured numerous natural disasters, witnessed our cities ablaze with the fires of extreme division and racial injustice, and experienced a siege of the United States Capitol by our fellow citizens. Many of us know that, despite our best efforts to address these issues, we cannot save ourselves. We need a Savior. We need good news from God that we can taste. We need preachers who so trust that Jesus is in the room with us that they can meaningfully proclaim Jesus as Savior and show the world that Jesus is with us everywhere we need God.

So do you make room for Jesus in preaching? Where is Jesus when you preach? In this book, I invite preachers to play a game of hide-and-seek with Jesus by using liturgical spaces to consider where Jesus is when we preach. I name places where, as a preacher, I found Jesus and Jesus found me. I then revisit some of these places as a way of proposing how to make room for Jesus in preaching. The church and the world win the game of hide-and-seek when preachers find Jesus in themselves. So does the preacher. The object of the game and of this book, then, is that preachers become yoked so closely and securely to Jesus that they humbly and reverently claim Christ's presence in the room and in themselves; make room for Jesus in preaching; and experience the grace, power, and joy that comes from preaching Jesus as Savior for no other reason than it is such good news.

Acknowledgments

Returning to Notre Dame provided a faith community in which my wife, Cathy, and I feel loved, valued, and respected, and a vocation in which I feel competent, at a time when Cathy and I truly needed both. I thank Timothy Matovina, chair of the Department of Theology, and Michael Connors, CSC, Director of the John S. Marten Program in Homiletics, for inviting me to spend a semester teaching preaching. Mike is a friend and wise collaborator of long-standing and the godfather of this book. I likewise benefited from conversation with Karla Bellinger, also of the Marten Program. I am grateful for the tutoring of my teachers and friends, Mary Catherine Hilkert, OP, in pneumatology and Robert Krieg, in soteriology, who generously shared their research and writing as well as their time. This book is also enriched by the exegetical insights of Raymond Pickett of Pacific Lutheran Theological Seminary and Walter F. Taylor Jr. of Trinity Lutheran Seminary.

My joy at returning to Notre Dame to teach was compounded by the invitation to write. I thank my editor, Beth Gaede, now of 1517 Media, for reaching out to ask what I was thinking, shepherding me through the review and approval process, and graciously partnering on this, our fifth book together. At Notre Dame, my writing was supported by the warm collegiality of Brian Daley, SJ; Michael Driscoll; and Max Johnson. I thank Sandy Schlesinger and our Synod

Executive Committee for honoring my vocation as teacher/ scholar as a gift to the church, and the synod staff, particularly Rosanne Anderson and David Sprang, for affording me time and space to pursue this project. I also thank Christopher Laughlin, Betsy Kamphuis, Ellen Schoepf, and Kurt Kusserow, for contributing to and reading chapter drafts and providing helpful questions and suggestions, and Andrew Gangle, Gary Bunge, and Rick Hoyme, for encouraging me to make the creativity and satisfaction book-writing brings me a priority.

I recognize Jesus as God's Agape Embodied in Cathy's self-less, sacrificial love for me, which makes writing and many other things I do possible. I am challenged to comprehend that Jesus's love *for me* exceeds Cathy's.

Chelsey Satterlee's mastery of English and her questions and curiosities greatly improved this book. Chelsey and I have come a long way from my reading to Chelsey to Chelsey editing my writing. During the eighteen months when Cathy and I did not see Chelsey because of the pandemic, I was grateful that this project gave me one more reason to pester her, and that Chelsey always responds to my texts and phone calls.

In writing this book, I experienced both the presence and the absence of my mentor and friend, John Allyn Melloh, SM. John taught me to teach preaching, guided my scholarship, and both challenged and advocated for me. In response to the first chapter of my dissertation, John instructed me to give it to my wife to read. "When Cathy understands it," John said, "then you can give it to me." John then explained that, more than writing a dissertation, I was going to learn to write books. I miss John, even as I am mindful that I am one of those carrying on his work. I dedicate this book to John in memoriam.

On my last day staring out the window of my Notre Dame office, as I prepared to return to the office of bishop, I found myself thinking about what I experience as the most poignant part of the charge I give pastors and deacons at ordination: "And be of good courage, for God has called you, and your labor in the Lord is not in vain."[1] I prayed out loud for myself what I usually pray silently as new pastors and deacons receive their stole: "Lord Jesus keep them yoked to you." I offer this prayer for you as you read this book. I also pray this book is an answer to my prayer for you.

+Craig Alan Satterlee
Feast of Saint Ambrose
342 Malloy Hall
University of Notre Dame

1

Yoked to Jesus

Where Is Jesus When You Preach?

In the Evangelical Lutheran Church in America, newly ordained pastors and deacons hear these words as red stoles are placed around their shoulders:

> Receive this stole as a sign of your work, and walk in obedience to the Lord Jesus, serving his people and remembering his promise: "Come to me, all who labor and are carrying heavy burdens, and I will give you rest. Take my yoke upon you, and learn from me; for I am gentle and lowly in heart, and you will find rest for your souls. For my yoke is easy, and my burden is light."[1]

I expect Jesus keeps pastors and deacons yoked closely and securely. So, I was stunned when a member of a congregation in my synod (diocese) quoted John 20:19 to me: "When it was evening on that day, the first day of the week, and the doors of the house where the disciples had met were locked for fear of the [Judeans],[2] Jesus came and stood among them and said, 'Peace be with you.'" And then the member asked, "Do preachers today believe Jesus is in the room with us

1

when we worship? Where do they think Jesus is when they preach?" In that conversation, I learned how much people want a preacher yoked so closely and securely to Jesus that they believe Jesus is in the room when they preach. Reflecting on this conversation, I realized how much I want to trust Jesus is in the room with us when I preach.

Do you believe Jesus is in the room when you preach? Better yet, in Johannine terms, do you *trust* Jesus is in the room when you preach? When you prepare your sermon, when you step up to the pulpit, when you open your mouth and look into the faces of the assembly, do you believe and trust Jesus is in the room with you?

My invitation—my challenge—to you is that you preach yoked so closely and securely to Jesus that the question becomes a conviction: Jesus is in the room when we preach. After all, as John tells it, no locked door can keep Jesus out. The disciples are locked away in fear of the authorities. As Luke tells it, the disciples become startled and terrified when Jesus shows up and think they are seeing a ghost.[3] Either way, the good news for both preachers and hearers is that Jesus comes to us in our fear and speaks a word of peace. Show up in people's fear and speak a word of peace in Jesus's name; there is a model for preaching!

Jesus shows the disciples his hands and his side—in Luke, his hands and his feet—to verify the crucified Christ is risen. So, too, we show disciples the crucified and risen Christ when we preach yoked to Jesus. Jesus empowers the disciples with the Holy Spirit. At its best, preaching empowers rather than exhorts or commands. Then, and only then, does Jesus send the disciples to first and foremost forgive. I have a hunch the issues that occupy us and the concerns that consume us and the world would be less paralyzing and divisive if we proclaimed Christ's forgiveness and peace. Meeting people in fear with a word of peace, showing them the crucified and risen Christ, empowering them with the Holy Spirit, and sending them to proclaim forgiveness—perhaps this is what it looks like to do what Jesus did because we are unmistakably aware Jesus is in the room with us.

"Seated at the Right Hand of the Father"

"Is Jesus in the room with you when you preach?" I suspect the doctrinally minded are finding my question a bit of a stretch. In the creeds, the church confesses that Jesus "ascended into heaven and is seated at the right hand of the Father." So, if you are not ready to put Jesus in the room with us, what does it mean that Jesus is seated at God's right hand when you preach? I do not believe Jesus is sitting idly by. Jesus is gifting, praying, sending the Holy Spirit, and drawing us and the cosmos to himself.

Seated at the right hand of the Father, Jesus is *gifting*. When a pastor or deacon is ordained, the bishop prays, in part: "We praise you that, having ascended into heaven, Christ pours out his gifts abundantly on the church, making some apostles, some prophets, some pastors and teachers, to equip your people for their work of ministry for building up the body of Christ."[4] One way or another, apostles, prophets, pastors (and deacons), and teachers all preach. Seated at God's right hand, Christ abundantly pours out his gifts to raise up preachers for the church. For most preachers, the Holy Spirit awakens in us natural talents—including gifts for preaching—improves them, and orients them toward God in the love and service of others.[5] In this way, Christ entrusts his gifts for preaching to you.

By *you*, I mean more than bishops, pastors, and deacons. I mean all God's people, all the baptized. Simply because it is true, I must acknowledge that some of the best preaching I ever received came outside of worship from preachers who were not ordained. With Martin Luther, I honor ordained ministry as Christ's gift and legacy to his church and part of the divine order, precisely because its chief responsibility is to preach the gospel and empower the proclamation of all the baptized as they live every day in the world. "The public ministry of the Word," Luther wrote, "ought to be established by holy ordination as the highest and greatest of the functions of the church."[6] Yet, God regularly reminds me of Eldad and Medad and Moses's wish: "Would that all the Lord's people were prophets, and that the Lord would put his spirit on them!"[7]

So, one of the charges given to the newly ordained is, in fact, given to all who in any way preach. Recalling First Corinthians 4:1, we say, "Think of us in this way, as servants of Christ and stewards of God's mysteries. Moreover, it is required of stewards that they be found trustworthy."[8] We all are responsible to be trustworthy stewards of whatever preaching gifts Jesus pours out upon us.

Seated at the right hand of the Father, Jesus is *praying*. In Romans 8:34, Paul writes of "Christ Jesus, who died, yes, who was raised, who is at the right hand of God, who indeed intercedes for us." Jesus intercedes for us. Take just a second and consider that, seated at the right hand of the Father, Jesus is praying for you when you preach. What do you imagine Jesus is praying? I suspect Jesus prays that through your preaching, people will know he loves them, forgives them, will come to them in their fear, and will bring them to new life. I imagine Jesus then prays the people will learn from him how to live so they and the world enjoy the abundant life he came to bring.[9]

Knowing that people pray for me when I preach both lightens the burden and makes it heavier. People's prayers lighten the burden because I know I am not alone; people are cheering the sermon on to the point they ask God to bless, sustain, and enliven my preaching. To think that one of those praying for me is Jesus deepens the grace, trust, and confidence I experience. People's prayers increase the burden of preaching because I am more aware of their investment in each sermon and their desire and hope for an encounter with Jesus; I do not want to let them down. To think one of those praying for me is Jesus, and Jesus desires and hopes the assembly encounters him through the sermon, makes the task of preaching more daunting as I feel the responsibility to preach Christ and am overwhelmed when I think my sermon might be the answer to Jesus's prayer.

Seated at the right hand of the Father, Jesus asks the Father to *send the Holy Spirit*. "I will ask the Father," Jesus promises, "and he will give you another Advocate, to be with you forever—the Spirit of truth."[10] Jesus sends the Holy Spirit to teach us, remind us what he said, testify to Jesus, and guide us into all the truth by reporting what the Spirit hears Jesus saying.[11] Jesus sends the Holy Spirit to guide our preparation, to open our hearers' ears, and to enliven our words, so preaching produces faith and inspires lives. Jesus sends the Holy Spirit to yoke us to Jesus.

Jesus draws us to himself. I do not think the right hand of the Father is all that far away. I just cannot fathom that God, who so loved the world that he gave his only Son, would send that Son away from the world God so loves. Perhaps we can see God's right hand from here. Full of the Holy Spirit, Stephen saw Jesus standing at the right hand of God.[12] Standing in the pulpit, I imagine God's right hand as up, perhaps way up, and to the right. Yet, we have scoured the heavens with the Hubble Space Telescope and have yet to spot Jesus seated at God's right hand. How can this be?

I have come to regard the right hand of the Father as a matter of time rather than space. Jesus ascended to that time when Christ reigns "far above all rule and authority and power and dominion, and above every name that is named, not only in this age but also in the one to come," when God "put all things under his feet and gave him as head over all things to the church, which is his body, the fullness of him who fills all in all."[13] Jesus does not sit docilely in the fullness of time, when Christ reigns all in all, passively waiting for us. Jesus draws, perhaps strenuously pulls, all creation to himself. "And I, when I am lifted up from the earth, will draw all people to myself."[14] One of the ways Jesus draws all people—all creation—to himself is through preaching.

Thinking of the right hand of God as a time rather than a place makes it very possible that Jesus is in the room when we preach in the same way Jesus is truly present in, with, and under bread and wine. But I understand preachers may not agree with me. I am content for preachers to leave Jesus at the right hand of the Father, so long as they understand Jesus is not passive. When we preach, Jesus is gifting, praying, sending, and drawing to himself.

Church Door

"Is Jesus in the room with you when you preach?" Some preachers do not believe he is. Like Jesus on the cross, preachers sometimes feel God has forsaken them.[15] Knowing otherwise and having faith does not always diminish this feeling. So, they look to the church door, convinced Jesus has left the building. Like many if not most preachers, I have known seasons—long, painful, dry seasons—when I was convinced Jesus went out the church door and left the building. Sometimes the building is my own heart, brought on by sin, doubt, unworthiness, despair, defeat, and the recognition the assembly cannot receive the gospel from me. Sometimes the building is the church, because the assembly has shown themselves to be "stiff-necked people, uncircumcised in heart and ears, forever opposing the Holy Spirit, just as their ancestors used to do."[16] Ask me where Jesus was when I preached during those times, and I would look to the church door and answer either "not here" or "far away."

So, what do preachers do when we are convinced Jesus has left the building? We go out the door and to a building where we trust Jesus to be. Often this means we become hearers of the Word. We go and hear good preaching. Some find it in a neighboring parish. Others find it on YouTube. We seek out a confessor or a spiritual director or a homebound member or a kid to speak grace to us. We open scripture with the sole purpose of receiving good news for us. We preach the good news we most need to hear; we preach it over and over and over again, as a call to Jesus to come to us. We do whatever we need to do to adjust and tighten the yoke, so we are closely and securely connected to Jesus, trusting Jesus to graciously yoke us to himself. And Jesus comes through the door. Slowly, unbelievably, mercifully, the season of abandonment ends. Jesus is back in the building. We may even realize Jesus never left the building, though it certainly felt that way.

Assuming we are yoked closely and securely to Jesus, I am increasingly convinced that when we sense Jesus is going out the door and leaving the building, it is because Jesus has indeed left the church building. Just as Jesus would not be confined to synagogues and brought the good news to people at the lakeshore, in homes, and beyond the margins, so Jesus leaves our church buildings to be in our homes, neighborhoods, workplaces, and communities. When we sense Jesus has left the building, we venture out into the neighborhood, because Jesus likes to hang out there, and so we spend time in places we expect Jesus to be. And we preach about Jesus in a way that encourages our people to join us in the places where we have found Jesus. After spending time in the neighborhood, we may find Jesus coming through the door of our building in new and unexpected ways and bringing friends with him.

Trusting Jesus is in the room with us, where do you say Jesus is when you preach? Can you name the place? Here is an interesting exercise to yoke preachers to Jesus. As part of preparing your sermons, play a game of hide-and-seek with Jesus in your favorite liturgical space and figure out where you find Jesus—or where Jesus finds you. Here are some places where I have looked.

Pulpit Bible

Perhaps the Bible on the pulpit is the place preachers first look for Jesus when we preach. After all, Jesus is the Word made flesh.[17] If Jesus is in the word when we preach, our task is to find Jesus in the Scripture readings as we prepare our sermons. This is certainly what Jesus taught his first preachers, the blessed apostles. Jesus said to them,

> "These are my words that I spoke to you while I was still with you—that everything written about me in the law of Moses, the prophets, and the psalms must be fulfilled." Then he opened their minds to understand the scriptures, and he said to them, "Thus it is written, that the Messiah is to suffer and to rise from the dead on the third day, and that repentance and forgiveness of sins is to be proclaimed in his name to all nations, beginning from Jerusalem."[18]

As preachers, we are to witness to *these* things. So we look for Jesus in the readings.

Coming home from Jerusalem to Emmaus, Cleophus and his companion remind us that Jesus comes to us in Scripture not in isolation but in conversation.

While they were talking and discussing, Jesus himself came near and went with them, but their eyes were kept from recognizing him. And he said to them, "What are you discussing with each other while you walk along?". . . Then he said to them, "Oh, how foolish you are, and how slow of heart to believe all that the prophets have declared! Was it not necessary that the Messiah should suffer these things and then enter into his glory?" Then beginning with Moses and all the prophets, he interpreted to them the things about himself in all the scriptures.[19]

As preachers, how do we break open the word with others, that together, we might find Jesus there? How do we open the word to find Jesus without imposing Jesus on the Scriptures?

Pulpit

Perhaps the last place preachers look for Jesus when we preach is the pulpit. Claiming Jesus is present in our own preaching somehow feels impious. Yet, as a Lutheran, I find comfort (and challenge) that Martin Luther calls preaching the *viva vox Christi* and the *viva vox evangeli*—the living voice of Christ and the living voice of the gospel.[20] Pope Francis says, "It is God who seeks to reach out to others through the preacher, and that God displays his power through human words."[21] Assuming we are striving to be faithful, what we declare for preaching generally we can dare to claim for our own. Christ speaks in and through our preaching. Jesus must be in the pulpit with us when we preach.

Of course, if Jesus is going to speak in our preaching, we need to give him a voice. In form, content, and delivery, Jesus stands front and center in the pulpit, and not in the back corner behind illustrations, issues, or instructions. We certainly do not place Jesus down the pulpit steps and a few feet away while we talk about something else. As we prepare our sermons, we ask, What is Jesus saying? How is Jesus saying it? Is this word from Jesus, or is this something I want or need or feel compelled to say?

Most important, for Jesus to speak in our preaching, we need to know Jesus, to be yoked to Jesus. This seems obvious. But it becomes all too easy to know *about* Jesus or to work for Jesus. Personally, I am much more comfortable thinking of myself as Jesus's servant than I am having Jesus call me friend. But Jesus calls me friend: "I do not call you servants any longer, because the servant does not know what the master is doing; but I have called you friends, because I have made known to you everything that I have heard from my Father."[22] I am one to whom Jesus gave his knowledge of God and his love without limit; I am one for whom Jesus laid down his life. Jesus has called me friend. So, I need to work on that friendship. Perhaps you do as well. Discerning where in the room Jesus is when you preach is a powerful way to strengthen friendship with Jesus. Putting Jesus front and center in our sermons is a powerful way we strengthen our people's friendship with Jesus.

Table and Font

Many preachers—and, I have learned, many parishioners—count on Christ to be present at the altar or table and in the baptismal font. They rely on Christ's presence in the waters of baptism, the declaration of absolution, and the bread and wine of the Eucharist as the safety net for the sermon. Preachers tell me that they take comfort that when they leave Jesus out of their sermons (yikes!), people will receive him in the

sacraments. Once upon a time, when I was a seminary professor, a colleague was preaching. The sermon had devolved
into a lecture and was running off the rails. All eyes were on
me, the preaching professor; I was doing everything in my
power not to react. Mercifully, another colleague sitting near
me touched my hand and whispered, "Sit back and listen to
the baptismal water." I took to sitting near the font.

As I observed above, some people speculate that, by relying
on Jesus's presence in the sacraments to proclaim the gospel,
preachers dedicate the sermon to something else. Rather
than bailing us out or freeing us to preach something else,
however, Christ present at table and font calls us to do our
best to proclaim Christ. We are to proclaim in our sermons
what Jesus promises in the waters of baptism, words of absolution, and bread and wine of the Eucharist:[23] Jesus naming
and claiming, Jesus forgiving and freeing, Jesus empowering
and sending, Jesus dying and rising. Jesus with us always,
Jesus bringing life.

Balcony

During my early years as a preacher, Jesus stood in the
balcony. Jesus was watching over the congregation and just
plain watching me. I had experienced a great big helping of the church's hesitation and speculation concerning
whether I could or should be a pastor, since I do not see
well and cannot drive a car. Having been given the chance,
I experienced both real and imagined evaluation. Imposter
syndrome on steroids!

My sense that I was being evaluated found expression in
my preaching. I recall being aware that, as the Nicene Creed
says, Jesus "will come again in glory to judge the living and
the dead." Matthew tells us what this will be like. "When the

Son of [Humanity] comes in his glory, and all the angels with him. . . all the nations will be gathered before him, and he will separate people one from another as a shepherd separates the sheep from the goats."[24] As the preacher, I felt compelled to get people to do something—feed the hungry, give the thirsty a drink, clothe the naked, care for the sick, visit prisoners, something.

Judgmental preaching aimed at getting people to do something did not go over well. The people did not like it, and I sensed Jesus was not happy either. I assumed Jesus's unhappiness stemmed from my inability to get people to respond. Thankfully, over time, patient parishioners reminded me of what I had been taught but forgot: Jesus is our Savior before Jesus is anything else. I had become so accustomed to looking for Jesus in the balcony that I had stopped looking for Jesus on the cross. As a result, my preaching about Jesus crucified and risen got smaller and smaller and smaller. My patient parishioners also helped me understand that when I stopped feeling judged and regarded Jesus first and foremost as Savior, I would feel less of a need to judge others or to protect them from God's judgment. I would be free to invite and inspire people to respond to Jesus's love in such a way that they would not be aware they were serving Jesus as they fed, clothed, welcomed, cared for, and visited.[25]

Who Jesus is to us and who we say Jesus is in our sermons matters. We proclaim Jesus as Savior before we name him as anything else. When I figured out that Jesus is Savior before he is anything else, and put this into practice, Jesus left the balcony. Jesus took his place among the least of these. And my preaching quite naturally gave the least of these a voice, speaking both to and for them. Rather than searching the balcony, I looked for Jesus on the edges and on the margins. And there he sat.

Pew

I am somewhat embarrassed that it has taken me until now to turn to the pews, to Christ's presence in the congregation. One of the reasons I so cherish *Fulfilled in Your Hearing: The Homily in the Sunday Assembly*, a publication of the United States Conference of Catholic Bishops, is that it starts with the assembly. And *The Use of the Means of Grace: A Statement on the Practice of Word and Sacrament* by the Evangelical Lutheran Church in America considers the assembly proclaiming the word before turning to preaching.[26]

Why do preachers take so long to encounter Jesus in their hearers? For sure, the courtship, the trust, the dance between the one in the pulpit and the many in the pew takes time to develop. So, both preachers and listeners need to be patient with one another. I advise pastors and deacons that it takes three years for a preacher and congregation to dance well together.

Encountering Jesus in the assembly is also about expectation. Preachers need to cultivate the expectation that Jesus tunes our hearers' ears at least as much as we nurture our trust that Jesus inspires our tongues. Preachers need to regard and approach the assembly as participants and partners in the proclamation of the gospel, treating them as such and teaching them that they are. The assembly's participation begins with responding to and interacting with the sermon and can extend, for example, to studying the readings with the preacher.

I have come to cherish the liturgy—the work of the people—as the assembly proclaiming the gospel to me. I no longer open a hymnal in worship, and I never read from the psalms. If I do not know the words to a hymn or psalm, I allow the assembly to sing for me, and I listen to their proclamation. I experience the proclamation of the gospel in the prayers when people use the same care in crafting words to name God that I use in creating the sermon. The same can be said of the whole of the liturgy—the assembly is proclaiming the gospel. So, at their best, homilies leave the assembly with a "Eucharistic attitude." *Fulfilled in Your Hearing* asserts, "The response [to the homily] that is most general and appropriate 'at all times and in every place' is the response of praise and thanksgiving (Eucharist)."[27]

As I look out upon the assembly, I find Jesus in four particular places. First, Jesus is certainly sitting among the faithful. As a bishop, I am always moved at worship services where I look out on vested clergy. I especially find Jesus sitting next to young people who, despite the state of the church and state of the world, are in worship, giving hope by their presence. Some of them are even considering how to answer God's call to public ministry. Mostly, I find Jesus sitting with congregational leaders, who volunteer for what turns out to be challenging work; they serve faithfully because they love the Lord and his church.

Second, sitting near the baptismal font, I have become mindful of Jesus among the crowd gathered around the congregation's Pool of Bethesda. These people are waiting. Some, like the man in John's Gospel who was paralyzed and actually waited at the Pool of Bethesda, are waiting for healing. Some, like Anna and Simeon, are waiting for the redemption of God's people. Some are waiting for an angel to trouble the waters on God's behalf.[28] Some have been waiting a long time. Seeing Jesus sitting among them reminds preachers that, sometimes, the only good news we have is that Jesus is with them as they wait.

Third, I find Jesus standing along the walls with the saints, with those who came before and those who will come after us, and with brothers and sisters beyond the walls in saints around the world. I hear them all speak in the creed. And I am especially mindful of the saints who stood in the pulpit before me and so stand in the pulpit alongside me. Writing in my ninth year as a bishop, I am increasingly mindful of the saints who will stand in the pulpit and lead the church after me.

Fourth, I see Jesus in empty pews, in the people who are not in the room. One Christmas Eve I preached that, if this was the night of Jesus's birth, the holy family would be in a stable or maybe a homeless shelter or with relatives who did not come tonight, not in church. I could not have imagined what good news this was for people in church worried about people they loved who were not in church. Perhaps we need to leave the crèche up all year so that Jesus might be with us in the room in a way that reminds us of his presence with people not in the room. Or perhaps this is the way we can look upon empty pews.

Wherever Jesus is sitting in the congregation, Jesus is listening to our sermons. How regularly does Jesus hear his name mentioned? Does Jesus recognize himself in what is preached? What does Jesus want the congregation to know most about him? How would our sermon preparation change if, each week as we write our sermons, we think of one member of the assembly, or one family, and imagine Jesus will be sitting with them as we preach?

Cross

On my fourth or fifth trip around the sanctuary, I realize I have forgotten to look up. Jesus said, "And just as Moses lifted up the serpent in the wilderness, so must the Son of [Humanity] be lifted up, that whoever believes in him may have eternal life"[29] Jesus is, of course, referring to his being lifted up on the cross. Just as Moses lifted up the bronze serpent and all who looked upon it were healed of the poisonous venom of snakebite and lived,[30] so all who look up to, look upon, trust in, or believe in Jesus on the cross will be healed of sin and all its manifestations, including death, and live. I had forgotten to look up, to look for Jesus on the cross.

The cross hangs prominently in our worship spaces. We carry the cross into worship. When does the cross become so familiar that we stop really seeing it? Why did I not look for Jesus on the cross first thing? I want to excuse myself because I cannot really see a cross on the wall: I am most connected to the pectoral cross around my neck. Still, I suspect there is something more. I learned that Jesus is Savior before Jesus is anything else when I made Jesus a judge in the balcony. How did I forget this lesson? Had I assumed the gospel? Had I presumed the gospel? Had I taken Jesus's cross for granted? Do I do this in my preaching? Do we all do this in our preaching?

"For Jews demand signs and Greeks desire wisdom, but we proclaim Christ crucified, a stumbling block to Jews and foolishness to gentiles, but to those who are the called, both Jews and Greeks, Christ the power of God and the wisdom of God."[31] Even when we are committed to preaching Christ crucified, how often we give way to signs and human wisdom, letting go of the power and wisdom of God. Before we look for Jesus anywhere else, before our preaching locates Jesus anywhere else, we look up to behold Jesus on the cross, and we preach so our people see Jesus as Savior. To make room for Jesus in preaching is to give prominent place to the cross.

The Walk to the Pulpit

I have looked in all these places and known that, at one time or another, Jesus has been there when I preached. But sometimes Jesus has not been there. So, where was he? One Sunday I was walking to the pulpit to preach and, as sometimes happens in a game of hide-and-seek, Jesus seemed to jump out and scare me half to death. In my bones, I knew Jesus walks me to the pulpit when I preach.

It turns out the walk I take to the pulpit with Jesus is the same walk Nicodemus took in John's Gospel. In the night before I preach, I come to Jesus with questions, just as Nicodemus came to Jesus by night with questions.[32] I have written my questions down in a homily manuscript. In prayerful conversation with Jesus, as I memorize that manuscript, Jesus transforms it from something I do to something the Spirit does through me, and the sermon is born from above.

Yes, going to the pulpit has begun to feel a bit like the walk Nicodemus took in John's Gospel, from coming to Jesus by night to going with Joseph of Arimathea to the tomb.[33] In my preaching, I strive to make the same bold and important declaration Joseph and Nicodemus made by requesting Jesus's body from Pilate, preparing it for burial, and laying it in a new tomb. Joseph and Nicodemus declare Jesus to be Messiah and King. They bury Jesus honorably, lavishly, royally. This is how I want to preach Jesus. I want to preach Christ with as much of myself as Joseph of Arimathea and Nicodemus gave to point beyond fear, shame, humiliation, violence, and death to Jesus's glorification and victory on the cross. My walk to the pulpit serves as the metaphor for the method of sermon preparation I use and teach.

Jesus Is in the Room When You Preach!

Jesus is in the room with you when you preach! Take some time. Go into your favorite liturgical space or take a virtual tour in your mind. Play a game of hide-and-seek with Jesus. In your seeking, trust Jesus to find you where you will grow as a preacher and where you need Jesus most. Expect Jesus to find you where your people can best receive him and where your people need him most. Continue to play hide-and-seek with Jesus, and you will find yourself yoked so closely and securely to Jesus that Jesus stands front and center in your sermon. You proclaim Christ crucified as the power and wisdom of God,[34] because to do otherwise feels like ignoring Jesus or treating him rudely. This feeling comes from the grace of finding Jesus in the preacher.

Assure your people you believe Jesus is in the room when you preach. Tell them where you believe Jesus is. Ask them where they think Jesus might be. Listeners report they listen to sermons more intently. Even better, listeners report they come to expect, since Jesus is in the room when we preach, Jesus is in the rooms where they work, play, study, and live— the classroom, the gym, the kitchen—and they wonder where Jesus is. They may even play their own game of hide-and-seek with Jesus and Jesus finds them in whatever room they are looking.

Asking where Jesus is when we preach leads many to wondering about the third person of the Trinity. Where is the Holy Spirit when we preach? In my experience, the Holy Spirit is impossible to locate; only in hindsight can we tell where the Spirit has been. The better question is: How do we welcome the Holy Spirit into our preaching?

2

Seated at God's Right Hand

How Do You Welcome the Holy Spirit?

"Preaching is supposed to be spiritual!" An exasperated student complained that my insistence that students learn a method of sermon preparation silenced if not suffocated the Holy Spirit. "Do not worry about how you are to defend yourselves or what you are to say," the student reminded me Jesus said, "for the Holy Spirit will teach you at that very hour what you ought to say."[1] The student assumed the Holy Spirit comes directly, individually, extraordinarily, and, most striking to me, outside of or apart from the training the church provides its preachers. Rather than teaching him to preach, the student wanted me to tell him where to find the Holy Spirit. "I want the Holy Spirit to tell me what to say!"

"Me too," I smiled, imagining how much easier life would be if the Holy Spirit poured a sermon into my head each Sunday. "I just haven't found that the Holy Spirit works that way."

Seated at God's right hand, Jesus sends the Holy Spirit.[2] How eager we are to welcome the Holy Spirit Jesus sends. Without the presence and power of the Holy Spirit, the sermon or homily, regardless of how entertaining, informative, insightful, or eloquent, remains merely words, a good speech.

Preachers and congregations name moments, even seasons when, despite their best efforts to faithfully preach and listen, the Holy Spirit did not show up. The faith community found itself famished for a morsel of the bread of God's word, parched for a swallow of living water, desperate for Jesus to send the Holy Spirit to empower his church's preaching.

Preachers and congregations also name moments and seasons when the Holy Spirit blew forcefully upon the church through preaching. With the presence and power of the Holy Spirit, the mere words of sermons, spoken and heard, were transformed into an experience of the gospel changing and even saving lives, an entrée into the reign of God in the here and now, and an encounter with the crucified and risen Christ.

No wonder we are eager for Jesus to send the Holy Spirit to enliven the church's preaching. We ask, "Where is the Holy Spirit when we preach?" If only we could find the Holy Spirit, perhaps we could also harness the Spirit, store up the Spirit, and, dare we say, control the Spirit. "I haven't found that the Holy Spirit works that way." In fact, pursuing the Holy Spirit can hinder being yoked closely and securely to Jesus. We do better to welcome the Holy Spirit, whom Jesus sends to his church.

Jesus says, "The wind blows where it chooses, and you hear the sound of it, but you do not know where it comes from or where it goes. So it is with everyone who is born of the Spirit."[8] Finding the Holy Spirit in preaching is like searching for the wind. Hopefully, the Holy Spirit is *everywhere* in preaching, from our initial reading of Scripture to our delivering and the congregation receiving the sermon. Ideally, the Holy Spirit permeates everything we do, the entire preaching event. To ask where the Holy Spirit is when we preach presumes that we can find, and that the Holy Spirit will be confined to, a specific place. "I haven't found that the Holy Spirit works that way." Instead, we welcome the Holy Spirit Jesus sends as we (1) stop searching for the Spirit, (2) preach Jesus, (3) align our expectations with the Spirit's mission in preaching, (4) notice signs the Spirit is at work, and (5) practice spiritual disciplines by which we actively welcome the Holy Spirit, whom Jesus sends.

Stop Searching for the Holy Spirit!

Whenever I ask where Jesus is when we preach, someone counters that we should be looking for the Holy Spirit, not Jesus. I encourage people to look, knowing that no matter how intently we look for tongues of fire above the preacher or how diligently we search, the Holy Spirit will not be found in a specific place. The Holy Spirit will not allow us to locate, let alone predict or guarantee, where the Holy Spirit will be. We cannot find the Holy Spirit for at least three reasons: (1) the Holy Spirit's nature makes the Spirit impossible to find, (2) Scripture provides no clues where to look, and (3) the mutuality of the Trinity prevents the Holy Spirit from standing out.

First, *the Spirit's nature makes the Holy Spirit impossible to find*. The Holy Spirit is elusive and complicated. When we search for the Holy Spirit, we are not entirely certain who or what we are looking for. Wading into the deep waters of pneumatology, the study of the Holy Spirit, leads quickly to the deeper waters of Trinitarian theology; soon many—including me—find we are in over our heads. More important, perhaps, relying on pneumatology for direction can leave us stuck in our heads. Jesus offered a short course in pneumatology to Nicodemus, explaining that to be born of the Spirit is to be "born again/from above." Nicodemus was confounded.[4] Contemporary scholars are equally confounding when they explain the Holy Spirit is central to theological reflection (and preaching) and the Holy Spirit does not replace Jesus at the center of theological reflection (and preaching). With

Nicodemus, we ask, "How can these things be?"[5] Rather than helping us find the Holy Spirit, pneumatology helps us understand why the Holy Spirit is impossible to find.

The Holy Spirit is impossible to find because the Holy Spirit is a spirit. Spirits among us become tangible when we consider team spirit, mob spirit, the spirit of affluence and white supremacy, generosity and diversity, violence, and the viral spirit of Covid-19. A spirit is without a definite "form" and "personality," making the Holy Spirit difficult to distinguish. "Spirit" is not a proper name. Using the language of the creeds, both the Father and the Son are also spirit.[6] Despite theological distinctions among the persons of the Trinity, including creating, redeeming, and sanctifying or sustaining, we cannot truly differentiate the presence of the Holy Spirit from that of the Father and the Son. The Spirit's elusiveness makes plain that, like being born, the Holy Spirit is not something we do but a gift we receive; the Holy Spirit is not someone we search for and find.

The Holy Spirit is not verifiable. One person's experience of the Holy Spirit is another person's experience of something else. In Acts, some "heard [the apostles] speaking in the native language of each." Others heard the apostles speak under the influence of another spirit; they "sneered and said, 'They are filled with new wine.'"[7] The subjectivity and hiddenness of the Spirit make all knowing that comes from the Spirit and all speech about the Spirit elusive.

Killian McDonnell, OSB, invites us to recognize that, by its very nature, the Holy Spirit is mystery; not mystery as a problem to be solved but "a sphere where the distinction between what is in me and what is before me loses its meaning and its initial validity."[8] Mysteries are more a presence we sense than a person we seek. Mysteries can only be hinted at and glimpsed momentarily but never permanently revealed. The Holy Spirit cannot be identified and viewed from a distance because the Holy Spirit is close, individually and communally personal, within rather than outside. Most often, we find the Holy Spirit through faithful hindsight and know then where the Holy Spirit has been.

Jesus is a more accessible mystery. Jesus is God's Word made flesh, the image of the invisible God, God with us.[9] Our shared humanity gives us a frame of reference as we contemplate locating Jesus in preaching. Rather than our finding the Holy Spirit in preaching, the Holy Spirit finds us when we are yoked closely and securely to Jesus.

A second reason we stop searching for the Holy Spirit in preaching is that *Scripture does not tell us where to look.* Metaphor is as close as we come to identifying the Holy Spirit. At Jesus's baptism, the Holy Spirit descended upon Jesus *like* a dove or *as* a dove.[10] On Pentecost, "from heaven there came a sound *like* the rush of a violent wind. . . Divided tongues, *as of* fire, appeared among [the disciples]."[11] Jesus speaks of being born of water and the Spirit.[12] Receiving the Holy Spirit is like a baby receiving birth.

The New Testament provides no developed teaching on the Holy Spirit. In fact, Scripture offers more questions than answers. In the biblical witness, is the Holy Spirit a power or a person? In Luke, Jesus tells the disciples to remain in the city until they are clothed with power from on high. In John, Jesus speaks of the Holy Spirit as the advocate whom Jesus will send to the disciples.[13] Is the Holy Spirit a presence distinct from Christ, as Luke's account of Pentecost suggests? Or does the Gospel of John indicate the Holy Spirit is the "personal presence of Jesus in the Christian while Jesus is with the Father"?[14]

Turning to the epistles, in 2 Corinthians 4:17, when Paul writes, "The Lord is the Spirit," what does Paul mean? Are the Lord and the Spirit one and the same? And how is it that Paul and other New Testament writers seem to have no awareness of the Pentecost event vividly reported by Luke? Rather than claiming he was anointed by the Holy Spirit, Paul names an encounter with the risen Christ as his apostolic credential.[15] While the New Testament writers were certainly confident of the Holy Spirit's presence, they did not systematically explain it or locate it, perhaps because locating the Holy Spirit is impossible.

I invite preachers to consider where Jesus is when they preach because, while Scripture provides no clues for finding the Holy Spirit, the Gospels assist us in locating Jesus. The details of Jesus's life tell us where we might look, including in the synagogue, among the marginalized, at table, and in places of suffering and death. In the Gospels, Jesus even tells us where to look for him—in the least of these, where two or three are gathered in his name, and in the breaking of the bread.[16] Scripture helps us imagine where Jesus might be when we preach.

Third, the Holy Spirit is impossible to find because *the mutuality of the Trinity prevents the Holy Spirit from standing out*. The three Persons of the Trinity, while distinct, do not contend for our attention. No "sibling rivalry" exists among them. The Persons of the Trinity are mutual, reciprocal, and communal. The work or mission of Jesus and the work or mission of the Holy Spirit are complementary and do not compete. McDonnell describes the mission of the Holy Spirit, and that of Jesus, as invisible, coextensive (extending over the same space and time), and simultaneous with one another.[17]

Some scholars describe the mutuality with which Jesus and the Holy Spirit carry out their missions by observing that the Holy Spirit does not manifest itself apart from Christ. According to these scholars, in Scripture both the revelation of the Holy Spirit and the bestowing of the Holy Spirit, who is uniquely the Spirit of Christ, always and only take place in and through Christ Jesus.[18] From this perspective, preaching about Jesus is essential to receiving the Holy Spirit in preaching. Apparently sharing this perspective, the *Augsburg Confession* condemns the teaching that we can obtain the Holy Spirit without the external word of the gospel, through our own preparation, thoughts, and works.[19]

Other scholars insist that, according to the Scriptures, the work of the Paraclete, the Spirit of Truth, is distinct from and as important as the work of Jesus. French Dominican Yves Congar, a preeminent theologian of the Holy Spirit, argues that the Holy Spirit and Jesus, whom Congar calls Word, are often together in Scripture and are hard to distinguish, because they are both involved in the same work. Congar also argues that the Word and the Spirit are not intermediaries, nor modalities through which a creative and provident God separately acts.[20] Without the work of the Holy Spirit, nothing can exist in history, neither the incarnation and reconciliation in Christ, nor personal faith, nor commitment to Jesus and his community.[21] Thus, Congar calls for "an appreciation of the role of the Spirit in the messianic life of Jesus, in the resurrection and glorification that have made him Lord and have caused the humanity hypostatically united to the eternal Son to pass from the *forma servi* to the *forma Dei*."[22] Congar encourages us to grasp the Holy Spirit's role in causing the humanity of Jesus united to the eternal Son to pass from the form of a servant to the form of God.

Scholars describe the Spirit's distinct work as the "point of contact" between God and humanity: "The Father touching history and the Church through Christ in the Spirit."[23] The Spirit, whom we individually and collectively experience in history, is the point of contact where the Father, through the Son, touches history and, therefore, the church and the Christian. The Spirit, then, is the universal point of contact between God and history, God and humanity, God and creation. At the same time, the Spirit is the point of contact where the world, the church, and the Christian enter the mystery of Christ, through which we access the Father.[24] The Spirit is the point of entry into the Christological mystery and life of the Trinity. The Spirit leads through Christ to the Father. Though the Holy Spirit is the "point of contact" and therefore central to the relationship between God and humanity, the work of the Spirit is neither superior to nor does it diminish Jesus's salvific work.

Whether we understand the Holy Spirit as manifesting itself in Christ or as the "point of contact" between God and the cosmos through Christ, the Trinity exercises control, so the centrality of Christ is not displaced. The mutuality of the Trinity makes the Holy Spirit inseparable from Jesus and impossible to find on its own. Rather than searching for the Holy Spirit, we preach with the power of the Spirit when we preach Jesus.

Preach Jesus!

Some preachers and hearers suggest we will preach in the power of the Holy Spirit if we devote more time to preaching about the Holy Spirit. They believe our inability to find the Holy Spirit in preaching is a consequence of too few sermons about the Holy Spirit. Some even regard the Holy Spirit as the forgotten Person of the Trinity. They suggest pneumatology replace Christology as the content of theological reflection and the Holy Spirit replace Jesus as the content of preaching, so the Holy Spirit overshadows Jesus in a kind of "pneumatological affirmative action," to compensate for the long concentration on Jesus at the expense of the Holy Spirit.

In terms of sermon content, the claim that the Holy Spirit is the forgotten Person of the Trinity may be valid. It may also be appropriate. However, the central good news of the gospel, in both the New Testament and the church, is Jesus Christ crucified and risen. Peter shows us this on Pentecost when he does not preach about the Holy Spirit, despite the sound of rushing wind, the tongues as of fire, and people hearing their own languages as the disciples spoke. Instead, Peter proclaims Jesus crucified and risen.[25] Peter's only mention of the Holy Spirit is actually a declaration about Jesus: "Having been exalted to the right hand of God, and having received from the Father the promise of the Holy Spirit, Jesus has poured forth this which you both see and hear."[26]

As the Pentecost event and Peter's preaching about it indicate, the Holy Spirit is central to the *Missio Dei* or mission of God but does not displace Jesus from the center. Jesus and the Holy Spirit both occupy the center of God's mission, each according to their proper function or mission, even while Jesus remains the content.[27] To preach Jesus neither neglects nor forgets the Holy Spirit. We certainly preach and teach the Holy Spirit when to do so strengthens our proclamation of Christ, as Peter did on Pentecost and, as Congar requests, by naming the Spirit's work in Jesus's life, death, and resurrection. Yet, to preach in the power of the Holy Spirit is to preach Jesus.

In addition to preaching Jesus, we teach ourselves and our congregations to expect, even anticipate, the Holy Spirit to come with power when the gospel of Jesus Christ is preached. We foster expectation and anticipation by leading our hearers to trust Jesus to send the Holy Spirit, by acknowledging the Holy Spirit's presence in the moment, and, looking back, by testifying to the Holy Spirit at work in preaching. One way we ready ourselves to welcome and preach in the power of the Holy Spirit is by considering the Holy Spirit's mission or function in preaching.

The Holy Spirit's Mission in Preaching

The Holy Spirit carries out a unique function in the *Missio Dei*, which includes preaching. McDonnell describes the Spirit's function or mission in relation to that of Jesus: "If Jesus Christ is the 'what,' the Spirit is the 'how.'"[28] Apropos for preaching, Congar explains the *what* and the *how* using the Trinitarian image of "the thought, the word, and the breath," commonly found in patristic sources. He considers "the thought, the word, and the breath" to be three dynamic and simultaneous components of the single act of speech and consistently refers to the Son and Spirit as *Word* and *Breath* of God.[29] As breath is related to word in speaking, so Congar distinguishes the Spirit's unique function or mission, without separating the Spirit from the Son.

Jesus "breathed on [the disciples] and said to them, 'Receive the Holy Spirit.'"[30] For Congar, *Breath* encapsulates an understanding of the Holy Spirit functioning as *activity*, *gift*, and *giving life*.[31] Congar finds in the term *Breath* natural associations with *activity* and *movement*—inhaling and exhaling. The *Breath* makes speech happen. Congar writes, it is the breath "that makes speech come forth and that carries it afar."[32] The *Breath* is the intangible power and energy that carries the good news of Jesus from the preacher to the congregation and from the church to the world.

Even as the *Breath* represents movement, Congar wants us to understand the Spirit is more than transmission. Congar therefore distinguishes between the "Spirit's *action*, a simple presence of cause, and the *gift*, the indwelling of the Spirit as a communication of grace that enables us to enter into a relationship of communion and familial intimacy with God."[33] Adrian Brooks describes the Spirit as a gift: "A word of love, breathed forth, dwells, grows and moves in us."[34] McDonnell describes the gift of the Holy Spirit dwelling in the believer as that very interior light that links the believer with the exterior light of God and spiritual realities.[35] We pray for this gift as we invoke the Holy Spirit at, for example, baptism, confirmation, ordination, and as part of preparing to preach.

As *Breath*, the Holy Spirit does not remain in us or in the world but is exhaled to *give life* to the gospel. "The Breath is the one who breathes forth the utterance of the Word far and wide; the Spirit ensures that Christ will continue to come in Christians throughout the course of history. As time unfolds, he constantly carries forward the truth which the Word contains.'"[36] Exhaled, the Spirit functions as the "Breath, the gush of air that wafts back to the Father."[37] This breath does not return to God empty.

The Spirit brings Christ to life in the world. In the creeds, the church confesses the Spirit's role in the Incarnation. The Spirit was also at work in the ministry of Jesus as the anointed Messiah.[38] Since Christ's ascension, the Spirit continues to bring life to the ecclesial body of Christ, "unceasingly" making "Christ's work real in the present."[39] For Congar, the Holy Spirit makes Christ present through the established structures of the church. (I hasten to add that, sometimes, the Holy Spirit makes Christ present in spite of the established structures of the church.)

Jesus as *Word* and the Holy Spirit as *Breath* work together as word and breath work together in speech. Congar concludes that there is no *Word* without *Breath*; it would remain in the throat and would address no one. The *Breath* is needed to carry the *Word* so that it can address the world. Likewise, there is no *Breath* without the *Word*: it would have no content and would transmit nothing to anyone.[40] The *Word* provides the content, the message, the tangible form. The Spirit never speaks of itself. The *Breath* and *Word* mutually inform and depend upon each other. As they work together, Jesus and the Holy Spirit, *Word* and *Breath*, each perform their own distinctive and essential function in the *Missio Dei*, which is the one work of God.

Signs of the Spirit in Preaching

That the Holy Spirit is elusive does not make it extraordinary. Signs of the Spirit's presence, in our lives, in the church, and in the world, surround us. We welcome the Holy Spirit by paying attention to signs the Spirit is at work in preaching. Unlike the Spirit itself, signs that the Spirit is working in preaching are so readily apparent that we might take them for granted. The Spirit (1) establishes preaching, (2) produces faith, (3) interprets Jesus's mission, (4) anoints the preaching event, and (5) yokes us to the Word.

First, *the preaching of the gospel is itself a sign of the Holy Spirit*, since preaching comes from God. Jesus Christ and the Holy Spirit act inseparably to establish what Congar termed the ecclesial means of grace—the Word, the sacraments, and the apostolic ministry.[41] In Luke, Jesus calls the disciples witnesses that the Messiah suffered and rose from the dead on the third day, and that repentance and forgiveness are to be preached in his name; Jesus assures the disciples he is sending what the Father promised. Jesus then tells them to wait until they are clothed with power from God. In John, Jesus tells the disciples he is sending them as the Father sent Jesus. Jesus then breathes the Holy Spirit into them.[42]

From the commissioning and empowering of the apostles, the institution of the proclamation of the Word, the sacraments, and the apostolic ministry occurred gradually throughout the apostolic era and over the course of Christian history. The church is built upon this foundation through the work of the Spirit and Jesus, and the cooperation of the Christian faithful.[43] As I said in chapter 1, seated at God's right hand, Jesus pours out gifts abundantly on the church and sends the Holy Spirit to establish, empower, and authorize all authentic preaching of the gospel.

That people have faith is a second sign the Spirit is at work in preaching. Paul writes, "No one can say 'Jesus is Lord' except by the Holy Spirit."[44] The *Augsburg Confession* provides one perspective on the reason God established preaching: to obtain faith. The Confession teaches:

> We receive forgiveness of sins and become righteous before God out of grace for Christ's sake through faith when we believe that Christ has suffered for us and that for his sake our sin is forgiven, and righteousness and eternal life are given to us. For God will reckon such faith as righteousness in his sight, as St. Paul says in Romans 3 [: 21–26] and 4 [:5].[45]
>
> To obtain such faith God instituted the office of preaching, giving the gospel and the sacraments. Through these, as through means, he gives the Holy Spirit who produces faith, where and when he wills, in those who hear the gospel.[46]

The *Augsburg Confession* summarizes the gospel as the good news "that we have a gracious God, not through our merit but through Christ's merit, when we so believe."[47] Moved by grace, God not only gives Jesus to suffer and die for us and all creation. God also establishes preaching, empowering preaching by the Holy Spirit, so we might believe that through Christ Jesus we are forgiven and made right with God.

God's purpose in establishing preaching is to secure faith in Jesus Christ. The Holy Spirit produces this faith. "Through these [the preaching of the gospel and the sacraments], as through means, [God] gives the Holy Spirit who produces faith, where and when he wills, in those who hear the gospel."[48]

The faith the Holy Spirit produces is more than belief in the claim of the gospel, more than trust in the promise of the gospel. The Holy Spirit is the source of a relationship with God, the hope of salvation, the only possibility of knowing the Father and the Son, and the font of our obedience.[49] Faith is a gift of the Holy Spirit; faith is not something we create, will, decide, or construct all on our own.

In his *Small Catechism*, Martin Luther explains the Third Article of the Apostles' Creed, which concerns the Holy Spirit:

> I believe that by my own understanding or strength I cannot believe in Jesus Christ my Lord or come to him, but instead the Holy Spirit has called me through the gospel, enlightened me with his gifts, made me holy and kept me in the true faith, just as he calls, gathers, enlightens, and makes holy the whole Christian church on earth and keeps it with Jesus Christ in the one common, true faith. Daily in this Christian church the Holy Spirit abundantly forgives all sins—mine and those of all believers. On the last day the Holy Spirit will raise me and all the dead and will give to me and all believers in Christ eternal life.[50]

When the Holy Spirit produces faith, Jesus "will sanctify those who believe in him by sending into their hearts the Holy Spirit, who will rule, and make them alive and defend them against the devil and the power of sin."[51] When the Holy Spirit dwells in our hearts, we love God with the very love with which God loves us. Our love for God flows forth in an absolute orientation to God that Congar described as holiness. The Holy Spirit perfects our human freedom such that there is complete concurrence between our own desire and will and the desire and will of God. We cooperate in disciplined synergy with God's grace. We follow the way of the cross. In so doing, we receive a host of spiritual gifts and fruits: love, joy, peace, patience, generosity, faithfulness, gentleness, and self-control.[52] The Spirit binds us to God, through Jesus Christ, and to one another, fostering a community in which we truly are members one of another.[53]

Confident of the work of the Holy Spirit, the *Augsburg Confession* declares "that this faith is bound to yield good fruits and that it ought to do good works commanded by God on account of God's will."[54] Lutheran Christians emphasize our cooperation with the Spirit's work of producing and responding in faith is neither instantaneous nor automatic. Rather, receiving faith and responding in faith are the daily living out of baptism. In baptism, "the old creature in us with all sins and evil desires is to be drowned and die through daily contrition and repentance, and on the other hand, daily a new person is to come forth and rise up to live before God in righteousness and purity forever."[55] Thus, receiving the gospel in preaching is not a one-time experience. The Holy Spirit continues to produce faith in us as we hear the gospel proclaimed throughout our lives.

The gospel proclaimed in a way that is meaningful and relevant is a third sign the Holy Spirit is at work. Rather than allowing the gospel to become a static doctrine or concept, the Holy Spirit interprets or provides a perspective on the paschal mystery or mission of Jesus, so God's saving work is relevant and meaningful to the faith community, church, and world at a given moment. As such, the Holy Spirit is the revelation of the Word, the message, or good news of Jesus that God gives through the preacher to a particular faith community on a given occasion. McDonnell says that through faith the Holy Spirit opens to every believer that horizon where the Spirit operates in a unique way, within which revelation is appropriated.[56]

McDonnell observes that the Johannine materials present the Holy Spirit giving knowledge about Jesus to those who believe.[57] This way of knowing is rooted in individual and community experiences and is not based on the reception of dramatic gifts and extraordinary experiences of the Spirit. Rather, in the Johannine writings, knowledge from the Holy Spirit comes through the quieter, more common inner experience, in both individuals and the community, which brings the presence of the Spirit into conscious awareness. Knowledge that comes from the Holy Spirit is comparable to, but distinct from, the experience of the Spirit in the "Abba, Father" passages.[58]

In First Corinthians, Paul understands natural knowledge and understanding as insufficient for knowing the mind of God. We know the mind of Christ through the Holy Spirit.[59] The knowledge that comes from the Holy Spirit, then, is beyond study, though study certainly contributes to the Spirit's revelation. In fact, the knowledge that comes from the Holy Spirit is informed and facilitated by traditional study. Knowledge from the Holy Spirit also comes from within the individual and community and is not received dramatically from outside. Asking, "What is the good news?" is shorthand for asking what particular gospel word the Spirit imparts to the preacher for a specific faith community on a given occasion.

Fourth, *the Holy Spirit anoints the preaching and hearing of the gospel*. Mary Catherine Hilkert, OP, calls the Holy Spirit "the passionate fire, the compassionate presence, and the strong driving wind empowering both the preaching and the hearing of the Gospel."[60] Hilkert distinguishes between the preaching and the hearing of the gospel and the preacher and hearers of the gospel. The Holy Spirit anoints the entire event in which the gospel is preached and not merely those who participate in it. Sometimes, the Spirit's anointing is forceful, like the sound of rushing wind on Luke's Pentecost, blowing faith communities where they do not want to go. More often, the Spirit's anointing is subtle, gentle, and intimate, as it was for the disciples in John's Gospel, when Jesus breathed on them and said, "Receive the Holy Spirit."

The Spirit's anointing begins long before the preacher utters the first word of the sermon. Ideally, the Holy Spirit is the "how"—the way the good news about Jesus is determined, the sermon crafted, and the delivery decided, rehearsed, and executed. In daily life, as well as in worship, the Holy Spirit also anoints the assembly with the capacity to hear the gospel of Jesus Christ and the desire to respond actively to that Word in faith, in daily discipleship, and in response to the events of the world.

The Holy Spirit anoints the preaching by working through the liturgy to prepare the preacher to proclaim and the assembly to receive the Word and by providing the first opportunity to respond to the good news in faith, prayer, and discipleship.[61] Changes in worship practice caused by the pandemic make me more attuned to the Holy Spirit anointing preaching through the liturgy of daily life as reported in the daily news broadcast, press conferences, inspiring stories of volunteers and first responders, and tragic notices of violence and death. The Holy Spirit anoints preaching through our awareness of relationships we can no longer take for granted, especially our relationship with God through in-person worship. As so often happens in prayer, when I ask Jesus to send the Holy Spirit to anoint my preaching, I become more aware of all the signs Jesus is sending the Holy Spirit, of how much bigger preaching is than my efforts, and of the grace and power with which the proclamation of the gospel is anointed.

Fifth, *the Holy Spirit yokes us to the Word.* The church confesses the Holy Spirit conceived Jesus Christ, uniting the Son of God to the humanity of Jesus. So too the Holy Spirit unites the Word of God to the church, the human body of

Christ, and through the church, to humankind. Scripture employs many images to describe this uniting. For example, as we have seen, Jesus invites us to take his yoke upon us and learn from him.[62] In John, Jesus declares, "I am the vine; you are the branches. If you remain in me and I in you, you will bear much fruit; apart from me you can do nothing."[63] Through the prophet Jeremiah, the Lord God declares, "I will put my law within them, and I will write it on their hearts; and I will be their God, and they shall be my people."[64]

Jeremiah makes plain that putting God's law within us—writing it on our hearts, yoking us to Christ, and connecting us to Jesus like branches to a vine—is God's activity and not something we accomplish on our own. The Spirit uses the word, proclaimed in sermon, study, and song, to yoke us to the Word.

We know the Spirit is working when, as Deuteronomy testifies, "the word is very near to you; it is in your mouth and in your heart for you to observe."[65] We experience the Spirit yoking us to the Word when references to biblical stories and characters become part of everyday conversation and we incorporate biblical phrases in our everyday speech. We experience the Spirit yoking us to the Word when individuals and especially faith communities make decisions based on Jesus's command to love one another, to love our enemies and pray for them, and to love our neighbors as ourselves.[66] We experience the Spirit yoking us to the Word when people leave the sermon to "preach sermons" of their own in their homes, schools, workplaces, and neighborhoods. We experience the Spirit yoking us to the Word when the stranger becomes the neighbor and justice and solidarity become expressions of faithfulness to Christ.

We certainly cooperate with and participate in the Spirit's yoking us to the Word. So, Paul writes to the Colossians, "Let the word of Christ dwell in you richly; teach and admonish one another in all wisdom; and with gratitude in your hearts sing psalms, hymns, and spiritual songs to God."[67] As we study the Bible, memorize passages, sing psalms, and participate in preaching, the Holy Spirit yokes us to the Word. Through the work of the Spirit, these activities become more than a way for us to acquire and internalize information, as we would when preparing for an exam, or experience admiration and inspiration, as we would from a work of art. Through the work of the Spirit, the Word becomes the language and images with which we think, hope, dream, and express ourselves. The Word provides our worldview and frame of reference. The Word becomes our guiding principles, not as an external law but as an internal compass. The Word stirs and teaches us how to speak of God to others and in the world, particularly in the public square. More than a text to be studied, the Bible becomes the book of our family stories, the characters in its pages our ancestors in the faith. The Spirit works through the proclaimed word to yoke us to the Word.

Welcoming the Holy Spirit in Preaching

Yves Congar stressed that our theologies of the Spirit will inevitably be inadequate. He believed it is more important to live in the Spirit than to try to articulate the Spirit's mystery.[68] When we stop searching for the Holy Spirit, preach about Jesus, and notice the signs the Holy Spirit moves, gifts, and gives life in and through preaching, we welcome the Holy Spirit. Preachers can open our arms in welcome even farther by practicing spiritual disciplines, through which we cooperate with the Holy Spirit.

Congar holds that cooperation of the faithful is essential, for the Spirit does not violate but rather elevates our existence as free and active subjects.[69] This understanding of the relationship between the Holy Spirit and humanity is different from understanding the preacher as an object into which the Holy Spirit pours a sermon. When we actively cooperate with the Holy Spirit, Jesus's words ring true: "Do not worry about how you are to defend yourselves or what you are to say, for the Holy Spirit will teach you at that very hour what you ought to say."[70] In the moment of trial, we find comfort in Jesus's words when we have cooperated with and learned from the Holy Spirit all along.

Preachers actively welcome and cooperate with the Holy Spirit by (1) taking Jesus's yoke upon them, (2) reflecting, (3) praying, (4) waiting, (5) testing and distinguishing, and (6) expecting. Preachers welcome the Spirit using different combinations and emphases of these disciplines during different seasons of preaching.

First, preachers welcome the Holy Spirit by *taking Jesus's yoke upon them*. William Willimon argues the preacher's chief homiletical-moral task is to be yoked so securely and joyously to the word that in the process of the proclamation of the word, we become the word, and it dwells in us richly.[71] Jesus certainly yokes us to his death and resurrection in the waters of baptism. As previously discussed, the Holy Spirit yokes us to the Word in preaching. As preachers, we welcome the Holy Spirit by intentionally taking Jesus's yoke upon us. The Christian tradition provides practices that help us, including asceticism, prayer, Bible study, fasting, almsgiving, spiritual direction, acts of charity, and advocacy. As a preacher, I find three additional practices especially helpful: (1) preaching from a place of grace, (2) participating in individual confession and absolution, and (3) embracing sermon preparation as a pilgrimage.

Preachers take Jesus's yoke upon them by putting ourselves in a place of grace when we prepare sermons and preach.[72] By a *place of grace*, I mean a place within us where God speaks, and we hear and listen. It is a state of mind and heart in which we are keenly aware of both our need for God's grace and God's gift of unconditional love, forgiveness, acceptance, and a second chance. Our place of grace is that chamber or room in our hearts where we come face-to-face with ourselves and with Jesus. A place of grace might be a memory of a time when we experienced God's grace as real, tangible, and immediate. Places of grace abide with us and are readily accessible to us. The more regularly we return to them, the more easily we return to them. When we recall and return to them, both our need for and God's gift of grace remain vivid and real; we may even experience God's gift of grace anew. Places of grace are true to us regardless of what others may think. The uncluttering, centering, prayer, and meditation by which we return to a place of grace and welcome the Holy Spirit are essential to how we prepare sermons and preach.

Preachers take Jesus's yoke upon them through regular confession and absolution. Returning to and preaching from a place of grace involves self-examination, confession, and forgiveness. Hilkert correctly asserts the Christian community, and especially those entrusted with a ministry of the word, are called to reflect on how their own lives and words may present stumbling blocks to the preaching and hearing of the Gospel. She observes, while the gospel itself is a kind of stumbling block, "ecclesial structures and the church's ministers of the word can present another kind of stumbling-block, a counter-witness which contradicts the words they preach."[73] Welcoming the Holy Spirit includes repenting of and amending those things in the life of the preacher and the life of the faith community that hinder the proclamation of Jesus as Savior.

Preachers take Jesus's yoke upon them when we approach sermon preparation and preaching as a pilgrimage. By *pilgrimage*, I do not mean a physical journey but a journey of spiritual significance to a place that is important to a person's beliefs and faith. Sermon preparation and preaching is a spiritual journey into the very presence of Jesus as Savior, when this good news is the goal of preaching. Approaching sermon preparation and preaching as a pilgrimage is very different from approaching sermon preparation and preaching as conducting research, preparing a speech or a lecture, persuading or recruiting, and certainly completing a task. Pilgrimage shapes sermon preparation and preaching so that we welcome the Holy Spirit, seek Jesus, arrive at his good news for his people, and preach as one returning from a significant spiritual journey.

Second, preachers welcome the Holy Spirit by *reflecting*. We reflect on when and where the Holy Spirit comes to us in sermon preparation. With our faith community and also with the church, we reflect on where and when the Holy Spirit comes in preaching. The purpose of this reflection is so we might become more aware of the Spirit's presence and especially attuned to welcoming the Holy Spirit when we are in those places where we received the Holy Spirit before. It leads to exploring how we understand and discern the Holy Spirit's presence. For example, we recognize an experience of the Holy Spirit is not identical with emotions, preferences, and aesthetics.

In sermon preparation, the Holy Spirit never comes to me when I sit staring at a blank computer screen. Over the years, I have learned to expect the Holy Spirit will come sometime after I seriously pray over and study the Scripture readings for preaching. The Holy Spirit comes as insights that bubble up from within me as I walk, take a shower, or am falling asleep. The Holy Spirit also comes to me in normal conversation when people say things that immediately connect with and even spark the sermon I am preparing. I once taught a student who welcomed the Holy Spirit as she cooked; her family loved the weeks she preached because they ate so well. The Holy Spirit came to another student as he drew the biblical story on which he was preaching. In time, he came to preach from his drawing rather than from a traditional manuscript.

The Holy Spirit is generous in providing revelation for preaching; however, the Spirit's generosity is fleeting. When we are not prepared to receive, the Spirit's revelation seems to quickly dissipate. I find it devastating when the Spirit provides a good news statement, sermon structure, or exact language for part of the sermon and I find the Spirit's revelation has vanished when I try to recall it later. I have learned to never be without, initially, a pad and pen, then a digital recorder, and now a recording app on my smartphone, so I am always prepared to welcome the Spirit's revelation.

Ideally, preachers do not reflect in isolation but with their faith community, since all individuals possess biases and presuppositions that may obscure our reflection. Reflecting on the Holy Spirit together as a faith community reveals and reminds us that the Holy Spirit is not anyone's individual or personal possession. In fact, Jesus promises to send the Holy Spirit to his community, the church. In the New Testament, Jesus does not send the Holy Spirit to individuals apart from the church. In both Acts 2 and John 20, the Holy Spirit comes to the faith community; Thomas, for example, was not present when Jesus breathed the Holy Spirit into the disciples. Thomas's reaction to the disciples' report that they had seen the Lord indicates he had not received the Holy Spirit.[74] While it is certainly possible Jesus sends the Holy Spirit to individuals apart from the church, such a revelation is extraordinary rather than normative and never intended to be used to discount others' revelations or against the faith community. Jesus might send the Holy Spirit to communities rather than individuals because his work is to draw us together. Together, communities can better distinguish and test whether what we receive is from the Holy Spirit or some other spirit, such as our American spirit of individualism.

Faith communities might begin reflecting together by considering ways the signs of the Holy Spirit discussed in this chapter are manifest among them. I value people considering what the Holy Spirit was doing during the sermon; this makes for a lively midweek conversation over coffee. This conversation about preaching is very different from asking whether people liked the sermon, got anything out of the sermon, or had a subjective experience of the Holy Spirit during the sermon.

Third, preachers welcome the Holy Spirit by *praying*. Prayer is attentiveness and receptivity in the presence of God. It includes both asking and listening. Ideally, sermon preparation and preaching becomes for the preacher a form of prayer. At the very least, preachers designate time to pray as part of sermon preparation. Welcoming the Holy Spirit through prayer is integral to sermon preparation; therefore, this will be a substantive time.[75]

Preachers welcome the Holy Spirit by asking. Preachers pray over the readings, asking for the fire of the Holy Spirit to kindle "the now meaning,"[76] the good news Jesus brings, in our hearts. We ask the Holy Spirit to open the heart of the assembly, so that God's Word falls on receptive ears. Preachers ask the Holy Spirit to remove from us and from our hearers all those things that would stand in the way of receiving the gospel. We pray for ourselves, asking the Holy Spirit to guide our preparation, help us maintain our role as a kind of "interloper" in the assembly, and grant us grace to differentiate our words from God's, so that we do not preach "what might be expedient, popular, burning in the preacher's heart, the correct answer, or best course of action, but not necessarily a word from God."[77] Preachers pray, asking and expecting the real movement of the Holy Spirit in themselves and in the assembly.[78]

Preachers welcome the Holy Spirit by listening. Preachers listen for the Holy Spirit breathing the Word, to the people they serve, to the world, to the occasion, and in their own lives before they utter a word. *Fulfilled in Your Hearing* reminds preachers that we are to be listeners before we are speakers, remaining open to the Lord's voice not only in the Scriptures but in the events of our daily lives and the experience of our brothers and sisters.[79] Preachers listen first because the primary speaker to, in, and through the Christian community is the living God through the presence of the risen Christ and by the power of the Spirit. Attentively listening to the Scripture and the people, *Fulfilled in Your Hearing* asserts, is perhaps the form of prayer most appropriate to the spirituality of the preacher.[80]

After listening to Scripture, our faith community, and the world, as we attentively and intentionally listen for the Holy Spirit to bring us the Word, we learn to distinguish our own voice from the Spirit using our own inner voice. When God spoke to Elijah, God was not heard in the earthquake, wind, or fire. Elijah heard God in a still, small voice.[81] As I reflect on this story in the context of listening to the Holy Spirit, I am convinced the still, small voice Elijah heard God speak with was his own. How often in prayer "the Advocate, the Holy Spirit, whom the Father will send in my name" uses our own inner voice to "teach you everything, and remind you of all that I have said to you."[82]

Fourth, *preachers welcome the Holy Spirit by waiting on the Holy Spirit.* "And see, I am sending upon you what my Father promised," Jesus tells the disciples just before ascending, "so stay here in the city until you have been clothed with power from on high."[83] After commissioning the disciples as witnesses,

Jesus tells them to wait on the Holy Spirit. Intentionally waiting on the Holy Spirit means preachers build time into our sermon preparation and our lives so the Holy Spirit has time to speak and act. Preachers will certainly begin sermon preparation early in the week and work through their routine at a leisurely pace. I teach preachers to give sermons time to incubate and pass on the wisdom I received: Sermons are prepared in slow cookers rather than microwave ovens. If we try to cook them too quickly, they come out half-baked. Many preachers have experienced the disappointment of rushing to prepare a sermon, preaching on Sunday, and having the sermon truly come together Monday afternoon when it is too late. If only we could have waited on the Holy Spirit.

Fifth, as I suggested when discussing communal reflection, *preachers welcome the Holy Spirit by distinguishing and testing what we receive from the Holy Spirit.* Congar provides an example of distinguishing the Holy Spirit. He cautions against confusing the Holy Spirit with either the breath that enlivens our bodies or the simple animation of nature, which we risk doing by stringing together Old Testament passages in which the word "spirit—breath—*ruach*" is found.[84] Congar resists considering the Spirit as breath as a purely immanent life force that permeates the universe and causes its evolution. The *Breath* is never an isolated breath, nor simply the animating life force that is present only in the world. It always carries forth the *Word*. The point is to resist assuming any "breath" is the Holy Spirit.

I am not infrequently asked what I would do if, as I was walking into worship, the Holy Spirit told me to discard the sermon I had prepared and preach something else. The inquisitor is often taken aback when I respond that I would ignore what I am hearing or feeling, because it is probably a spirit other than the Holy Spirit. The *Holy* Spirit is the Spirit of Christ, the Spirit of Truth, the life-giving, gift-bringing, suffering Spirit who empowers us to resist what Charles L. Campbell calls the powers of death at work in the world.[85] These spirits work through concrete, material institutions, structures, and systems—including the church—to rebel against God by making idols of themselves and placing their own desires above God's purpose for humanity and creation. White supremacy, fear, survival, affluence, discrimination, division, exploitation, hate, and my own ego are but a few examples of these spirits.

I find it possible, even likely, one of these spirits would attempt to diminish or derail preaching Jesus by cajoling me to discard my sermon and preach something else. If I trust my routine of sermon preparation and have faithfully prepared, the Holy Spirit will have had ample opportunity to determine and shape the message. I certainly nuance the sermon I prepared when something significant happens the night before I preach. Completely discarding my prepared sermon shortly before preaching can be only the work of another spirit—my own needs, emotions, anxieties, and passions; or apprehension about the congregation's reaction; or an agenda other than proclaiming Jesus; or "the devil and all the forces that defy God, the powers of this world that rebel against God, and the ways of sin that draw [us] from God."[86]

The author of First John writes, "Beloved, do not believe every spirit, but test the spirits to see whether they are from God; for many false prophets have gone out into the world. By this you know the Spirit of God: every spirit that confesses that Jesus Christ has come in the flesh is from God, and every spirit that does not confess Jesus is not from God."[87] Preachers test messages we receive with the church to avoid the temptation of concluding the Holy Spirit imparts a word to us individually that is apart from or unavailable to the church. Congar reminds us that in both the Gospel of John and the Pauline epistles, the Holy Spirit is promised and given to the church rather than to individuals.[88] Jesus promises, "The Father will give *you* [plural] the Spirit."[89] Paul proclaimed, "The love of God is poured forth in *our* hearts through the Holy Spirit who is given to *us*."[90] Elizabeth Groppe adds, "This is not to say that the Holy Spirit is operative only within the life of the Church. To the contrary, Congar affirmed the Holy Spirit is present wherever there is truth."[91]

Distinguishing the Holy Spirit is a second reason preachers welcome the Holy Spirit in community rather than isolation, since testing the Holy Spirit is an ensemble rather than a solo act. Paul reminds us, "To each is given the manifestation of the Spirit for the common good. To one is given through the Spirit the utterance of wisdom, and to another the utterance of knowledge according to the same Spirit, . . . to another various kinds of tongues, to another the interpretation of tongues."[92] We need each other to listen to the Spirit for the common good. Commentaries, creeds, colleagues, and conversations with people very different from us all assist us in testing what we receive from the Spirit.

Sixth, *preachers welcome the Holy Spirit by expecting the Spirit to act in all the ways Jesus promised.* Expecting the Holy Spirit is more than a feeling. We expect the Holy Spirit as a reality when we develop a method of sermon preparation we trust and rely on. Preachers do well to embrace method as a way of welcoming and cooperating with the Holy Spirit. As the Spirit does not come to the church haphazardly but through the means of grace, so too the Spirit does not come to the preacher haphazardly but through a means of sermon preparation. So, method is a friend and not a constraint. A method, an orderly way of proceeding, guarantees some result. Ideally, that result is the goal of preaching, to proclaim Jesus as Savior. As the Holy Spirit works through a homiletic method, we can expect the Holy Spirit to bring us to the good news of Jesus as Savior that is meaningful to the faith community in the world at a given moment in time.

Practicing these spiritual disciplines to welcome the Holy Spirit adds another layer to a method of sermon preparation. If a method of sermon preparation tells us *what* to do, spiritual practices that help us welcome the Holy Spirit tell us *how* to do it. Spiritual disciplines for preaching are therefore best practiced as an integral part of sermon preparation. Of course, the surest way to welcome the Holy Spirit is to choose proclaiming Jesus as Savior as the goal of preaching.

3

Pulpit

What Is the Goal of Your Preaching?

What is the goal of your preaching? What purpose does your preaching serve? Each Sunday, as you exit the pulpit, what do you hope has happened? On Sunday afternoon or Sunday night, as you close your eyes and think back to your sermon, what causes your sleep to be sound or restless?

I sleep soundly when I preach Jesus. My denomination defines preaching as "the living and contemporary voice of one who interprets in all the Scriptures the things concerning Jesus Christ."[1] Preaching Jesus is our call, privilege, and responsibility as public ministers of Christ's church. Preaching Jesus is also a preacher's choice.

What is the goal of your preaching? Your goal is more concrete and precise than a universal ideal—to proclaim the gospel or to preach the word of God. Your goal is the core message that fills your heart, guides your life and ministry, and stands front and center in your pulpit. You may uncover your goal by reviewing six months of sermons or asking parishioners what they heard from you in the last six months. Some say every preacher has but a single sermon and preaches endless varieties of this message. If this is true, your single sermon is your goal.

Knowing the goal of our preaching, what we hope to accomplish when we stand in the pulpit, provides a clear path for interpreting Scripture and determining the message we preach. Our goal guides the form we give our sermon, the language we select, and the delivery with which we preach. Our goal gives us courage to preach—or to refrain from preaching—a message that is difficult or challenging, popular or pleasing. Our goal comforts us when people "having itching ears"[2] criticize our sermons or desire them to be different, and when we pay a personal price—people being upset, withholding their offerings, leaving our church, or something more sinister—for our preaching. When we do not know the goal of our preaching, we may find ourselves "tossed to and fro and blown about by every wind of doctrine,"[3] preaching a message or in a manner we do not intend, approve of, or agree with.

What is the goal of your preaching? If your goal is to preach the word of God, what Bible verse best summarizes that word? If our goal is to "make disciples, . . . teaching them to observe all that I have commanded you,"[4] our sermons will be instruction. If our goal is for people "to do justice, and to love kindness, and to walk humbly with your God,"[5] our preaching will be moral exhortation. If our goal is to "comfort, O comfort, my people,"[6] our preaching will reinforce the status quo. If our goal is to herald the news "The time is fulfilled, and the kingdom of God has come near; repent, and believe in the good news,"[7] our preaching will call or invite people to turn and be part of God's reign. If our goal is that people decide to open the door of our hearts to Jesus, "Listen! I am standing at the door, knocking; if you hear my voice and open the door, I will come in to you and eat with you, and you with me,"[8] then our sermons will be crafted so that people hear him knocking. If our goal is to "set before [the people] life and death, blessings and curses," our sermons will lay out the contrast and encourage people to "choose life."[9] All these goals are legitimate, even laudable. Yet, they are secondary, since the primary goal of Christian preaching is to be "the living and contemporary voice of one who interprets in all the Scriptures the things concerning Jesus Christ."[10]

Preach Jesus!

I indicated in the preface that the goal of my preaching and teaching of preaching is summarized in First Corinthians 1:22–24: to proclaim Christ crucified or to preach Jesus. I strive to guarantee one place Jesus will be when I preach is in the pulpit, because I intentionally put Jesus there in the sermon.

Paul declares "Christ the power of God and the wisdom of God."[11] In Christ, God deliberately chooses to reveal God's own self and exercise divine power, the goal of which is salvation, the redemption and reconciliation of humanity and all creation. To preach Jesus or, in Paul's words, to "proclaim Christ crucified," is to facilitate God's power to change all things for the better, upend the status quo, restore life and the world to what God intends, and transform death into new life.

The irony is that human power and wisdom render Jesus and the cross the last place humanity expects to discover God's ultimate wisdom and power. We therefore pursue human power and wisdom in our attempts to know God and find our way to God. In preaching, these include proving, convincing, persuading, coercing, and changing the subject altogether. However, Jesus thwarts or relieves us of our attempts to figure out and find God. In Jesus, God chooses to know us as one of us and comes to us in the worst situations and circumstances, as is exemplified in the cross. Preaching

Jesus announces that God is with us and, in Christ, raises us from death to new life.

At its best, preaching Jesus raises the dead; that is, through preaching Jesus, God brings people from death to new life. I do not believe that preaching Jesus will literally resuscitate a corpse. I do believe that whenever the church gathers, people in the assembly are struggling with or are lost in some form of death. Within us and around us, we battle death-dealing powers and realities. We discover the weakness, even the futility, of human power and the limits, even folly, of human wisdom. We need God to come to us and raise us and restore us. We preach Jesus, we proclaim Christ crucified, because it is the power and wisdom of God to bring us new life.

When I say that the goal is to proclaim Christ or preach Jesus, I intend more than including a passing reference, a brief mention, a formula, or a doctrine in the sermon. Proclaiming Christ Jesus in a theoretical or theological manner is insufficient. We preach what in chapter 2 I called "the now meaning,"[12] the good news Jesus brings, in our hearts. To proclaim Christ or preach Jesus is to interpret or provide a perspective on Jesus's life, death, and resurrection that is relevant and meaningful to the faith community, church, and world at a specific moment in time. Preachers cannot do this without standing securely on Scripture, theology, tradition, and doctrine, and being yoked closely and securely to Jesus.

I also intend more than preaching *about* Jesus. To preach Jesus is to participate in and facilitate an encounter with the risen Christ for preacher and assembly alike. This preaching begins with trusting, if not knowing, Jesus is in the room when we preach. This preaching cooperates with the Holy Spirit in evoking in the assembly an experience of Jesus standing among us, greeting us with peace, showing us his hands and his side, breathing the Holy Spirit into us, and sending us to extend his own ministry of forgiveness and reconciliation. Or this preaching cooperates with the Holy Spirit to evoke the experience of Jesus opening our minds to understand the Scriptures to witness to the Messiah's suffering, death, and resurrection, and sending us to proclaim repentance and forgiveness of sins in his name. This preaching helps people "taste" grace or the gospel and experience the real presence of Christ in, with, and under the words of the sermon spoken and heard.

Preaching Jesus means explicitly naming Jesus in a way that my friend Mary Catherine Hilkert describes as "naming grace found in the depths of human experience."[13] Preaching Jesus leads the community to name Christ's gracious presence in their midst. For example, as bishop, my proclamation of Jesus must include naming how I see Jesus graciously at work in every congregation where I visit and preach. Word, water, bread, and wine are reliable touchstones. Yet, I try to find something particular to each congregation; sometimes this is challenging. But the effort leads me to view the congregation and its situation not through its difficulties but through the lens of grace revealed in Jesus Christ. I hope the congregation will see itself in the same way.

Preaching Jesus means proclaiming Christ as Savior before naming Jesus anything else. In all three of the synoptic gospels, a moment comes when Jesus asks the disciples, "Who do people say that I am? . . . But who do you say that I am?"[14] The disciples offer some very impressive answers: John the Baptist, Elijah, Jeremiah, one of the prophets. Peter answers, "the Messiah, the Son of the living God."[15] Jesus declared the other disciples' answers human and Peter's answer a revelation from God. With too much regularity, when we preachers answer Jesus's question, we offer human answers, including prophet, teacher, miracle worker, healer, and example, and never announce the divine revelation that Jesus is Messiah and Son of the living

God. We assume the gospel, presume the gospel, and look to Jesus to show and tell us how to respond to the gospel.

This concern is not new. In *A Brief Introduction to What to Look for and Expect in the Gospels*, Martin Luther distinguishes between proclaiming and moralizing.[16] Luther writes, "Be sure, moreover, that you do not make Christ into a Moses, as if Christ did nothing more than teach and provide examples as the other saints do, as if the gospel were simply a textbook of teachings or laws." Luther is not saying Jesus is not our teacher and example. Indeed, we should grasp Christ, his words, works, and sufferings as an example we should follow and imitate. In the words of First Peter, "Christ suffered for you, leaving you an example, so that you should follow in his steps."[17] So, Luther says, as we see Jesus pray, fast, help people, and love them, we should too, both for ourselves and for our neighbors.

"However," Luther adds, and it is quite a *however,* "this is the smallest part of the gospel, on the basis of which it cannot yet even be called gospel." On this level, Christ's life remains his own and does not contribute anything to us. Luther instructs us to grasp Christ at what he calls "a much higher level." "Even though this higher level has for a long time been the very best," Luther says, "the preaching of it has been something rare." For Luther, before we make Jesus a Moses, we proclaim Christ as "the great fire of the love of God for us, whereby the heart and conscience become happy, secure, and content."

Preaching Jesus has taken on a new urgency for me since I came to the office of bishop. As an American Lutheran bishop, I am an itinerant preacher. Unless prevented by the Covid-19 pandemic, I preach in a different congregation every Sunday—sometimes more than one. Even preaching in a prepandemic average of fifty-seven congregations per year, it takes me three years to worship with the 115 congregations under my care. If I am lucky, I will get two or three chances to speak with my people of Jesus's life, death, and resurrection in a way that matters. So, itinerancy begets a certain sense of urgency. When I am at my best, I am clear that, regardless of what other agendas are playing out during my visit to a congregation, and there are often many, my primary goal is that people go away from worship saying, "The bishop preached the gospel." I approach each sermon with the awareness that I have only a handful of opportunities—perhaps as few as two—to proclaim Christ and preach Jesus into my people's lives. I preach Jesus as Savior because everyone has a finite number of opportunities to proclaim and receive this good news, and every opportunity may be our last. As we determine the goal of preaching, recognizing that our ministry is not open-ended can have a significant impact.

Preaching Jesus is a choice that preachers make every time we sit down to prepare a sermon. I believe that for Christian preachers preaching in Christian congregations, preaching Jesus is the best and even the only choice. Preaching Jesus is our call, privilege, and responsibility as public ministers of Christ's church. Preaching Jesus yokes both preacher and congregation to Jesus, welcomes the Holy Spirit, and fulfills God's purpose in establishing preaching—to produce faith. Preaching Jesus is what the church expects us to do. Choosing Jesus as the goal of preaching can therefore seem obvious, even instinctive. Regrettably, it is not.

Choosing Jesus as the goal of preaching is not always wise, safe, easy, or automatic. Paul declares preaching Christ crucified a stumbling block and foolishness.[18] Over time, preachers discover Paul speaks truth. As I lead continuing education events, perhaps the most animated, even agitated, conversation I hear among preachers is about whether and how we include Jesus in sermons. Preachers wonder whether Jesus must be the subject of *every* sermon, why we cannot trust or even expect the congregation knows Jesus and therefore begin preaching from that starting point, and if certain Sundays, seasons of life and ministry, and occasions call for pursuing a goal other than preaching Jesus. I am all too familiar with the temptation to avoid the stumbling block, play it smart, and preach on a matter that at the moment seems more urgent and important than preaching Jesus. Yes, putting Jesus front and center in the pulpit calls for a conscious, weekly choice.

Stumbling Blocks to Preaching Jesus

Most preachers do not decide to escort Jesus to the rear of the pulpit or evict Jesus altogether from the sermon. That choice, often unconscious, is more a matter of erosion. Confronted by several stumbling blocks, our goal for preaching may change with time and circumstance. Choosing or recommitting to Jesus as the goal of preaching requires preachers to undertake the spiritual work of coming to terms with the stumbling blocks and foolishness of preaching Christ and discovering how preaching Jesus responds to and perhaps overcomes them as the power and wisdom of God. Preaching Jesus can seem foolish and become a stumbling block when to do so (1) interferes with other goals and agendas, (2) fails to get results, (3) challenges our interpretation of Scripture, (4) exposes false gods, (5) makes exclusive claims, and (6) surrenders to Jesus. Jesus directs those who would be his disciples to "count the cost."[19] Counting the cost is equally essential for preachers who would make Jesus the goal of preaching. Preaching Jesus certainly pays these costs, but not necessarily in ways we might hope, expect, or desire.

Interfering with Other Goals and Agendas

Preaching Jesus can be a stumbling block when doing so *interferes with other goals and agendas.* Some goals and agendas come from the preacher; others are imposed on the preacher. All preachers bring goals and agendas to preaching—our particular emphases, passions, projects, causes, and directions. Over time, preachers may experience preaching these topics as increasingly important, especially when people, systems, and circumstances cause us to grow impatient or become justifiably outraged, or when we are convinced our agenda is a word from the Lord. With the prophet Jeremiah we declare, "If I say, 'I will not mention him, or speak any more in his name,' then within me there is something like a burning fire shut up in my bones; I am weary with holding it in, and I cannot."[20] Almost imperceptibly, our agenda, including our feelings about it, becomes the lens through which we interpret Scripture and circumstance, and arrive at and preach our message.

Other goals and agendas are imposed on the preacher. Preachers feel the pressure to explain Scripture, speak to specific situations, explore the human condition, address social issues, expound on their congregations' mission statements, respond to pastoral concerns, raise money, and inspire their congregations to do what it takes to grow. The bishop's office and denomination expect preachers to push their priorities, church institutions want preachers to highlight their mission, and the world needs preachers to call people to respond in love for the neighbor. And preachers are to do all this while attracting more people and not alienating the people who are there.

Unless the preacher remains attentive, other goals and agendas find or force their way into the pulpit. Jesus is assumed or presumed as the reason and motivation for a particular agenda, though the connection to Jesus may never be evaluated or articulated explicitly. We may even preach another agenda in place of rather than on account of Jesus, especially when Jesus gets in the way. Eventually, some listeners are likely to complain the preacher's personal agenda, the denomination's agenda, politics, or (preserving or undermining) the culture removed Jesus from the sermon altogether.

Even as the fire of our agenda burns within us, especially as other agendas are imposed upon us, we choose preaching Jesus rather than any agenda as the goal of preaching because *Jesus frees and empowers us to preach about everything.* No subject is off-limits for Jesus. For example, a quick survey of the Sermon on the Mount[21] finds Jesus addressing social structure, anger, adultery, divorce, enemies, integrity, judgment, money, and retaliation, as well as fasting, prayer, and profaning the holy. Following Jesus's own example as a preacher, every issue is fair game for preaching; no topic is out of bounds. To say otherwise is to conclude Jesus agrees with our understanding of the topic, Jesus has nothing to say about the topic, or some topics or areas of life are outside or beyond Jesus's reign.

Jesus, the mystery of faith, is such a simple message. "Christ has died. Christ is risen. Christ will come again." Jesus says, "And I, when I am lifted up from the earth, will draw all people to myself."[22] Jesus also says, "I am the light of the world."[23] When we lift Jesus up in preaching and contemplate his life, death, and resurrection through the lens of specific Scripture, issues, and circumstances, at its best, the wisdom and power of this good news are revealed. At the same time, proclaiming Jesus enlightens the specific Scripture, issues, and circumstances that surround God's people as they live their lives and come together as church, as well as the issues facing the world. The good news of Jesus authorizes and empowers preachers to address any and every subject.

The good news of Jesus also informs, directs, and limits both what preachers say and how we say it. "I will do whatever you ask in my name," Jesus promises, "so that the Father may be glorified in the Son."[24] Preaching Jesus helps to ensure our agenda and the manner in which we accomplish it are consistent with and grounded in Jesus and pursued in Jesus's name. Preaching Jesus means becoming humble and obedient as Jesus was, in this instance, by subordinating our agenda to Jesus or, more likely, by yoking our agenda closely and securely to Jesus, and making this connection explicit. In sermons, we draw a clear and direct line from Jesus to the agenda or subject.

If we cannot draw such a line, either what is being sought is inconsistent with Jesus, we are not yet ready to preach on the topic, or we need to consider whether preaching is the best way to address the subject. In making this determination, preachers must steel themselves to resist other goals that would replace Jesus as the goal of preaching and people who advocate for them. Resisting is especially difficult when goals are godly, urgent, and impactful and those advocating for them are important and influential. Preachers are therefore helped to resist when we are yoked closely and securely to Jesus. Yoked to Jesus, we remain cognizant that when we pursue another goal in preaching, we yield to someone or something else the place that belongs to Jesus.

Preachers maintain preaching Jesus as the goal by recognizing that, while preaching is special and prominent, it is not our only means of communication. Pastors and deacons today regularly use newsletters, podcasts, blog posts, and social media to communicate with their congregants and the world. When Jesus is the goal of preaching, leaders can use other means of communication to advocate for and pursue other goals that flow from and are in keeping with Jesus proclaimed from the pulpit. Preaching Jesus also limits how we accomplish any agenda, in the pulpit and out, because our manner and means must be consistent with Jesus. Jesus precludes employing fear, intimidation, coercion, or manipulation, for example, because Jesus did not use these tactics himself. Both our message and manner are to be consistent with asking in Jesus's name.

Most important, perhaps, preaching Jesus calls the church and its preachers to recognize the pulpit is neither a personal soapbox nor a *tabula rasa*, an absence of preconceived ideas or predetermined goals. Though lacking inclusive language, John 12:21—"Sir, we wish to see Jesus"—inscribed on many pulpits is as much direction and expectation as prayer. To choose preaching Jesus as our goal, especially when a fire from God burns within us, requires an active faith in which we are yoked closely and securely enough to Jesus that we trust Jesus to accomplish his agenda and empower his church to participate in it.

Lack of Results

Preaching Jesus becomes a stumbling block when it *fails to produce needed or desired results*. Church leaders frequently look to preaching to draw large crowds, raise lots of money, bring about social change, transform lives, and so generate the positive results the church seeks. Those seeking these kinds of results want clear, quick, profound, and lasting outcomes that remain under their control. People may even come to measure preaching, using the yardstick of the results they need or desire.

After all, Jesus's preaching produced positive results. According to Luke, the results of Jesus's preaching include ten lepers and a man who was blind receiving healing, Zacchaeus climbing down from his tree, and a crowd of 5,000 following Jesus to a deserted place to hear him preach. We can name preachers who produced similar results and imagine the same for ourselves.

Yet Jesus explicitly rejects the results we often seek. When Satan tempts Jesus with the world's preferred results, Jesus chooses faithfulness to God. And Jesus does not promise or guarantee these results to those who follow him. Instead, God intends Jesus to confound human wisdom and overturn human results. Jesus therefore warns, "If any want to become my followers, let them deny themselves and take up their cross and follow me."[25] Preaching Jesus is a stumbling block because dying and rising, rather than avoiding death, openness to self-sacrifice, sharing patiently in affliction, resisting the lure of power, foregoing influence and status, and refusing to compete according to the rules of the world, all of which Jesus modeled on the cross, are not the results we desire or seek. The results Jesus brings are the slow, subtle, small, and patient changes that the power of God produces.

Pursuing the results we want and need, we may tone down preaching that includes denying ourselves, taking up our cross, and following Jesus. We may turn away from the stories of creation, deliverance, freedom, abundance, empowerment, and life with and in God, contained in Scripture and embodied in Jesus Christ, as the governing narratives of our individual, ecclesiastical, and common life.

In their place, we turn to and preach the tall tales that we believe will generate the results we desire. These are stories of scarcity, of saving for a rainy day, of needing to work harder to do better, of being the best and winning the congregational or denominational or whatever-it-is competition. We turn to the cultural stories of the separation of faith and citizenship, of people getting what they deserve, of everything happening for a reason, of bigger is better. We preach messages of nostalgia for the past, fear of the future, and resistance to change. Or we preach messages about making a difference, about it all being up to us to make the world better. And we find biblical language with which to express these fables. We use all of these stories to pursue the results we want because the story of Jesus dying and rising may take us somewhere we don't want to go.

Mostly, rather than preaching and living out of the biblical narrative of being "baptized into Christ's death, buried with him by baptism into death, so that, just as Christ was raised from the dead by the glory of the Father, so we too might walk in newness of life,"[26] we preach messages that bolster our resolve never to die. The problem, of course, is that everything dies, including the people we love, the churches we serve, the things we cherish, the institutions we revere, and we ourselves. If we are honest with ourselves, the results we seek are often self-serving rather than Christ-centered. Even if we achieve them for a time, the results we seek are fleeting. The results we seek will perish.

Rather than change our message to obtain results that are temporary and may be incongruent with Jesus, we navigate the stumbling block by changing both our expectations and the results we seek, and celebrating the ways preaching Jesus makes the world better. First, we change our expectations of preaching. We acknowledge that Jesus bringing life out of death, rather than avoiding, negating, or sidestepping death, has always been a stumbling block, even for Jesus. The gospels report people did not always respond positively to Jesus's preaching because Jesus did not give them what they expected or desired. After Jesus's first sermon, the people of Nazareth drove Jesus out of town, and led him to the brow of the hill on which their town was built, "so that they might hurl him off the cliff." John reports that after Jesus finished preaching on the Bread of Life, "many of his disciples turned back and no longer went about with him."[27] Both Matthew and Mark report that Peter rebuked Jesus when Jesus predicted the results of his ministry would be rejection, suffering, death, and resurrection.[28] By the end of Mark's Easter, every one of Jesus's disciples has abandoned him.[29] We should not be surprised when preaching Jesus does not generate the human results we seek.

Second, we reevaluate the results we seek through preaching. Since people are inundated with messages about status, success, growth, financial security, certainty, and the hope of living forever, we can trust that people attending to Christian preaching are truly seeking Jesus. Perhaps they know the fallibility of other messages; perhaps they know their need of God. Perhaps they have exhausted themselves chasing after human results or attained those results and found them wanting. So they seek Jesus. Regrettably, congregations seeking human results want to speak about their church rather than Jesus. Ask those folks about Jesus and they tell you about their church, about how much they love their church, about how much their church is a family. They tell you about their pastor, about how great or cool their pastor is. Except the question was about Jesus. I used to think that if we could get people to come to church, they might come to know Jesus. Now I am convinced that if we can help people come to know Jesus, they just might come to church. We need to attend to people's questions about Jesus rather than preserving our church.

Third, we celebrate ways preaching Jesus makes the world better. In addition to producing faith, preaching Jesus resists the powers of death that work to oppose God, secure their own survival, dominate humanity, and bring chaos to the world.[30] Might Covid-19 be such a spirit? Mammon certainly is. Preaching Jesus is a critical act of nonviolent resistance to these destructive powers. As God began the first creation through the Word, God inaugurates the new creation through Jesus Christ, the Word made flesh. Jesus, as the incarnation of the Word, embodies God's way not merely in his life but most specifically in his choice of preaching as the means to the reign of God.[31] Regardless of how people respond to sermons, the proclamation of Jesus is itself a way the Christian community resists all those forces trying to divide, dishearten, and disassemble both the community of faith and the world God intends.

Preaching Jesus also empowers people to be their best. A wise pastor observed the suspension of in-person worship during the pandemic had a detrimental effect on the behavior of members of the congregation who could not or did not participate in worship virtually. It appears that hearing Jesus preached has a salutary effect on the way people behave and interact, which makes the world better. We call this salutary effect *sanctification* or *daily dying and rising with Christ*. It is a fruit of the Spirit that grows from faith when Jesus is preached; the pastor noticed the absence of this growth in people who had not heard Jesus preached recently. By making people more Christlike, preaching Jesus makes the world better.

When it comes to results, we do better to think of the cumulative effect of preaching, the small but significant ways sermons change people and faith communities, and through them the world, over weeks, years, and lifetimes. While the single sermon rarely overturns the hearer's worldview, the cumulative effect of small, transforming proclamation— and subsequent conversion—makes preaching an immensely important part of the ministry of the church.[32] Thus, the ministry of the Word requires a company of preachers who preach in a congregation's pulpit and people's lives over the course of many years. The preaching that takes place in the pulpit must also be partnered with the preaching of all Christians, who preach Jesus with words, through relationships, and in how the congregation lives.

Challenges Our Interpretation of Scripture

For Christians, the Bible is sacred, the norm of our faith and life, because the Bible proclaims Christ crucified as the power and wisdom of God. Thus, for Christians, to preach the word of God is to preach Jesus. Wherever we look in the Bible, we find God doing what God does in Jesus: bringing light out of darkness, life out of death, freedom out of oppression, and hope out of despair. Or, put another way, the Bible tells how, again and again, God establishes a covenant with God's people, God's people break that covenant, God remains faithful and forgives, and the covenant is renewed. Jesus, the Word made flesh,[33] is the sweeping story of God's saving activity, recorded in Scripture, lived out in a human life. So, the gospels attest that Jesus fulfills the Scriptures.[34]

Since, for Christians, to preach the word of God is to preach Jesus, my "goal verses" include words of Jesus. From John 12:32, I strive to preach Jesus's radical, all-inclusive grace. In John 10:10, Jesus says, "I came that they may have life, and have it abundantly." While denying ourselves, taking up our cross, and following Jesus[35] are the realities of discipleship in this world, Jesus wills and works to bring abundant life. This good news—God drawing creation to Godself and blessing creation with abundant life—is the story of Scripture. Therefore, for Christians, to preach the Bible is to preach Jesus.

This claim causes preachers to stumble. I am regularly "advised" that approaching Scripture as proclaiming Jesus challenges biblical interpretation in several ways. First, preaching Jesus inevitably leads to not treating all Scripture equally. The church draws out of Scripture an assemblage of texts that speak of or to God's salvation in Jesus Christ. While Scripture is the ultimate pool from which readings are drawn, the church has historically remembered a fairly limited number of readings. While the Bible provides the rule of faith (canon), the texts read in worship provide the proclamation of faith.[36] Passages that proclaim Jesus are weighted more heavily and deemed more important than passages that do not; passages that contradict the proclamation of

Jesus become even less important. The concern is that this approach does not embrace the entire Bible and so obscures the proclamation of God's word. We overcome this stumbling block by recognizing that, in practice, all Scripture is never of equal importance, except perhaps when studying Scripture academically.

Second, preaching Jesus subordinates a text's original intent to the church's interpretation of the text as a proclamation of Christ. Readings are lifted out of their historical and literary context in Scripture and placed in the context of the Christian year and the other pericopes read in worship. The greater context of readings is not the books in which they are found but the Sundays, feasts, seasons, and segments of the Christian year on which they are read. The immediate context is the worship life of the church, where they are related to the other readings, the liturgy of the day, and the assembly at prayer.[37]

The reason for this stumbling block may be an understanding of the Bible as an anthology or even a unified volume whose books, chapters, and verses each possess a single meaning or correct interpretation, which can be determined. To preach Jesus is to respect Scripture as overflowing with revelation rather than to reduce a passage to a single interpretation. Ambrose of Milan (d. 397) viewed Scripture as a mystery. Borrowing from Origen, he uses the image of the well to describe the enigmatic nature of the word of God. Guided by the Holy Spirit, who certainly works through exegetical study, we can always draw fresh water from the well of Scripture.

Preaching Jesus means Jesus Christ is the fresh water we draw from the deep well of Scripture; we interpret Scripture through Jesus or through the grace, reconciliation, and abundant life Jesus reveals and establishes. As part of sermon preparation, preachers consider the biblical and historical context of the passages they are preaching on. In choosing to preach Jesus, preachers include insights and information about the readings that facilitates or enhances preaching Jesus. Preachers do not include information about the reading that does not contribute to proclaiming Jesus for its own sake, as one would in a Bible study, since Jesus is Lord even of Scripture, especially in Christian preaching.

In Isaiah, for example, God declares, "The righteous one, my servant, shall make many righteous, and he shall bear their iniquities."[38] Isaiah's fourth "servant song" proclaims the suffering of God's servant for many. Isaiah's suffering servant is the suffering community of exiles, whose distress atones for all Israel and brings God's salvation to the nations. Yet on Good Friday, when this reading is included in worship, Christians understand that Isaiah's suffering servant can only be Jesus, who was lifted up from the earth and drew all people to himself.[39] Isaiah provides a way of understanding and proclaiming the significance of Jesus's death on the cross.

To further overcome the stumbling blocks of honoring the entire Bible, its historical context, and original intent, preachers teach the Bible with the same commitment with which we preach Jesus. Familiarity with the entire Bible and a passage's historical context and original meaning makes Christians better listeners to sermons. Yet, the goal of preaching is to preach Jesus. Moreover, the worship context and communication dynamics of the sermon make the pulpit less than ideal for teaching the Bible. Preachers therefore commit to teaching the Bible in settings akin to the classroom, with time frames longer than twenty minutes and opportunity for interaction, questions, and dialogue. Preachers do well to teach the Bible to all ages and at various levels of familiarity and comfort with Scripture. Preachers teach the Bible regardless of attendance. I encourage preachers to teach (at least) one Bible study a week.

Preaching Jesus can also be a stumbling block when it dis-abuses us of the idea that the Bible is about us. Preachers instinctively look to Scripture to discover how we are to serve God, emulate Jesus, and—empowered by the Holy Spirit—respond in the world. When this becomes the message of the sermon, preachers teach our congregations this is how Scrip-ture is to be read. This anthropocentric approach to Scrip-ture is enhanced when things happen in the church, world, and people's lives that demand our response, and we need direction. For good reason, preachers might address these situations and circumstances, and give needed direction, by explaining the Scriptures in light of them. Unintentionally, Jesus is shuffled into the shadows as we, as human beings, and our concerns step into the spotlight of the sermon.

Some are concerned that preaching Jesus will result in offering God's grace without naming our need of God's grace or how we are to respond to God's grace. They fear preaching Jesus will minimize and even eliminate important messages from God we need to hear about ourselves. Scripture's nam-ing of sin, prophetic edge, concern for social justice, and call to repentance will be lost.

Regardless of how important preachers find a particular message in Scripture or how zealous we are to preach it, what matters is that God's people receive it. Rather than moving instinctively to how God wants them to repent or respond, the people in the pews are instinctively aware of the vast difference between them and God. They know that God is righteous, and they are not. They know that Jesus is Jesus, and we are us. Most of us are not willing to embrace crucifixion, and none of us has figured out how to do resurrection for ourselves. People therefore want to know who God is, what God is like, and what Jesus is doing, before we tell them how God expects us to live or behave or what work God has for us to do. Research indicates that people seem at times desperate to hear about God, and people are not hearing all they want to know about God from the pulpit.[40] Preaching Jesus tells people who God is and what God is like, opening them up to receive God's message about themselves and the world. The issue behind these concerns is not so much whether we preach Jesus but how we preach Jesus.

Exposes False Gods

Preaching Jesus exposes false gods, or false notions of God, regardless of how much we cherish them. Perhaps people not hearing all they want to hear about God from the pulpit is the reason I encounter so many gods for whom Jesus is a stumbling block. Both within and outside sermons, these gods are of the build-your-own variety. Inside sermons, I hear about the vague and squishy kind of god, who loves diversity and works for social justice. I hear sermons about the moral compass kind of god, who calls us to do (or not do) and to be (or not be) this or that. I hear sermons about the Magic Mirror kind of god, who always sees us at our best, loves us just the way we are, and assures us we are enough. The church has a history of preaching the fire and brimstone kind of god, who would just as soon zap us out of existence for the slightest infraction of the sin du jour.

Outside sermons, I increasingly hear of the god who uniquely blesses the United States, not to be a blessing to the world but to be privileged and protected; this god blesses reducing the church to a backdrop, the Bible to a prop, and the cross to a flag stand for Old Glory. I also hear about a god intent on separating the sheep from the goats, insiders from outsiders, those who are right from those who are wrong. This god seems content to use chaos, discord, and hate to solidify and reinforce the dividing line. I hear about the god of the pandemic, who desires people to be in worship; this god miraculously protects those who have faith to come to church from getting sick with Covid-19. For this god, faith and science stand in opposition.

We choose preaching Jesus as the goal of preaching because *Jesus reveals God*. In the epistle to the Colossians, Paul calls Jesus "the image of the invisible God."[41] That Jesus reveals God is a prominent theme in John's Gospel. John's prologue declares, "No one has ever seen God. It is God the only Son, who is close to the Father's heart, who has made him known."[42] When Philip asked Jesus to show the disciples the Father, Jesus answered, "Whoever has seen me has seen the Father. How can you say, 'Show us the Father'? Do you not believe that I am in the Father and the Father is in me? The words that I say to you I do not speak on my own; but the Father who dwells in me does his works. Believe me that I am in the Father and the Father is in me."[43]

When we preach Jesus, we proclaim the good news celebrated in the proper preface for Christmas: "In the wonder and mystery of the Word made flesh you have opened the eyes of faith to a new and radiant vision of your glory; that, beholding the God made visible, we may be drawn to love the God whom we cannot see."[44] Preaching Jesus to reveal the invisible God demands that preachers periodically pause to consider whether and how we are creating God in our own image because it is easier, popular, or more effective to preach about a god of the build-your-own variety. Preaching Jesus reminds us of the problem with this kind of preaching: None of these gods is God.

Preaching Jesus to reveal the invisible God does not get stuck in a single or favorite portrait of Jesus. Preaching Jesus takes in the whole picture. For years my students were enamored with the truth-telling, table-turning, troublemaking embracer of the marginalized. They were less keen to consider that, if they only preached this Jesus, their ministry was likely to have a three-year run that culminated in their crucifixion. More important, preaching only this or any single portrait of Jesus distorts the image of God Jesus reveals.

Exclusive Claims

Preaching Jesus is a stumbling block when to do so involves making claims that exclude. For example, Jesus says, "All things have been handed over to me by my Father; and no one knows the Son except the Father, and no one knows the Father except the Son and anyone to whom the Son chooses to reveal him."[45] Again, Jesus says, "I am the way, and the truth, and the life. No one comes to the Father except through me."[46] Some preachers and congregants find preaching Jesus a stumbling block when Jesus appears to place anyone beyond God's love and outside God's salvation. Other preachers and congregants find preaching Jesus a stumbling block when it does not take these exclusive claims seriously.

We stumble when we need some to be "in" and some to be "out" and look to Jesus to tell us who's who. We stumble when we attempt to determine and name the limits of God's grace, the boundaries of God's reign, and the criteria of God's welcome and judgment. We stumble when, with every good intention, we attempt to offer answers and convince our hearers our answers are correct. We stumble because none of these are preaching Jesus.

Jesus's exclusive claims present a particular stumbling block as we consider people of other faiths. To preach Jesus, to preach like Jesus, is to respect all people as created in God's image, endowed by the Creator with gifts and seasoned by life with experience. Even more, we respect people of other faiths as people of faith. Their faith may be different from

Christianity, but through their faith, they also have a relationship with God. This recognition may rightfully silence us and instill in us a desire to learn about other faiths. This is especially true as Christians build relationships with Jews and Muslims, since all three traditions claim to worship the God of Abraham, though in significantly different ways. Learning about other faiths certainly is of God and enhances preaching Jesus.

As I stumble over claims about Jesus that seem to exclude, I am helped by remembering that preaching Jesus includes both witnessing to Christ—the "make disciples, baptize, and teach" of the Great Commission (Matthew 28:19–20)—and loving our neighbor—the "do to the least of these" of the Great Commandment (Matthew 22:34–40).[47] As witnesses to Christ, our testimony is bold. Jesus is the Word of God, through whom everything was made, becoming a human being and living a human life. Through Jesus's life, death, and resurrection, God reconciles all things to Godself and brings forth a new creation. Jesus does this as God's free gift, without imposing any requirements or conditions. As we boldly witness to Christ Jesus, we embrace First Peter's admonition, "all of you must clothe yourselves with humility in your dealings with one another, for 'God opposes the proud, but gives grace to the humble.'"[48] When our testimony is bold in terms of good news and humble in spirit, we witness to Jesus as those yoked to him and eager to share this good news.

As we witness to Christ Jesus, we need to decide whether we are saved by Christ or by our belief in Christ. If we are saved by Christ, Jesus's promise to draw all people to himself[49] is powerful and freeing. Jesus does not promise to draw some people, only those who believe a certain way. Jesus promises to draw *all* people to himself. "For God so loved the world that God gave the only Son."[50] To preach Jesus is to announce God's global, even cosmic, redemption of which every individual and community is a part and in which every individual and community can participate. To preach Jesus is to make this announcement with humility, as good news. To preach Jesus is to trust Jesus to do what Jesus promises to do.

Trusting Jesus to keep his promises, we preach Jesus as both the subject and the actor of the sermon. For, while we preach Jesus, only God brings people to faith. To preach Jesus is to trust the Holy Spirit to "produce faith, where and when it pleases God, in those who hear the Gospel."[51] To preach Jesus is to trust that Christ's presence brings people from death to life, from sin to grace, from fearful to forgiven, from trapped to transformed.

To preach Jesus is to preach in a manner congruent with Jesus's intention to draw all to himself. Jesus said, "I am the way, and the truth, and the life. No one comes to the Father except through me."[52] Too often this verse is used to exclude. But Jesus says these words to his disciples to assure them that he is the way, that they are safe, that their fate is secure. We might think of a parent assuring one child, "Of course, I love *you*." In no way does this statement say to another child, "I do not love *you*." Just before declaring himself the way, Jesus speaks of his Father's house having many dwelling places. To preach Jesus is to declare God has room enough for everyone. When Jesus was lifted up, he drew all people to himself. Perhaps this is why, in Matthew, Jesus speaks of making disciples of all nations. Jesus is telling the church his intention is that everyone—all nations—knows that, on the cross, Jesus drew them into God's embrace.

As an expression of our witness to Christ and as an extension of Jesus's own ministry, preaching Jesus also includes an invitation to participate in Jesus's own work of reconciliation by loving God and loving and serving the neighbor, which Jesus makes concrete in the Great Commandment (Matthew 22:34–40). Paul asserts, "in Christ God was reconciling the world to himself. . . and entrusting the message of reconciliation to us. So we are ambassadors for Christ, since God is making his appeal through us."[53] "As a faithful response to Christ's message of reconciliation, we seek right, peaceful, and just relationships with all our neighbors, including those of other religions and worldviews."[54] Preaching a message that excludes is inconsistent with loving the neighbor.

Preaching Jesus, then, is an invitation rather than an answer. Jesus came to proclaim and inaugurate the reign of God, which is nothing less than the world running the way God intends. We can understand the gospel as inviting us into the grace-filled mystery that is the life and work of God rather than as making exclusive claims or giving us all the answers that we are to convince others to agree with or accept. Preaching Jesus as invitation leads us to understand the life and work of God as still unfolding and expanding rather than already defined and determined.

Surrenders to Jesus

Preaching Jesus surrenders to Jesus, which can be a stumbling block when Jesus becomes a challenging companion. Jesus may describe his yoke as easy and his burden as light, but we all know times when they were difficult and heavy and carrying them brought trouble. In preaching, Jesus can be a stumbling block when, surrendered to in a sermon, Jesus is out of our control, alienates people, and exposes the preacher.

We may stumble when Jesus appears out of (our) control. The Gospel of Mark verifies there are times when Jesus will. Once when Jesus came home to rest, the crowd that gathered around him was very large and many demanded Jesus heal them, to such a degree that Jesus and his disciples could not even eat. Some people observing Jesus said, "He has gone out of his mind" and accused Jesus of being possessed by Beelzebub. When his family heard this, they set out to seize Jesus. When his family arrived, Jesus refused to see them; instead, Jesus named those who do the will of God as his true family.[55] Even as he appeared out of control, Jesus was doing God's will by responding to the large crowd with healing. God's will revealed in healing, freedom, and grace regularly appears out of our control. We need to expect this and be ready.

Preaching Jesus involves being yoked so closely and securely to Jesus that there is no tug-of-war for control; preachers do this by claiming our place as witnesses, disciples, and those joined to Jesus's death and resurrection. Then we know the grace of Jesus being in control and us not. We know the wisdom of allowing Jesus to be Jesus, even as we open the Bible to the gospel reading for the coming Sunday and think, *I wish Jesus hadn't said that* or *I wish Jesus hadn't done that*.

Preaching Jesus means accepting that Jesus alienates people and not being caught off guard when Jesus does. The good news Jesus brings is not good news for everyone, which is why Jesus was crucified. For example, Jesus healed the sick,[56] good news unless you think people should get what they deserve. Then Jesus healing just anyone is troublesome. Jesus healed on the Sabbath. We all know what we should be doing on the Sabbath—going to church. Is Jesus saying we do not have to go to church and Jesus will still heal us, because God still loves us? If healing is not enough, Jesus forgives sins.[57] Jesus forgives everyone for everything. Jesus does not expect people to be sorry or tell us how sorry Jesus expects us to be. Jesus does not put conditions and qualifications, protections and precautions, on forgiveness. In fact, Jesus eats with outcasts and sinners.[58] Jesus even likes outcasts and sinners. Love so radical is alienating.

Jesus feeds 5,000 with five loaves and two fish.[59] His perspective is abundance rather than scarcity, and that we have more than enough for everyone. When we feel righteous because we do not kill, steal, or cheat, Jesus invites us to sell all we have, give the money to the poor, and follow him.[60] That the reign of God has an economic and material dimension is alienating for those who prefer Jesus confine himself to our souls and spiritual lines. Most alienating of all, Jesus says being Number One means being last of all and servant of all.[61]

Unless we pick and choose what we say about Jesus, only preaching our favorite stories and images, or the ones that do not cause trouble, Jesus is bound to alienate someone. It is therefore essential we preach what we receive from Jesus through Scripture and not what we impose upon Jesus by reading it into Scripture. We must also craft sermons so that we stand with our people and receive a word from Jesus rather than using a word from Jesus to stand against our people. As much as we might long to channel John the Baptist, preaching Jesus means honoring the people to whom we preach as those Jesus came to save.

Preaching Jesus is a stumbling block when Jesus exposes the preacher. Preaching Jesus can expose the gap that always exists between the message proclaimed and the life and character of the preacher. For example, to authentically preach Jesus as Savior reveals, at least to the preacher but probably to others, the preacher's own need to be saved. Boldly calling the congregation to follow Jesus in lives of sacrificial love of God and neighbor reveals the preacher's inability or unwillingness to completely embrace the life of sacrifice and love they call for.

Speaking only for myself, even as I know myself to be a sinner, I do not want everyone knowing and naming my sins. Even as I cling to the saving grace of Jesus made tangible in Word, water, bread, and wine, I struggle to trust it is for me. As I seek to live a godly life, I struggle with the Jesus who exalts those obviously morally inferior to those he directly or indirectly castigates.[62] I struggle to trust Jesus, who forgives anything, who dies for everyone, who raises me to new life just when I become resigned to my many graves. I struggle with trusting the Jesus who bids me to follow him because I appreciate having a place to lay my head. I worry about providing for my family, and I am not ready to die. Yes, I struggle trusting Jesus. So, sometimes, I place my trust in and preach something else.

Paul writes, "But we have this treasure in clay jars."[63] Again, speaking only for myself, I find God gives grace, insight, and power when I examine and attend to the "clay jar" of my life, not in the pulpit but through confession, spiritual direction, and therapy. I have come to understand the spiritual work of being yoked to Jesus in a healthy way as an essential part of preparing to preach. Our calling is to witness to Jesus. There is no more powerful witness than one who knows themselves saved by Jesus's grace, experienced Jesus bringing life out of death, and struggling to faithfully follow him.

Paul also writes, "For we do not proclaim ourselves; we proclaim Jesus Christ as Lord and ourselves as your slaves for Jesus's sake."[64] Preaching Jesus is always about the treasure and not the clay jar. No witness ought to overshadow Jesus. Even John the Baptist counseled his disciples, "He must increase, but I must decrease."[65] Early on, I looked to my own life to illustrate and punctuate the gospel, probably because mine was the only experience I had to draw on. As the years went by, I became more restrained. I came to understand that my life is not that extraordinary; essentially, I do my job, love my family, serve my God, and try to have fun. I also came to understand that pointing to myself in the pulpit invites people to look to me everywhere else, which eventually disappoints everyone. I receive enough attention without shining a spotlight on myself, a spotlight that might cast Jesus into the shadows. Now, I strive to be transparent in the pulpit. I surrender my identity to the office I hold through even the vestments I wear, and I pray people will not so much see me as see through me to Jesus.

Preaching in a different congregation every Sunday, I need to familiarize myself with the pulpit, especially the steps leading into the pulpit, so that I do not stumble. Familiarizing ourselves with the ways preaching Jesus is truly a stumbling block prevents preachers from tripping as we step into the pulpit. When preaching Jesus becomes a stumbling block, we do not abandon this goal. The issue is not whether we preach Jesus but how we preach Jesus. Turning to the cross, we contemplate how Jesus saves.

4

Cross

What Is the Gospel?

"What is the gospel?" I ask this question of every pastor and deacon our staff considers as a candidate for a congregation in our synod (diocese). I ask candidates to imagine themselves sitting in a coffee shop, sipping their cappuccino or chai (or eating breakfast in the Main Street Café or stepping out of the locker room at the YMCA), dressed in a clerical collar. A young adult approaches and asks if they are a pastor (or priest). When the pastor answers they are, or when the deacon explains what a deacon is, the inquisitor asks, "What is the gospel? I keep hearing about the gospel. What is it?"

I make the inquisitor a young adult and the setting a coffee shop so the pastor or deacon must respond in the moment, spontaneously and without forethought. I am not interested in a pat answer. I seek more than the doctrinal construct, theological formula, or definition learned in seminary that pastors and deacons are prone to provide a bishop. I want a voicing of the gospel that I hope will be accessible to real people, concrete in terms of everyday experience, and relevant to real life.

I hope the pastor's (or deacon's) response to the inquirer in the imaginary coffee shop is good news from God about God's nature, intention, and action for us and for the world. I hope the response includes and names Jesus. I hope I hear about Jesus's death and resurrection, as well as his life. I hope Jesus is identified as Savior before Jesus is lifted up as teacher, example, role model, or anything else. I hope the pastor or deacon shares how Jesus saves in a way that connects with the young adult in the imaginary coffee shop. When this happens, and especially when it does not, I learn the message from and about God *this* pastor or deacon lives by, ministers from, and likely preaches. Asking what the gospel is, first to preaching students and now to pastors and deacons, I have also learned that everyone expresses the gospel uniquely because Jesus's life, death, and resurrection is a holy mystery, and not a doctrine, theory, or formula.

The Mystery of Faith

Jesus's death and resurrection is a holy mystery. Both the New Testament and the church describe God's self-disclosure in Jesus Christ as *mystery*. Paul speaks of "the mystery of Christ."[1] Roman Catholics call Jesus's passion, death, and resurrection the "Paschal mystery," and Lutherans "proclaim the mystery of faith—Christ has died, Christ is risen, Christ will come again" as part of their celebration of the Eucharist.[2] The gospel is a mystery because God's self-revelation in Jesus Christ is an experience of God's intervention in history that requires interpretation. "But when the fullness of time had come, God sent his Son, born of a woman, born under the law, in order to redeem those who were under the law, so that we might receive adoption as children."[3] Since the dawn of creation, encountering humanity and all creation is God's way of making Godself known. The

Bible recounts God's history of self-revelation. "The highpoint of God's history of self-disclosure, according to Christians, is the Lord Jesus, the Christ, God's Word made flesh (Jn 1:14)."[4] Mystery is hidden and enigmatic, transcending simple conception and complete comprehension, extraordinary and unfamiliar. Anyone who has recalled, reflected on, and related an encounter knows how quickly we move from describing to interpreting and assigning meaning. The Gospel writers illustrate this tendency to interpret in their accounts of Jesus's passion, death, and resurrection. In the garden, John's account of Jesus stepping forward and declaring himself "I AM" to the detachment of soldiers and temple police who came to arrest him is very different from Mark's portrait of Jesus throwing himself on the ground and praying that, if it were possible, God would remove this cup from him.[5] On the cross, Mark's report of Jesus's last words, "My God, my God, why have you forsaken me?" is a far cry from Jesus's final pronouncement, "it is finished," in John.[6] Mary Magdalene going from the tomb and announcing to the disciples, "I have seen the Lord," is the complete opposite of the women fleeing from the tomb and saying nothing to anyone because they were afraid.[7] The New Testament includes four perspectives on Jesus's death and resurrection, five with Paul, because, rather than a single interpretation that can be encapsulated in a doctrine, the gospel is a mystery.

To preach Jesus's death and resurrection, to proclaim the mystery of faith, is to explore and reflect upon a holy mystery and not to explain and apply concepts, formulas, or doctrines. Preaching Jesus is diminished when preachers equate the death and resurrection of Jesus with a specific interpretation. Any single interpretation confines rather than expands the meaning and relevance of Jesus's passion, death, and resurrection. A single interpretation speaks to some but not all. When preachers are uncomfortable or disagree with what they think is the only interpretation of the gospel, Jesus's death and resurrection may disappear from sermons altogether as Jesus is presented as something other than Savior. Therefore, whether in the coffee shop or the pulpit, every preacher needs to be able to voice God's good news in Jesus Christ by answering the question, "What do you mean by the gospel, the Paschal mystery, the mystery of faith?"

The Gospel in Fifty Words

What do you mean by the gospel? I strongly encourage preachers—and assign preaching students—to answer this question by writing a fifty-word summary of their understanding of the gospel. I urge not using words like *incarnation*, *justification*, and *remission*. Fifty words are easily memorized and therefore easy to internalize. I recommend preachers post this statement where they prepare their sermons and find a way to include this message in every sermon they preach. Former students of mine report their fifty words continue to hang on their computer or bulletin board years after they wrote it in preaching class.

"Do I have to go to the cross every time I preach?" I am frequently asked. I do. I was taught every sermon should answer the question of what difference it makes that Jesus died and rose. While some highlight the incarnation, I find that without the death and resurrection, Jesus gets reduced to just another wise teacher or holy role model. I need Jesus the Savior before he is anything else. But the main reason I try to get to the cross and resurrection in every sermon is that I have a hunch someone in the house is in some way dying. Perhaps once upon a time you spent a long season struggling with spiritual, vocational, or relational death and, like me, found that there is nothing worse than when the preacher is afraid, unwilling, or incapable of going to Jesus's cross.

I find it beneficial to periodically revisit my fifty words to discover how my experience and expression of Christ's death and resurrection may have changed. As I prepared this chapter, I asked myself what I mean by the gospel. I arrived at these fifty words: "Jesus, whose words are spoken and works done, whose body was broken and blood shed, died on the cross and rose from the dead that we and all creation know God's love, trust God's forgiveness, share Jesus's abundant life, and participate in Christ's work of reconciling the world to God." I would like to add that Jesus is God's gift and God's Word enfleshed and that we participate in Christ's work of reconciliation empowered by the Holy Spirit, but that would make sixty-one words!

Every preacher's fifty-word statement of the gospel is unique. Yet preachers do not write them either alone or on a blank slate. The gospel we preach is in keeping and conversation with the church, as a continuation of the gospel proclaimed by the church. Preachers therefore ground their gospel statements in Scripture as the word of God. Many preachers also represent churches that confess and teach the Apostles', Nicene, and Athanasian creeds. As a Lutheran Christian, my gospel statement is to be consistent with the confessions of the Lutheran church.

While creating a fifty-word gospel statement is individual work, preachers undertake it in a faith community. In preaching class, students share their gospel statements in small groups for reaction, reflection, and revision; pastors could do the same with colleagues or parishioners. Preachers certainly benefit from conversation with people in coffee shops and cafés, as well as congregations, about questions people are asking, issues they are facing, concerns they are raising, and their need and desire for God.

These conversations reveal that no fifty words can hold the entirety of the gospel; these conversations also help us know what is particularly important to each of us, what we may overlook, and how we might express the gospel more accessibly, graciously, or relevantly. In light of these conversations, preachers might contemplate the holy mystery and formulate their fifty words by engaging the writings of theologians to discover ways others in the church, past and present, express the meaning and significance of Jesus's death and resurrection.

How Jesus Saves: Classic Models

Soteriology, the theological study of salvation, assists us as we determine what the gospel means by providing perspectives on God's saving mystery in Jesus Christ. God's self-revelation in Christ is once and for all. However, the church's understanding of God's self-disclosure in Christ has unfolded over the centuries. As it explores and proclaims the gospel, the church benefits from distinct yet overlapping theologies, which Christians in earlier eras generated in response to the question of how Jesus saves. Today, emerging voices within the church offer new insights into God's gift of salvation in Jesus Christ.

Robert A. Krieg, who teaches theology at the University of Notre Dame, asserts that, today, the church embraces at least five classic models of "the Lord Jesus as the bearer of salvation, as the God-man who has opened the way for all people in the Spirit to receive salvation, that is, personal wholeness in union with God and in communion with other people and the rest of God's creation"[8] Krieg names these models (1) the Representative, (2) the Victim/Victor, (3) the Reconciler/Innocent Penitent, (4) God's Agape-Embodied, and (5) the Substitute. To varying degrees, each type or model enjoys acceptance among the various Christian traditions. Each model or type illuminates aspects of the saving mystery of Jesus Christ that the others do not bring into focus. Thus, they overlap and exist side by side. I do not claim this is an exhaustive list. Rather than settling on a single or even a closed set of interpretations on how Jesus saves, the church welcomes fresh perspectives and insights.

In addition to these classic models, the church benefits from the work of contemporary women theologians and the indigenous models of salvation from African, Asian, and Latin American churches. Mindful that this is a book on preaching and not soteriology, I am challenged to offer only brief sketches of the five classic models, followed by an admittedly terse sampling of contemporary insights from liberation, Black, feminist, and womanist theologies and the LGBTQIA+ and disabilities communities.

The Representative

Christ, the Representative, presents Jesus as representing God to humanity and humanity to God. According to Paul, God chose Jesus, God's Word-made-flesh, as humanity's "new head" or personal representative, succeeding and replacing humanity's initial head, Adam. Paul writes, "Therefore just as one man's trespass led to condemnation for all, so one man's act of righteousness leads to justification and life for all. For just as by the one man's disobedience the many were made sinners, so by the one man's obedience the many will be made righteous."[9] The first Adam brought sin and death; the second Adam, Jesus Christ, brings us to new life in relation to God.[10] In this way, God chose Jesus "to re-head" or "to gather up" all creation.

As humanity's new head, Jesus makes it possible for us and all creation to respond to God's gift of creating and saving love and grow into the life God intends. Paul writes: "For since death came through a human being, the resurrection of the dead has also come through a human being; for as all die in Adam, so all will be made alive in Christ."[11] Thus, God "set forth in Christ, as a plan for the fullness of times, to gather up [re-head] all things in him, things in heaven and things on earth."[12]

Irenaeus of Lyons (130–200 CE) developed Paul's metaphor into this model of how Jesus saves: Jesus Christ is "the God-man who came among us on God's behalf (Jn 1:14) and lived, acted, spoke, and suffered on behalf of our best or truest selves; he is now drawing us and all of creation to our fullness in God's life (2 Pet 1:3–4)."[13] For Irenaeus, Jesus Christ saved us by being our representative, the New Adam, who lived in unswerving faithfulness to God, even unto death on the cross, and so became the first fully grown human being.

As God's Word-made-flesh, Jesus is *God's* personal representative in creation and history. Jesus embodies God's saving mystery in his own life, death, and resurrection. Jesus speaks on God's behalf, conveying and representing God's compassion and forgiveness. On the cross, Jesus accepts us as we are and chooses to identify with us in all things, including with what our sins bring upon us. Jesus thereby witnesses to the God who comes down from heaven and undergoes suffering, heartache, and death with us. Through his suffering, death, and resurrection, Jesus gives us hope in God's future presence among us in suffering, as Jesus remains on the cross for as long as humankind itself is being crucified. Now, Jesus brings God's compassion and forgiveness about in our lives. In this perspective, Jesus not only acted once and for all on the cross; Jesus remains committed to walking with us in this world and leading and loving us into God's new creation, when God will bring every human person to the fullness God intends.

Jesus is also *our* representative to God. Jesus represents our best, truest selves to God by remaining completely faithful to God. In living unceasingly and completely faithful to God, Jesus reversed the sin, the unfaithfulness of the first Adam, and so became the new Adam. Jesus became the Savior who speaks on our behalf in accepting God's forgiveness and initiates a new beginning for the human family and creation in relation to the Creator. As our representative, Jesus is intent on our reaching the full humanity and personal wholeness God envisions for us as unique individuals and communities. Jesus empowers us to do this by showing us how to live in faithfulness to God and strengthening us with the Holy Spirit.[14] As our "teacher,"[15] Jesus affirms, forgives, strengthens, and challenges us to become the persons whom God intends and to live into a loving relationship with God, which includes representing God to others and representing others to God.

We learn to preach Jesus as Representative by drawing upon our experience of being personally represented by our parents, family, friends, teachers, and employers. Like these people, Jesus accepts each of us as irreplaceable and empowers us to become our true selves, to attain our unique identities as God intends. Jesus does this for communities as well as individuals. To have faith, then, is to follow Jesus as a representative of God to humanity and humanity to God. As representatives, we relate to God in Christ as we participate in politics and social action on behalf of human rights and human dignity, and not exclusively or even primarily by participation in the institutional church.

The Victim/Victor

Jesus is the innocent victim whose death on the cross makes him the victor over Satan, sin, and death. Jesus says of Satan, "But no one can enter a strong man's house and plunder his property without first tying up the strong man; then indeed the house can be plundered."[16] To "tie up" Satan, Jesus, though innocent, allowed himself to be executed on the cross, thereby entering "the strong man's house" or Satan's dominion of death. Jesus overcame Satan through innocent suffering and "plundered his property," namely, freeing humanity held captive by Satan in sin and death. We can grasp this model by reflecting on human experiences in which innocent people suffer and are overcome by evil and their defeat unfolds into a victory for themselves and others.

Understanding Jesus as Victim/Victor grows out of Christians' reflection, since the second century,[17] on the New Testament's testimony about the cross, as a curse on the one hand and a ransom on the other.[18] In some passages, Jesus saved us by succumbing to evil in death but then victoriously overcoming it. In other texts, Jesus allowed Satan to seize him as the "ransom" in exchange for which Satan frees the descendants of Adam and Eve.[19] By the fourth century, this model had assumed two distinct, though related, themes: Jesus defeating Satan for our freedom and Jesus buying us back or redeeming us from Satan.

Both articulations of Jesus as Victim/Victor maintain the biblical understanding of God as the Creator of all things through God's Word, Jesus Christ. The world, full of joy and sorrow, triumph and tragedy, love and hate, "is not a co-authored project between a good but less-than-omnipotent God and a well-matched demonic counterpart."[20] God has no competitor. Evil is God's gift of freedom to accept or reject the Creator misused or misdirected. Wrongly directed freedom comes to its fullest expression in Satan. In response, God remains intent on bringing good, even out of evil.

In his treatise *The Trinity*, Augustine of Hippo (d. 430) gives a succinct statement, based on Romans 5, on salvation as

God's pure gift and on Jesus's freeing the descendants of Adam and Eve from Satan's hold.[21] Jesus saved us by allowing Satan to put him to death on the cross, after which Christ overcame Satan, sin, and death by rising to new life. Salvation, like creation, is solely the Triune God's pure gift of love. In Paul's words: "God's love has been poured into our hearts through the Holy Spirit that has been given to us."[22]

Augustine states that human captivity to Satan occurred because the sin of Adam and Eve "subjected man [sic] to the devil through the just wrath of God."[23] In the name of justice, God allowed sinful humanity "to be delivered" into Satan's hands. However, God did not angrily turn away from humanity after the "Fall" but steadfastly intended humanity's reconciliation with God. Therefore, God continued to reach out in love to humanity and Satan as they remain members of God's creation. In emancipating humanity from Satan's control, God could not simply use power as both the devil and fallen humanity prefer to pursue power over justice. Instead, God chose to overcome Satan using justice, intending that humanity would similarly imitate Christ in overcoming evil.[24] God therefore sent God's Son to bring justice that prevailed over evil and the devil.

God's saving act occurred when Jesus permitted Satan to seize him and have him killed by crucifixion. By not using power to resist, Jesus acted with justice against Satan, even though Satan acted with injustice by executing Jesus, an innocent victim. After seizing the crucified Jesus, the devil "found nothing in [Christ] deserving of death, and yet he had killed him. It is therefore perfectly just that [Satan] should let the debtors he held go free, who believe in the one whom he killed without being in his debt. This is how we are said to be justified in the blood of Christ."[25]

For Augustine, Jesus's victory involved more than rising from the dead; in allowing his innocent blood to be spilled, Jesus canceled the debt brought on by our sin. Augustine writes: "This was the justice that overcame 'the strong man,' this the rope that 'tied him up' so that 'his furniture' could be 'carried off' (Mt 12:29), and from being 'the furniture of wrath' in his house together with him and his angels, could be turned into 'the furniture of mercy' (Rom 9:22)."[26] Though Jesus overcame Satan, evil persists as Jesus reveals and inaugurates God's reign in a world with values and powers opposed to God.

The Reconciler

Jesus is the Reconciler through whose death all human beings "were reconciled to God."[27] Jesus reconciled humanity to God when, in Paul's words, "being found in human form, he humbled himself and became obedient to the point of death—even death on a cross."[28] In *Why God Became Human*,[29] Anselm of Canterbury (1033–1109 CE) proposed that Jesus saved us by living and dying in complete repentance for our sins, although he himself was sinless and had no reason to repent. In so doing, Jesus restored the honor due to God from human beings because of our disobedience, thereby reconciling humanity to God.

From Anselm's perspective, which was based on feudal society, humanity needed to "make amends"[30] for disobeying and so dishonoring God by performing acts of apology, restitution, reparation, and generosity. Since we could not sufficiently do this for ourselves, God became human "to make amends" to God on our behalf.[31] When Jesus suffered and died on the cross, he offered to God the perfect reparation for humanity's disobedience. By being faithful to the Father unto death, Jesus so honored God that he reversed our unfaithfulness, released our potential faithfulness, and restored the way for us to be reconciled with God in Christ through the Spirit.[32]

Anselm's proposal rests on the universal human experience of an act of wrongdoing disrupting the harmony or "justice"[33] in a family, community, or organization. This disruption results in relationships, social systems, and a world afflicted by manipulation, exploitation, and distrust.[34] This dysfunction is an affront to God, who intends humanity's fulfillment and happiness in union with God as realized in the mystery of Christ's "person" and "work,"[35] and dishonors God's community of love.

In response, Anselm argues, God can either exact punishment on sinful humanity or accept an act of reparation or compensation from us. God cannot simply forgive humanity's disobedience; God's mercy cannot erode God's justice. Rather, God's mercy must facilitate the realization of justice, since God intended that harmony and right relationships characterize creation, and that justice characterizes humanity. Moreover, Anselm notes, for God to simply forgive leaves the offender empty because such forgiveness denies humanity the chance to "repay" a great debt. Such emptiness is not part of God's reconciling plan. Similarly, God does not punish or penalize humanity because, while eternal damnation would certainly suffice for restoring the order of creation, it would also subvert God's plan that humanity shares in God's own life and nature.[36]

Therefore, the only option is for God to accept an act of reparation or compensation from humanity. Unfortunately, humanity lacks the inner resources to restore our right relationship with God and consequently with self, others, and the earth. For this reason, Anselm argues the only One to save humanity needed to be fully divine, so he can make the amends appropriate to God the Father, and fully human to truly act for humanity in relation to God. Jesus cannot save us if not truly God, and Jesus has no obligation to save us if not truly human.[37] Thomas Aquinas adds that the Son's act to make amends can "count" on behalf of those who are so united to him in love as to be "one person."[38] Therefore, God the Father sent the Son to become human so Jesus could reconcile humanity to God by performing on our behalf an act of reparation appropriate to God the Father.

Anselm asserts Jesus could make appropriate amends for us in relation to God only by a supreme act of obedience. Jesus's sinless life, lived in perfect love of God and neighbor, is certainly valuable, except that such a life is expected of Jesus and every human being. However, Jesus can give himself to the Father through death, a consequence of sin that Jesus, being sinless, does not owe. In choosing such a death on the cross, Jesus aligned his will to God's foremost desire—humanity reconciled with God. Jesus voiced this act of commitment in the Garden of Gethsemane: "Abba, Father, for you all things are possible; remove this cup from me; yet, not what I want, but what you want."[39] God the Father willed that God's Son make amends for the disobedience of Adam and Eve by remaining obedient to God's justice unto death. Dying on the cross, Jesus freely chose to undergo the once-and-for-all act of reconciling humanity in relation to God, self, others, and creation. It remains for us to undergo the radical change from being estranged in Adam to becoming reconciled in Christ.

God's Agape-Embodied

Jesus Christ, as Agape-Embodied, is God's selfless love made flesh.[40] According to Peter Abelard (1079–1142 CE), Jesus, truly God and truly human, saved us by living and dying on the cross to reveal and realize in human life God's self-sacrificing love for us. Paul writes, "For I am convinced that neither death, nor life, nor angels, nor rules, nor things present, nor things to come, nor powers, nor height, nor depth, nor anything else in all creation, will be able to separate us from the love of God in Christ Jesus our Lord."[41] In response to God's Agape, humanity selflessly loves God, ourselves, one another, and creation. Thus, Jesus fulfills God's covenantal love recorded in Scripture.

God intended Jesus's entire life, culminating in his crucifixion and death, to demonstrate and actualize in human life God's Agape or selfless love toward us. "God's 'matchless grace' was realized among us when 'his Son received our nature, and in that nature, teaching us both by word and by example, persevered to the death and bound us to himself even more through love.'"[42] Throughout his entire life, Jesus manifested God's love by preaching good news, teaching the reign of God with authority, healing, casting out demons, forgiving sins, and loving the unloved. Jesus manifested God's love most unambiguously in his passion, death, and resurrection.

Jesus's death on the cross is his gift of himself, on God's behalf, to God's people. Jesus remained true to himself as God's Agape-Embodied, knowing that his opponents would subject him to a horrific death. By freely giving his life for our well-being, Jesus reveals the depth and persistence of God's love for us, which God gives as pure gift. Rather than overpowering Satan or satisfying God's honor, in his life, death, and resurrection, Jesus "bound us to himself even more through love."[43] As God's Agape, Jesus's living of selfless love unto death was the act by which God demonstrated God's love for us. "But God proves his love for us in that while we were still sinners Christ died for us."[44]

Jesus did not somehow change God's heart, mind, and will toward humanity: Jesus changed humankind's heart, mind, and will toward God. By the love revealed in his life, death, and resurrection, Jesus inaugurated a new existence in which humanity relates to God, self, others, and creation out of selfless love. Jesus's act of love inspires humanity to greater selflessness toward others and dares us to endure anything for his sake. Of course, we can ignore God's gift of selfless love in Christ Jesus. However, when we trust that Jesus lived and died for us, Christ's Passion causes us to love God more because God's Agape "frees us from slavery to sin," and "gains for us the true liberty of the sons [and daughters] of God, so that we may complete all things by his love rather than by fear."[45]

Jesus as God's Agape-Embodied stresses that Jesus's entire life, culminating in his death on the cross, was the manifestation and actualization of God's covenant love with God's people. We can appreciate Jesus as God's Agape-Embodied by recalling people whose selfless love culminated in deaths that revealed their longstanding commitment to self-giving love transforming the lives of others to love selflessly. First responders running into a burning building, healthcare workers fighting Covid-19, and schoolteachers using their bodies to shield children from a shooter help us to understand Jesus as God's selfless love made flesh. More common but no less profound, selfless love is frequently manifest in the relationship between two spouses and the love parents give to their children.

The Substitute

The first Christians looked to Jesus as our *Substitute*. In the New Testament, Jesus's followers interpret Jesus's life, death, and resurrection through the lens of Isaiah's fourth Servant Song.[46] John Calvin (1509–64 CE) developed the model of Jesus as our *substitute*, saving us by taking our place on the cross. In his crucifixion, Jesus underwent for us God's condemnation of sin and was then raised by God to the new life that we now share through faith in Christ. Paul writes, "We entreat you on behalf of Christ, be reconciled to God.

For our sake [God, the Father] made [Jesus, the Son] to be sin who knew no sin, so that in him we might become the righteousness of God."[47] Jesus's suffering and death is his act of substitution.

In his *Institutes*, John Calvin uses two biblical images to interpret Jesus as Substitute: Christ as cultic priest-victim and Christ as penal Suffering Servant.[48] Drawing on Hebrews, Calvin presents Jesus as the perfect high priest who went into God's presence and offered the ideal sacrifice, himself, to atone for our sins,[49] thereby appeasing God's anger and reinstating us in God's favor. God the Father willed that Christ, the Son of God, "should be at once victim and priest, because no other fit satisfaction for sin could be found, nor was any one worthy of the honour of offering an only-begotten son to God."[50] Jesus was the cultic substitute, the priest and the victim whose crucifixion was the perfect act of recompense and appeasement and satisfaction.

At the same time, Jesus is humanity's penal substitute. Drawing on the passion narratives, interpreted using Isaiah 52:13—53:12, Calvin portrays Jesus as the one truly innocent human being who was judged guilty and punished. Calvin refers to the gospels and Isaiah 53:7 to depict Jesus as a sheep before its shearers. Obediently yielding to his Father's will, Jesus freely chose to submit to this humiliation. Calvin notes that Jesus's condemnation before Pilate teaches us the punishment to which we were liable as sinners and criminals was inflicted on the innocent, righteous One. Jesus suffers for our crime, not his own. For Calvin, Jesus is *"our substitute-ransom and propitiation."*[51] As God's servant upon whom "was the punishment that made us whole, and by his bruises we are healed,"[52] Christ as Substitute undid evil, appeased God's anger, and bore the punishment of humanity's sin by becoming the scapegoat of all sinners and freely submitting to suffering and death.

The only appropriate response to the crucified Lord as substitute is Christian faith. Calvin asserts that salvation and justification require the act of faith, which "may find in Christ a solid ground of salvation."[53] Faith embraces Jesus as the true "Prophet," who teaches us perfect wisdom; the true "King," in whom we are "clothed with his righteousness"; and true "Priest," who by his own holiness secures the favor of God for us.[54] This faith is a necessity: it makes it possible for God to transfer Christ's righteousness to us.[55] As we turn to Christ in faith, we must recall that Christ took our place on the cross, so that we may not spend our lives "in trepidation and anxiety, as if the just vengeance, which the Son of God transferred to himself, were still impending over us."[56] We must "never lose sight of [Jesus's] sacrifice and ablution" so that "these may take deep root and have their seat in our inmost hearts."[57]

We consider Jesus as Substitute by recalling times in our lives when someone took our place or carried out a task on our behalf, so we did not need to try to do or endure something. In those instances, we benefited from a person or group freely acting or suffering for the sake of our well-being, with no expectation that afterward we do or endure what the substitute experienced.

Contemporary Insights into Soteriology

More recent models of how Jesus saves hold that "the Christian proclamation of salvation must address the stark reality of the suffering that characterizes the lives of billions of people across the globe."[58] They ask what it means for people who live in situations of injustice, deprivation, and oppression to confess Jesus as Savior. They answer Jesus saves through God's solidarity and liberation. I offer glimpses of this perspective from examples of liberation, Black, feminist, womanist, queer, and disabilities theologies.

Liberation Theology

For Gustavo Gutiérrez, the good news of salvation in Christ must address the experience of the poor, primarily the economically poor. In *A Theology of Liberation*, Gutiérrez defines salvation as the communion of human beings with God and one another, which grounds and embraces all human reality, transforms it, and leads to its fullness in Christ.[59] Thus, Gutiérrez does not distinguish between salvation history and a separate secular history. Gutiérrez writes, "Rather there is only one human destiny, irreversibly assumed by Christ the Lord of history."[60]

Humanity needs to be saved from sin, a breach of communion with God and one's fellow human beings, which is the ultimate cause of poverty, injustice, and oppression. This sinful state is personal, societal, and systemic. Gutiérrez argues sin requires liberation on three levels, which are intertwined.[61] (1) Social and political liberation frees the poor from oppression and forms a just economic and political order. (2) Psychological liberation empowers people to assume conscious responsibility for their lives and their destinies, by moving either away from self-preoccupation toward concern for others or toward greater self-possession and creative initiative. (3) Liberation from sin brings total freedom because sin is the ultimate root of injustice and oppression.[62]

Gutiérrez considers the incarnation key to how Jesus saves. Jesus was born into lowliness and service "in the midst of the overbearing power exercised by the mighty of this world; an irruption that smells of the stable."[63] Moreover, Jesus lived in Galilee, far from the center of religious and political power. The message of God's universal love for humankind comes from "among the poor and despised."[64]

Gutiérrez argues that we should not isolate and consider the cross apart from Jesus's public ministry, where Jesus identified with the least members of society and disclosed the God of life to them through healing, forgiveness, and table fellowship. Jesus turned things upside down by manifesting a new understanding of power as service rather than domination. "Jesus's death is the consequence of his struggle for justice, his proclamation of the kingdom, and his identification with the poor."[65]

Although the victim of an unjust act, committed by those in power, Jesus is not a passive victim. Jesus takes up his cross in radical fidelity to his mission and shows that God is close to all the crucified of history.[66] Jesus's death "was an act of radical solidarity with all humanity,"[67] which "brought him down to the deepest level of history at the very moment when his life was ending."[68] Jesus also maintains abiding communion with the Father, even in his moment of greatest agony. "He who has been 'abandoned' abandons himself in turn into the hands of the Father."[69] The message of the cross is one of "communion in suffering and in hope, in the abandonment of loneliness and in trusting self-surrender in death as in life."[70]

The resurrection confirms Jesus's mission as the Father endorses the gift of life that Jesus offered in his public ministry. "The raising of Jesus is the sign of God's liberation breaking into the world; it reveals that the God of life is more powerful than the forces of death."[71] Christians are called to bear witness to the resurrection through their commitment to their sisters and brothers, especially by their preferential option for the poor.

Black Theology

In *The Cross and the Lynching Tree*, James Cone recontextualizes the cross by connecting the death of Jesus to the history of the lynching of Black Americans.[72] Cone asserts that the cross and the lynching tree interpret each other. The cross needs the lynching tree to remind us of the reality of suffering. The lynching tree needs the cross to amplify hope. Yet, it is impossible to comprehend both the brutality and the beauty of the cross without standing in solidarity with those who are poor and powerless.

Cone insists that Christian faith provides resources for resisting and overcoming the evil that continues in our midst. Building on the Jesus as Victim/Victor model, Cone demonstrates that Jesus the Victor's promise that physical death is not the end can sustain the strength to persevere in the face of evil. Terrorized by lynching, which Southern whites used to dehumanize and remind Black Americans of their subordinate social status and powerlessness, Black Americans found strength in the Gospel's message of liberation that "lifts our spirits to a world far removed from the suffering of this one." Drawing on their faith, Black leaders "faced their deaths, sustained by the conviction that this was not the end but the beginning of a new life of meaning."

Yet, Cone reminds us, the "gospel is more than a transcendent reality." Jesus the Victim reveals God's reign is also "an immanent reality—a powerful liberating presence among the poor right now in their midst." When the gospel is experienced in "concrete signs of divine presence in the lives of the poor," the gospel "liberates the powerless from humiliation and suffering."

For Cone, God's reign is both "already" and "not yet." The "not yet" provides hope in the face of immediate, unthinkable evil. The "already" assures us that God has not abandoned us in the present evil, but dwells amid the oppressed, strengthening the downtrodden as they demand justice. We resist evil by heralding Jesus as Victim and Victor. "The cross was God's critique of power—white power—with powerless love, snatching victory out of defeat."[73]

Feminist Theology

Elizabeth Johnson considers how Jesus saves from the experience of oppressed women, past and present, who have been subjugated in male-dominated societies, where sexism is pervasive. Feminist theology emphasizes God's self-emptying love, empowerment, and solidarity in suffering. The incarnation and Jesus's public ministry are as essential to salvation as Jesus's death and resurrection.

Johnson begins by considering God's self-emptying in creation. Conceiving of God as Holy Wisdom (Sophia),[74] Johnson asserts that self-emptying "is the pattern of Sophia-God's love always and everywhere operative."[75] In creation, God expresses self-emptying love by making room for creation to be or exist by constricting divine presence and power.[76] Creation reveals God empowers people through God's faithful presence to and solidarity with them. Women's experience discloses that divine power is power with rather than power over. We experience God's faithful presence in God's ability to enter in compassionate solidarity and to freely suffer with another. This divine suffering represents an excellence, not an imperfection, in God and is a free, active suffering, not one imposed from outside.[77] In Jesus, we experience God's solidarity with humanity. In the incarnation, Holy Wisdom becomes flesh, self-emptying to participate in the beauty and tragedy of human history. The incarnation is "God's plunging into human history and transforming it from within."[78] Christian belief in the incarnation assumes that the transcendent God is "capable of personal union with what is not God, the flesh and spirit of humanity."[79]

Johnson agrees that Jesus's public ministry is essential to Christ's saving work. "While the climax is Jesus's faithful love to the point of death and resurrection, the repair of the world is signaled in his entire life as salvific."[80] Jesus was "sent to announce that God is the God of all-inclusive love who wills the wholeness and humanity of everyone, especially the poor and heavy-burdened. He is sent to gather all the outcast under the wings of their gracious Sophia-God and bring them to shalom."[81] God's passion for the wholeness of creatures is manifest in Jesus's healing and exorcism. Jesus gathered those deemed beyond God's reach into communion with himself and, therefore, with God through his table fellowship. In doing this, Jesus made possible relationships marked by mutuality rather than domination.

Jesus's death on the cross is the consequence of Jesus's ministry, which was "committed to the flourishing of life in solidarity with others."[82] Jesus remained faithful to his mission, even embracing a terrifying death. "The friendship and inclusive care of Sophia are rejected as Jesus is violently executed, preeminent in the long line of Sophia's murdered prophets."[83] In Jesus's resurrection, God's "pure, beneficent, people-loving Spirit seals him in new unimaginable life as pledge of the future for all the violated and the dead."[84] This transformation in the Spirit releases the presence of Jesus throughout the world and shows that Jesus's death on the cross was "neither passive, useless, nor divinely ordained, but is linked to the ways of Sophia forging justice and peace in an antagonistic world."[85]

Christians tell the story of Jesus's life, ministry, death, and resurrection because this memory leads believers to active solidarity with people who are suffering, living and dead, especially the deceased who have been victims of oppression.[86] "The grace of salvation in Christ calls forth human cooperation in the work of salvation, graced human acts that 'allow fragments of well-being to gain a foothold amid historical meaninglessness and suffering.'"[87]

Womanist Theology

Womanist theology[88] rejects understanding Jesus as a substitute, representative, or "surrogate" sufferer because these understandings divinely validate surrogacy as an acceptable way for people to relate to one another. This is particularly important to Black women forced into surrogacy during and following the era of the transatlantic slave trade.[89] Womanist theology further resists any tendency toward spiritualizing suffering, pain, and oppression and challenges the glorification of servanthood. Thus, womanist theology emphasizes the vast difference between the forced, oppressive servitude of Black women and Jesus's sacrificial, redemptive servanthood.

Jesus's sacrificial act is the tragic outcome of his confrontation with evil.[90] Jesus suffered and died at the hands of a system of oppression.[91] The cross is a sign of human violence against Jesus by the evil forces in the world that oppose Jesus's healing, liberating power.[92] Thus, the cross in no way reflects or condones suffering from forced servitude, which is oppressive rather than redemptive or salvific.[93]

Jesus's act of self-sacrifice was not forced servitude, but service borne of God's love and mercy. In Christ's suffering, God chose to be in solidarity with humanity, especially those who are poor, outcast, sick, and dysfunctional.[94] Jesus's crucifixion is the price Jesus willingly pays for identifying with poor, outcast, abject and despised women and men in the struggle for life.[95] God's power and glory are revealed in the cross as Jesus refuses to be dehumanized by suffering. Jesus thereby empowers humanity to reject passive suffering, and struggle against oppression. The resurrection becomes the fulfillment of the struggle for liberation.[96] Thus, Jesus's crucifixion was rooted in God's salvific love, reflecting God's love for humanity in a profound way and proclaiming that humans are not destined for suffering but for partnership with God.

Some womanist theologians seek a source of redemption in Jesus other than his suffering. They look to Jesus's incarnation as the empowering of Black women, in that the purpose of the incarnation was for God's Son to "make a way out of no way."[97] Womanist theologians emphasize Jesus's humanity to demonstrate Jesus's solidarity with poor, oppressed Black women. Jesus defied the patriarchal expression of masculinity, which employs coercion, power, exploitation, and exclusion of others. Moreover, Jesus stretched solidarity to the point of challenging us to love our enemies, choosing women as disciples, overturning patriarchal structures, and practicing masculinity through emptying himself of all that would subvert authentic human liberation.[98] Humanity is redeemed as God, through Jesus's ministerial vision, gives humankind "the ethical thought and practice upon which to build positive, productive quality of life."[99] Jesus's ministerial vision points not to death but gives hope to those attempting to right the relations with self, others, and God. "Humankind is, then, redeemed through Jesus's ministerial vision of life and not through his death."[100]

Queer Theology

In *From Sin to Amazing Grace*,[101] Patrick S. Cheng argues that theologies of sin and grace are particularly problematic to the *LGBTQIA+ community* because they have been defined in the West by a "crime-based" model. In this view, sin is a crime against God requiring punishment, and grace is acquittal and rehabilitation from that crime. Cheng outlines the development of this model from Augustine to John Calvin. He argues that the crime-based model is rooted in "a deep-seated fear of collective punishment" by God and that same-sex and gender variant acts have often been considered the cause of such punishment.[102] Thus, Cheng concludes this model is "inadequate and maybe even dangerous for LGBT people."[103] Cheng argues the doctrines of sin and grace should not be avoided but reframed or reinterpreted. He reframes sin and grace from "crime-based" to "Christ-centered." Sin is "immaturity" and grace is *theosis* or "becoming more like God."[104]

Cheng's Christ-centered model empowers the LGBTQIA+ community and others, seeking to live faithfully to God and to themselves, to interpret sin and grace using the framework of a queer understanding of Christ. Cheng presents seven models, offered by queer theologians, for understanding Christ: (1) Erotic Christ, (2) Out Christ, (3) Liberator Christ, (4) Transgressive Christ, (5) Self-Loving Christ, (6) Interconnected Christ, and (7) Hybrid Christ. Cheng demonstrates how each understanding of Christ redefines sin and grace. While space prevents me from discussing all seven models, I will briefly summarize Cheng's first two models.

First, the Erotic Christ model expands on the understanding of "erotic" to be a desire to deeply connect with another person in ways other than for our own satisfaction. In this model, Jesus, as the Erotic Christ, becomes the embodiment of God's desire to connect and have a relationship with humanity. Jesus, therefore, is not an object for God's self-satisfaction, but is a manifestation of God's love for us. Cheng proposes sin as exploitation or using another person as an object for our own stimulation and satisfaction and not taking their needs or desires into consideration. Grace, therefore, is the awareness and understanding that we have a relationship with each other and creation. This understanding allows us to feel authentically and deeply connected to others and to God.

Second, the "Out Christ" model presents the person of Jesus Christ as God's "coming out" to humanity; God reveals Godself most fully through Christ. Through this lens, sin is the "closet" and grace the "courage" to come out. Thus, coming out of the closet is understood as part of *theosis*. By sharing our most authentic selves with others, we become more like the God who desires authenticity and openness.

Theology of Disability

Nancy Eiesland proposes that the cross and resurrection of Jesus reveal the image of the Disabled God. Jesus as Disabled God makes sense of the "normal" experience of embodiment of *people who live with disabilities* and supports and participates in their struggle for liberation.[105] Eiesland argues that traditional images of God, especially those that lead to views of disability as either a blessing or a curse, are inadequate. The Disabled God is neither an omnipotent and self-sufficient nor a pitiable suffering servant. God is a survivor, as one of those whom society would label "not feasible," "unemployable," with a "questionable quality of life."[106]

Eiesland encounters this image in Luke's account of the resurrected Jesus's appearance to his disciples; Jesus reveals himself by showing the disciples his injured hands and feet.[107] Jesus, risen, comes to his disciples "embodied, as we are—disabled and divine."[108] Eiesland suggests that Jesus reveals the Disabled God and shows that divinity (as well as humanity) is fully compatible with the experience of disability. The *imago Dei* includes pierced hands and feet and side.

As evidenced in Jesus's answer to the disciples' question about the reason the man was born blind,[109] the Disabled God rejects the notion that disability is in any way a consequence of individual sin. Jesus did not sin, yet on the cross, Jesus became disabled. The invitation to touch Jesus's hands and side shows that taboos against disability are to be rejected as well.

The accounts of the crucifixion and resurrection lead Eiesland to reject the notion that God has absolute power;

she argues instead that God is in solidarity with people with disabilities and others who are oppressed. Jesus reveals a God who has experienced and understands pain and rejection. Eiesland suggests that the Disabled God emphasizes relationality over hierarchy, values embodiment in all its diversity, and provides a profound example of inclusion, love, and acceptance.

The resurrected Christ is seldom recognized as a deity whose hands, feet, and side bear the marks of profound physical impairment. "Christians do not have an able-bodied God as their primal image. Rather, the Disabled God promising grace through a broken body is at the center of piety, prayer, practice, and mission."[110]

What About Preaching Sin?

"What is the gospel?" Frequently, the pastor or deacon in the imaginary coffee shop immediately steps out of the role-play to protest the impossibility of sharing the gospel without knowing more about the young adult posing the question. The pastor or deacon objects that we cannot explain how Jesus saves without knowing what someone needs to be saved from. In sermons, the preacher might tell people what they need to be saved from; the shorthand answer is *sin*. Jesus saves us from sin.

"What about preaching sin?" I am regularly asked, often by younger preachers. Sin is serious stuff. Theologically speaking, sin dishonors God. Sin breaks our relationship with God, ourselves, one another, and creation. Sin leads to death. I am sometimes criticized for not giving sin more time in sermons and for being soft on sin to the point of making grace cheap. Perhaps this is true; however, I have several problems with preaching sin.

One of my problems with preaching sin is personal. Naming individual, communal, and societal sin is challenging because I stand on feet of clay. More than thirty years of preaching, serving, and leading leave me mindful of my individual and corporate sinfulness in ways I sometimes can hardly bear. With feet of clay and certain of my own sinfulness, I prefer preaching Jesus because that is the good news I need to hear. We preach sin by regularly traveling the spiritual path of contrition, confession, absolution, and amendment of life in a manner that holds us accountable to someone else. Of course, if we do not know our own sin and need of Jesus, we ought not be preaching at all.

My second problem with preaching sin is theological. Christian theology since Augustine has been rightly wary of any stark dualism between good and evil, since God created *all* things and called them good.[111] To make too much of the powers of evil bestows on them a status they do not possess—equality with God. Besides, the church has used accusations of sin and demon possession to target powerless people, including people who are sick or disabled. Most important, threats of spending eternity cut off from God in unquenchable fire as punishment for bad behavior here on earth tends to drown out proclamation of God who loves the whole world and desires that all be saved. We cannot preach sin and Jesus as equals.

Third, too often, preaching sin leaves us knowing we need to do better and not knowing we need Jesus. Instead of leaving us crying to Jesus to rescue and raise us from death to new life, we resolve to rely on our inner resources to do better so that we will no longer feel bad or called out in the sermon. And, if we try very hard, the preacher tells us in the final thirty seconds of the sermon, Jesus will help us. Doing our best and helped by Jesus, we vow, we will get ourselves together. Or, like a wounded animal, we growl, bare our teeth, and try to defend ourselves from accusation and attack. But we cannot domesticate sin into a personal problem we can deny or solve, even with Jesus's help. I suspect people who know themselves to be sinners do not need to be reminded, and people who do not know themselves to be sinners cannot be convinced. Besides, if sin is something we can fix, and in so doing save ourselves, we do not need Jesus to save us.

Fourth, in more ways than they can count, most people get sin "preached" at them all week long. This "preaching" is effective; it leads people to throw up their hands and implore God to help them. The last thing people need is for the church to be one more place where they feel bad about themselves—better to stay home. To paraphrase Jesus, if your church causes you to stumble, cut it off.[112] Preaching sin is holding up a mirror so people recognize themselves, not hurling an accusation that causes them to duck and stop listening. To preach sin is to speak for people to God as well as to people on God's behalf.

Fifth, the church has sins of its own it needs to address. It is easy to rail against the denomination and other Christian traditions. How about congregations claiming their own sins? For instance, if people do as James 5:16 directs and confess their sins in church, forgiveness and reconciliation cannot be assumed; in fact, the church might no longer be safe for them. In so many faith communities, when someone's sin is known, justice tempers mercy, accountability conditions grace, righteous indignation replaces prayer, consequences mute genuine repentance, and, sometimes out of necessity, the church forgets it is in the business of forgiveness. To preach sin, the faith community owns its own sinfulness and strives to be a place of forgiveness and reconciliation.

Finally, preachers are often unclear what they mean by *sin*. They do not define *sin*. Do we mean evil, disobedience, brokenness, shame, self-centeredness, arrogance, unworthiness, despair, fallenness, fear, failure, or finitude? How do we know in any given sermon? Other preachers make sin too small by using the word to promote their own agendas. If Jesus had to die on a cross to forgive me for failing to compost or voting for a political candidate who is not pro-life, we have a petty God. We need to say what we mean by *sin*. We need to name our need for Jesus.

While preachers must name sin and our need for Jesus, he strikes fear in this preacher when he warns, if one places a stumbling block in front of a believer, or if one stumbles, it is better to drown with a millstone or cut off a body part than go to hell.[113] Perhaps we need to ponder God's righteousness and the risks to ourselves if our failures to love and forgive our neighbors, our distortions of the way of Christ, our too narrow understandings of the truth, and our rush to pronounce judgment turn out to be roadblocks to those who would enter Jesus's community as they try to find the way of faithful living. We preach sin by naming the roadblocks in the way of responding to and following Jesus. Or we name what we need Jesus to save us from because we cannot save ourselves.

Our Need for Jesus

What do we need Jesus to save us from because we cannot save ourselves? If I were to visit that imaginary coffee shop when the young adult asks what the gospel is, I might answer, "The gospel is the good news that Jesus saves us and the world." Then I might ask, "What do you think the world needs to be saved from?" Musing on this imaginary encounter while the news plays in the background, my imaginary young friend gives me a list of very real things we need Jesus to save us from because we cannot save ourselves. This list is not exhaustive; I share it in no particular order.

We need Jesus to save us from *death*. Prior to the pandemic, I had come to believe that what happens at the hour of death, whether we meet a God of judgment or a God of mercy, was not most people's ultimate concern. I had wondered whether we had come to accept death as the natural conclusion of life, which, regrettably, sometimes occurs prematurely or tragically. As the Covid-19 death toll in the United States approached 500,000, we experienced death's unshakable hold, which we can certainly deny but on our own cannot defeat. We can also deny the reality of climate change to the point that we are unconcerned with defeating it; we can deny the truth that the death of our planet will bring extinction.

Jesus bringing life out of death so that death does not have the last word has become more relevant and important as recent world events—including a global pandemic, war in Ukraine, and school shootings—reveal that death is tragic, senseless, and immense. I increasingly need to hear that through his ministry of curing and restoring, Jesus demonstrates God will bring wholeness and healing and that God will not abandon us in suffering and sickness.[114] God raises Jesus to show "death is swallowed up in victory." Trusting in Jesus, we can declare, "[God] who raised Christ from the dead will give life to your mortal bodies also through his Spirit that dwells in you," and "after my skin has been thus destroyed, then in my flesh I shall see God."[115] We need Jesus to save us from death.

We need Jesus to save us from the *devil*. Debating the existence of a literal devil misses the point: The devil is evil personified. Far too many people encounter evil personified as part of life—evil within, evil around, evil in others, evil in institutions and systems, evil even in institutions and systems we honor and (long to) trust. Jesus overcomes and outwits the devil. So, Jesus says of his death, "Now is the judgment of this world; now the ruler of this world will be driven out."[116]

We need Jesus to save us from *damnation*. I am not talking about being thrown into "the outer darkness, where there will

be weeping and gnashing of teeth,"[117] which is questionable.
I am talking about the damnation of being thrown out of
relationships, families, communities, society, and the church
with no opportunity or ability to earn or be given a chance
to return. We need Jesus to restore us. Jesus restores Zacchaeus, the woman caught in adultery, the woman at the well,
and Peter to the community.[118] When we are damned, Jesus
restores us to God and to the family of God, which in some
instances transcends the church.

We need Jesus to save us from *disobedience*. I intend more
than moral infractions of the Ten Commandments. I mean
our way of thinking we know better than God, who desires
our best and directs us on how to be our best, so the world
might be its best, the world God intends. We need Jesus to save
us from the devastating consequences of individually and
corporately doing what we think best rather than what God
directs. On the cross, Jesus frees us from needing to prove
ourselves and be at the center of everything so that we can
love God, ourselves, our neighbor, and God's good creation.

We need Jesus to save us from *decline*. Our church declines
numerically and in terms of its influence. Our nation declines
in its standing in the world. Our faculties and the faculties of
those we love decline, to the point that we can no longer see
or walk or think or remember. Decline causes us to become
afraid. Jesus tells us not to fear. Jesus assures us that God
remembers us. God will never forget us. "Are not five sparrows sold for two pennies?" Jesus asks. "Yet not one of them
is forgotten in God's sight. But even the hairs of your head
are all counted. Do not be afraid; you are of more value than
many sparrows."[119] Jesus willingly accepts death on the cross
to show us how much God loves us. God's love for us is so
deep that, even when our abilities, accomplishments, and
memories decline, and even when they are lost, even lost to

us, they are never lost to God. Neither are we. Our "names are written in heaven."[120]

We need Jesus to save us from *destruction*. With increasing regularity, and frequently without warning, we are forced to behold just how fragile our accomplishments, institutions, and monuments truly are. Jesus said of the temple, "Do you see these great buildings? Not one stone will be left here upon another; all will be thrown down."[121] History shows this is the fate of everything humanity accomplishes. In our lifetime, we have seen not only the toppling of the Twin Towers but also the siege of the United States Capitol and the threatened collapse of our democracy. The teacher of Ecclesiastes declares, "I saw all the deeds that are done under the sun; and see, all is vanity and a chasing after wind."[122] It is God's pleasure to give us the kingdom in Jesus, "an unfailing treasure in heaven, where no thief comes near and no moth destroys."[123]

We need Jesus to save us from *division*, perhaps more than anything else. We are divided by race and in our politics. Even public health is a cause of division. We can measure our division using the metrics of economics, for example, the 1 percent and the 99 percent. We are even divided over what constitutes the truth. Common ground appears impossible to find; compromise is regarded as anathema. Polarization and tribalism are the norm. We have lost our ability and our appetite to overcome our division. We need Christ to make us one.

Jesus gives us a new identity we can embrace, a future we can live into, and power to do both. Jesus unites us as God's children: "There is no longer Jew or Greek, there is no longer slave or free, there is no longer male and female; for all of you are one in Christ Jesus."[124] Christ empowers us to strive to overcome rather than contribute to division by claiming this identity for ourselves and regarding others, first and foremost, as also one with us in Christ. We regard no one from a human point of view. For "if anyone is in Christ, there is a new creation: Everything old has passed away; see, everything has become new! All this is from God, who reconciled us to himself through Christ, and has given us the ministry of reconciliation; that is, in Christ God was reconciling the world to himself, not counting their trespasses against them, and entrusting the message of reconciliation to us"[125]

We need Jesus to save us from *derision*. We need Jesus to save us from scorn, mockery, distain, ridicule, disrespect, and contempt. We need Jesus to save us from scorning, mocking, distaining, ridiculing, disrespecting others, and regarding them with contempt. We use all these synonyms to feel the damage we inflict. Sometimes we deride another individually. Sometimes we deride one another because we possess particular characteristics or belong to particular groups. Derision brings shame.

Jesus knows what it is to be scorned, mocked, and derided. Pilate's soldiers mocked Jesus. Those who passed by the cross derided Jesus, calling on him to come down from the cross and prove he is the Son of God. The chief priests, scribes, and elders mocked him in the same way. Even those crucified with Jesus taunted him.[126] Jesus is present in human derision. Jesus is with us when we are derided; Jesus asks God to forgive us when we deride. Jesus replaces our shame with God's love and restores us to God's image.

We need Jesus to save us from *detestation*. The root of division and derision is hatred. We need Jesus to save us from hate. Jesus responds to hate with self-giving love, laying down his life for his friends. Jesus rejects violence, declaring that "all who take the sword will perish by the sword." Jesus responds to the manifestation of hate that is the cross by asking God to forgive.[127] On the cross, Jesus submitted to hate. In the resurrection, Jesus declared that hate will not stand; hate will not win. Grounded in Jesus's love, forgiveness, and life, we are raised to reject violence and respond to hate with forgiveness and love as Jesus did.

Working our way down this list, we may find ourselves despairing. We need Jesus to save us from *despair* by giving us a reason to hope. The good news is that Jesus is the reason to hope. In Jesus, the things that cause us to despair are birth pangs. Faced with wars, uprisings, famines, and earthquakes, Jesus instructs us not to lose hope but anticipate the birth pangs of God's coming reign. So, we "may not grieve as others do who have no hope."[128]

We need Jesus to save us from *defenselessness*, from powerlessness. I am not sure Jesus does. I am sure Jesus redefines power. On the cross, Jesus transforms power. In his ministry, Jesus rejects human power. Jesus frees us from human power and invites us to live by a different power structure, where the last shall be first and the greatest of all will be the servant of all. In so doing, Jesus gives us different criteria to use in determining how powerful we truly are. Jesus gives us different power.

We could go on. I, for one, need Jesus to save me from spiritual *depletion* and to raise me to resilience. In my experience, Jesus does this by yoking me closely and securely to himself. More precisely, Jesus yokes himself closely and securely to me in my depletion, and me to him in rising with resilience. My role is to not conjure resilience, but to own my depletion.

Deciding what we need Jesus to save us from, because we cannot save ourselves, will vary from sermon to sermon, depending on what is happening in people's lives, as well as in the community and the world. The consistent message is that we need Jesus to save us, and Jesus does.

Conclusion

"What is the gospel?" The inquisitor stood across the bistro table waiting. "God became human in Jesus and gave himself to the world, to be with us in everything, even the most horrible death; to draw the world to the life God intends; and, by God's Spirit, to free and empower us to live God's abundant life now, because God loves us." Sipping my espresso, I quickly counted my words; there were fifty. While I was feeling proud about myself, I realized all I had actually done was reflect on John 3:16 in light of John's Gospel. Our proclamation of the gospel comes from and through the Scriptures. So, we turn to the pulpit Bible and consider how to interpret Scripture to preach Jesus.

5

Pulpit Bible

How Do You Interpret Scripture to Preach Jesus?

I was to preach the final sermon in the congregation's 187-year history. Standing in the pulpit prior to the service and grasping the sides of the large Bible to center myself, I became spiritually aware that I was not alone; I was cognizant of the faithful who had gathered around the stories in that pulpit Bible for almost two centuries. I stood with all those who had read and preached from the pulpit Bible. I recalled how my first senior pastor, who began pastoral ministry in this congregation, returned to this pulpit thirty-five years later for an anniversary celebration. He told me that he spied a note he had written years before while turning the pages in the pulpit Bible. As I looked out at the then empty pews, I reflected on all the saints over 187 years who had heard God's Word read and the gospel preached from that pulpit Bible.

The Bible is neither a book we read nor an ancient document we study. The Bible is the collection of God's family stories, and the characters in its pages our kin in the faith. God's family gathers to hear these stories; the story we want to hear most of all is the story to which all the other stories point: the story of our brother and Savior, Jesus.

It merits repeating that, for Christians, the Bible is sacred, the norm of our faith and life, because the Bible proclaims Christ crucified as the power and wisdom of God.[1] Thus, for Christians, to preach the word of God is to preach Jesus. Scripture serves to proclaim Christ. In chapter 1, I highlighted Luke 24:25–27 and Luke 24:44–47 to demonstrate that Jesus taught his first disciples the task when interpreting Scripture is to find Jesus. This is also our task as we prepare sermons, since our goal is to preach Jesus. Undertaking to teach, explain, defend, or demythologize the Bible in the sermon can overpower preaching Jesus, though we certainly do these things as part of proclaiming Christ.

I am grateful that the Bible is more than a book for both personal and practical reasons. If the Bible were only a book, an ancient document we study, I would be in serious trouble. I am to the point in my preaching ministry that I can publicly admit that translating Hebrew and Greek and decoding the textual variants and specific manuscript evidence to distill the singular meaning of a text is simply too visual an endeavor for me. Were it not for some gracious scripture professors in seminary, I suspect I would be doing something other than preaching today. One professor in particular, finding me overwhelmed and distraught over my inability to exegete due to my visual challenges, made it her mission to help me "fall in love with the Bible again."

I am also grateful the Bible is not a history book, a law book, a science book, or a magic book that offers a single, unified perspective. I am gratefully relieved to know it is inconsistent with Scripture itself to approach the Bible as one of these volumes and get caught up in the heated, divisive debates that often arise from scouring the Bible's pages in search of answers to questions and resolutions to issues the Bible never intended to address. Both defending and demythologizing the

Bible as science, history, or anything else can overpower the greater message of Jesus as Savior and, if undertaken, should therefore be reserved for an occasion other than preaching.

For Christians, the Bible is most alive and life-giving when we approach and interpret it to proclaim Jesus. In this chapter, I lay out how preachers can faithfully do this. These are the conclusions of a preacher, teacher of preaching, and bishop, not a biblical scholar, which I neither allege nor pretend to be.

God's Family Stories

To preach Jesus, we approach the Bible less as a book and more as a collection of God's family stories, which for Christians, are united in Jesus Christ. Despite what we sometimes think, God did not publish a book to communicate with humanity. God's communication of Godself to humankind is through events, in time and space; that is, God communicates Godself in the way human beings can receive and understand. The Bible is the written record of God's initiative and activity in human history and the world, as well as in our individual lives. We can think of this written record as a collection of God's "family stories" or memories. Like our own family stories, God's family stories were held in the memory of God's people and passed on as each generation told them to the next for a long time before they were ever written down.

God's family stories, like the stories our families tell, are not made up; they are true. Yet, the way God's family passed these stories on is not historically or scientifically objective. Other parts of God's family tell the story of the same events differently. This happens because, by their nature, events in time and space are neutral; they can be understood and interpreted in many ways, from a variety of perspectives. Interpretations come from those who experienced the event and those who reflect on reports of the event. To claim events as meaningful, to make events our own and give them significance, demands that we interpret them.

In time, the family or community that experienced an event and claims it as its own accepts an interpretation. In the process, a neutral event in time and space always gives rise to a story that is "slanted" according to the community doing the interpreting. The story becomes "scripted" so that it is consistently told in a uniform way. The community or family can hold these scripted stories to be real and true, even while understanding that other families or communities can recall, interpret, and tell the events in these stories differently.

The scripted stories eventually get written down, so they are not forgotten or lost. The popularity of online genealogy sites indicates our need to preserve family stories. When God's people feared their family stories and memories would be lost, they wrote them down and eventually collected them in books. The Hebrew Scriptures were written when Israel was exiled in Babylon (sixth century CE); the New Testament was written in the first century CE, when those who knew Jesus were dying. In both instances, the critical stories of God's people were written down. What we have in Scripture, then, are the scripted stories of the events of God.

The Gospel of Luke alludes to this process. Luke writes, "Since many have undertaken to set down an orderly account of the events that have been fulfilled among us, just as they were handed on to us by those who from the beginning were eyewitnesses and servants of the word, I too decided, after investigating everything carefully from the very first, to write an orderly account for you, most excellent Theophilus."[2] The common memory of the Christian community needed to be kept alive to ensure the Christian community's ongoing history. Thus, the stories were written down. Reporting on Christian worship in the second century, Justin Martyr (c. 155 CE) can therefore call the gospels "the memories of the apostles."[3]

The Christian story is God's communication of Godself in the events of the life, death, and resurrection of Jesus Christ. The Christian community "slants" the stories in the Bible to proclaim salvation in Jesus Christ because Christians understand the gospels and the epistles as reporting the fulfillment of "everything written about [Jesus] in the law of Moses, the prophets, and the psalms."[4] We read the Bible, especially in worship, to retell the stories and so pass on the memories of our salvation in Jesus Christ. Secondarily, we share how these stories form and nurture us as God's family in Christ, inviting and empowering us to live in the world today.

Scripture, as God's holy Word, is not held in the written Bible, even when read individually. Scripture as God's holy Word is held in the communal memory of the church. As a community, we return or reconvert the Bible into the oral stories from whence it came. The stories in the Bible, as God's word, are spoken, not silent; aural, not visual. Their memory is communal, not individual; their interpretation is shared, not solitary or localized.

Part of the preacher's task is to study the Scripture to bring the story to life so that the community can experience the event of God's initiative and action in Jesus Christ today. When this happens, rather than reading from a book, Scripture becomes a communal event in which the voice of Christ, together with apostles and prophets who point to Christ, are heard. In this hope, in the liturgy, we respond to the readings, "The Word of the Lord" and "Praise to you, O Christ." Moreover, when we read Scripture individually, we do so as part of God's family, mindful that we need one another to interpret and understand God's holy Word. We can cultivate this awareness of being part of God's family by reading Scripture aloud so that it comes to us from outside us by exiting through our mouth and returning to us through the ears.

Finally, like every family, God's family has lots of stories. Families do not consider every story and memory equally but tell some stories and pass on some memories more than others. As God's "family stories," Scripture is not weighted equally; some parts of the Bible are deemed more valuable than others. For example, many Christians consider John 3:16, "For God so loved the world," the most important verse in the Bible, the "canon within the canon." At the same time, many Christians prefer to ignore and even delete John 8:44–45, where Jesus calls Jews children of the devil, a murderer and liar, who choose to do their father's desires. Since these words contradict John 3:16 and fuel anti-Semitism and hate, Christians tell the biblical stories that honor and proclaim Jesus. For Christians, Jesus is the Word.

Jesus Is the Word

"In the beginning was the Word," the Gospel of John declares, "and the Word was with God, and the Word was God. He was in the beginning with God. All things came into being through him, and without him not one thing came into being."[5] God *said*, "Let there be," and there was.[6] And the Word has been speaking life ever since.

To Noah, the Word said, "Never again! Never again shall there be a flood to destroy the earth."[7] The Word promised to make great nations of both Hagar's and Sarah's sons. To Moses, the Word commanded, "Lift up your staff, and stretch out your hand over the sea and divide it."[8] God's Word declares, "I will write [my law] on their hearts; and I will be their God, and they shall be my people."[9] The way God chose to write God's law—God's Word—on our hearts was to give God's Word a human heart all his own. So, "the Word became flesh and lived among us."[10]

As God declared to Moses from the burning bush, so Jesus, the incarnate Word, announced to the world, "I AM! I AM!" "I AM the bread of life, the light of the world, the gate, the vine; the good shepherd; the resurrection and the life. I AM the way of the truth that leads to life." In the garden, when we came to kill him, Jesus declared, "I AM he." From the cross, Jesus, knowing that all was now complete, proclaimed, "I am thirsty" to fulfill God's will.[11] Speaking words of hope to us, the risen Christ declares, "I am the Alpha and the Omega, the first and the last, the beginning and the end."[12]

Jesus participated in God's every initiative and action in human history, whether as preexistent Word, God incarnate, or ascended Lord. As the Second Person of the triune God, Jesus is everywhere in Scripture. For Christians, the event of Jesus's life, death, and resurrection is God's most significant initiative and action in human history, to which the biblical events that precede it point and from which the biblical events that follow flow. "The life and history of Israel, the saving work of Jesus, and the mission of the early church as these events are proclaimed in Scripture [are] connected to one another. . . as the single, continuing story of God's saving activity in Jesus Christ."[13]

We can imagine God's single, continuing, saving activity as a *stone dropped in a pond*. Some think of history as linear; others think of history as cyclical. If we think of history as a pond, God stands above history and at its center, creating all history from the center outward in many directions. We can think of God's salvation history recorded in Scripture as occurring before and after God dropped a stone in the pond. As parts of God's one salvation history, both directions move in such a way that the two directions parallel and mirror one another as figure and fulfillment.

The stone that God drops is the event of Christ's life, death, and resurrection. Like a stone dropped in a pond, Christ sends ripple effects both forward and backward in time. The backward ripple effects are recorded in the Old Testament as figures of Christ. This view of history is evident in First Corinthians 10:1–4, for example, where Paul calls Israel passing through the sea "baptism" and declares that the rock from which they drank was Christ. The forward ripple effects are Christ present and active in history since the ascension, in the church's worship, for example, where Christ continues to reconcile and save.

To preach Jesus is to see and to help God's Christian people see Scripture as a whole, as the single story of God's saving activity in Christ, a story that continues in our day and will be brought to completion when Christ comes again. Preachers lead the church to understand itself in biblical terms and see itself as a continuation of God's saving work recorded in the Bible. We do this by demonstrating how the various events recorded in the Bible are all united in the saving activity of Jesus Christ and how this saving activity continues beyond Scripture in the Christian life.

To preach Jesus is to respect Scripture as overflowing with revelation rather than to reduce a passage to a single interpretation. One of those revelations is Jesus Christ. Whereas Saint Ambrose called Scripture a deep well, Martin Luther suggests Scripture is a rich and inexhaustible mine in which we find the wisdom of God. Luther then compares Scripture to the manger and swaddling clothes in which Jesus lies. Not everything in Scripture is the treasure. Some of it is more swaddling clothes and manger. But it is the loftiest and noblest of holy things because of the treasure it holds.[14] For Christians, and especially for Christian preachers, that treasure is Jesus Christ.

Christ in Scripture

Looking for Jesus in Scripture is, indeed, a treasure hunt. My preferred way of hunting for clues for locating Jesus is to ask, "What's the good news?" When I find God's good news in a reading, Jesus is never far away. I find Jesus in Scripture explicitly, implicitly, typologically, and as a lens for interpretation.

Christ's Explicit Presence

Jesus, as God's incarnate Word, is *explicitly* present in the gospels. The gospels bear witness that Jesus brings and embodies God's good news—teaching, healing, welcoming, casting out demons, and dying and rising—with God's power. Preachers diligently honor the unique perspective on Jesus that Matthew, Mark, Luke, and John each present. We are careful not to conflate gospel stories and inadvertently preach about Jesus in a way that is not held either in Scripture or in the memory of the church. This can be challenging, since the church certainly combines Matthew's and Luke's accounts of Jesus's nativity. I once heard the gospel accounts of Jesus's passion stitched together so the cock crowed four times! Yet, most often in preaching, blending the gospels is much subtler, and the congregation may not even notice. Preachers can preserve each Gospel writer's perspective by comparing the same story across the gospels, noting what they share in common and what is unique to each.

Preachers consider the gospel as a whole to understand and interpret a specific reading contained therein. Preachers benefit from the whole picture by, for example, periodically reading aloud or listening to an entire gospel in a single sitting. When studying a particular reading, we use a concordance to understand how a given word in the passage is used in other places in the gospel. Preachers also gain insight by attending to how a particular story is anticipated and reflected at other places in the gospel.

Christ's Implicit Presence

Jesus, as ascended Lord, appears *implicitly*, for example, in the epistles. My work as a bishop gives me new appreciation for the epistles. While the church considers the epistles sacred Scripture, they originated as letters from an apostle and overseer to very real congregations. In this regard, the epistles remind me of letters I regularly write.

Jesus is never the explicit subject of my letters to congregations; none have asked me to settle a dispute over the two natures of Christ, for example. Yet, implicitly, as a referent and touchstone, Jesus is always the subject of those letters. During the pandemic, many of my letters responding to demands that I immediately tell congregations to return to in-person worship included a reflection on Jesus's sacrificial love and his new commandment to love one another as Jesus loved us.[15]

At this point in my ministry as bishop, I am able to reread some of my letters years after writing them. When I do, I realize the importance of recalling a congregation's specific context and situation at the time of my writing. In my letter, I have only one side of the correspondence; I need to recall or retrieve the other side. Recalling this context allows me to better understand how Jesus was at work in the congregation, how I hoped Jesus would be at work, or how the congregation could respond to Jesus being at work in the congregation at that specific time.

I find this a helpful approach to discerning Jesus's implicit presence in the epistles. Before I approach the epistles as intended for the church of all times and places, and especially for the church I serve today, I read and study the epistles as bishop's letters to specific congregations, at specific moments in time, intended to assure or challenge by pointing to Christ's presence in their faith community. I want to know the situation the epistle writer is addressing, how the writer names Christ as present, the implications of Christ's presence for the community, and how all this corresponds to situations in the congregations I oversee and serve.

Christ's Presence as Figure or Type

The sermons of the church fathers or doctors reveal Jesus's presence in Scripture in what patristic preachers call *figure* and modern scholars call *type*.[16] Our image of a stone dropped in a pond as a way of understanding Christ's presence in Scripture helps us understand that the church doctors assume the realities of the Old Testament are figures of Jesus's person and actions in the New Testament. This "science of the similitudes between the two Testaments" is *typology*.[17] Types contribute to a prophetic understanding of Scripture. They show how Old Testament events point to present fulfillment or present instances are fulfilled prophecies. In this way, types relate to the Christian sense of a providential history leading to the fulfillment of God's reign.

Typology is biblical; that is, this "science of the similitudes" is a way Scripture interprets itself. The foundation of typology as a method of interpreting Scripture was laid in the Old Testament during Israel's exile in Babylon. The prophets proclaimed that, in the future, God would perform for Israel deeds of power analogous to and even greater than those God performed in the past. God will bring a new flood that will annihilate the sinful world but preserve a faithful "remnant" to inaugurate a new humanity.[18] God will initiate a new exodus in which God will set humanity free and lead God's redeemed people to a new paradise.[19]

The New Testament shows that the events recorded in the Old Testament are fulfilled in the person of Jesus of Nazareth. Jesus is the new Adam who inaugurates the future paradise.[20] Jesus is the new flood that realizes the destruction of the sinful world.[21] Jesus accomplished the true exodus, which delivered the people of God from the power of the devil. The accounts of the transfiguration in the synoptic Gospels, for example, are an echo of Moses ascending Mount Sinai.[22]

To establish the truth of their message, the apostles used typology to show that Christ continues and goes beyond the Old Testament. Peter speaks of Noah's baptism.[23] The author of Hebrews relates the tabernacle on earth with the one in heaven.[24] Paul writes: "These things happened to them to serve as an example, and they were written down to instruct us."[25]

The doctors of the church interpret Isaac, Joseph, and Jonah as types that point to and proclaim Jesus Christ. Stories told during the Easter Vigil—including creation, the sacrifice of Isaac, crossing the Red Sea, the valley of dry bones, and the rescue from the fiery furnace—can all be approached as types of Jesus's death and resurrection and ought to be on this holy night when, at length, the church tells its family story.

The difference between typology and contemporary methods of interpretation is that typology assumes both God and the supernatural or transcendent realm are part of the "historical" world, not confined to "private" experience. Like all ancient exegesis, whether pagan, Christian, or Jewish, typology assumes that scripture is the work of God, acting in and through human authors and events, and that God is precisely the source of its meaning. Typological interpretation therefore approaches the Bible as a whole, rather than as verses, chapters, pericopes, and books. In this regard, typology is neither "unbiased" nor "scientific."

Apostles, Gospel writers, church doctors, and, indeed, the church can apply typology by allowing, even expecting one event or image to give meaning to another. The characteristics and attributes of one reality or event correspond to another because the two events constitute the single reality of God's saving work. Rather than moving in a single, forward flow of time, history is a pond with God at the center, actively bringing about eras and events that reflect upon and correspond to one another, in the creating and redeeming will of God.

Christ Present as Interpretive Key

Of course, the Bible includes passages in which Christ simply is not present. As we look for Jesus in these texts and do not find him, we are careful not to use baseless allegory, tangential allusion, or anything else to insert, even force, Jesus into passages where Jesus is not present and does not belong. While Jesus may be the rock from which the Israelites drank in the wilderness, Jesus is not hiding under every rock in the Old Testament. Rather, in these instances, Christ functions as a *hermeneutic key* or an *interpretive lens*. While a text's original meaning informs our proclamation, the gospel determines the message we preach. At the same time, we remember Jesus fulfills and neither invalidates nor negates God's promises found in the Hebrew Scriptures.

For me, the gospel is the promise of John 3:16, John 10:10, John 12:32, and Romans 3:28. In Lutheran preaching, God's promise is justification by grace through faith apart from works. This promise is the norm for the content of Lutheran preaching. Whatever promises from and fulfilled in Jesus resonate with you, these promises provide a hermeneutic key or interpretive lens for preaching Jesus from Scripture, even when Jesus may go unnamed in the sermon. For preaching is the place where God's promises are spoken and not where Scripture is explained.

Jesus Christ as interpretive lens leads us to discount some passages of Scripture. For example, Leviticus declares that no one who is blind or has a blemish of the eye shall come near the altar to make offerings to the Lord.[26] People sometimes quote this text to "prove" that persons with disabilities should not be pastors (or bishops) since we are forbidden by God from celebrating the Lord's Supper. In response to this claim, John's Gospel counters, "His disciples asked him, 'Rabbi, who sinned, this man or his parents, that he was born blind?' Jesus answered, 'Neither this man nor his parents sinned; he was born blind so that God's works might be revealed in him.'"[27] We will not always find words of Jesus that directly respond to a passage that contradicts the gospel; however, to interpret a text through the lens of Christ Jesus is to consider how, in his words and actions, Jesus responds to and interprets that passage. After all, the Sermon on the Mount shows Jesus has a penchant for reinterpreting Scripture.[28]

Jesus is the key. Jesus is the lens. Stated another way, our fifty-word statement of the gospel aids in interpreting Scripture *so that* we preach Jesus. Or, more specifically, our fifty-word statement of the gospel helps us guard against interpreting and preaching a passage where Christ is not present in a manner that is inconsistent with or undermines God revealed in Jesus Christ.

To learn to interpret Scripture through the lens of Jesus or the gospel, preachers might ask what their—and their congregation's—"canon within the canon" is. Be sure that the verses selected are God's promise and not a command. Then preachers might use this "canon" to consider what ten verses they cannot live without and what ten verses they would remove from the Bible if they could. In this process, preachers learn firsthand that not all Scripture is equal for preaching Jesus.

Preaching Jesus and interpreting Scripture through the lens of Jesus obligates preachers to determine the reason we would preach from portions of the Bible that do not point to, reveal, or proclaim Jesus Christ. In an interreligious context, for example, preachers might choose to proclaim God's grace, mercy, forgiveness, or hope from Scripture Jews, Muslims, and Christians hold in common. When deciding to preach from passages where Christ is not present, however, preachers vigilantly guard against both using Scripture to warrant, bolster, and justify a message they want or feel compelled to preach and preaching a sermon for a purpose other than proclaiming Christ crucified. Preachers employ a variety of tools to locate Jesus in Scripture and to look through Jesus as our interpretive lens.

Tools for Interpretation

Opening the pulpit Bible—or any Bible we turn to when intending to bring a message to the pulpit—begins with recognition that this Bible is distinctive. The pulpit Bible is a combination of a study Bible and a devotional Bible. The pulpit Bible is also the church's Bible, overflowing with meanings, associations, and memories that form and sustain both Christians and congregations. The pulpit Bible is also the world's Bible, ideally bearing witness to God's love for all creation in Jesus Christ as those who do not yet know or consider themselves as belonging to God's family hear or overhear God's promises.

Opening and immersing oneself in the pulpit Bible takes all these realities seriously and therefore calls for a distinct approach and set of tools. I find that (1) prayer and (2) study need to complement each other. Preachers cultivate (3) a holy imagination, in part by (4) speaking the Bible, and check that imagination against the (5) memories and teaching of the church. Both (6) typology and a (7) law/gospel paradigm reveal Jesus and facilitate hearing the "now meaning," good news, and promise for Christ's people and for the world today. This jumble of practices come together in proclamation. Here, I pull apart the jumble and consider them one by one. Except for beginning and ending with prayer, I am not advocating a particular order for using these tools.

Prayer

Fulfilled in Your Hearing declares that preachers are, above all else, to be prayerful.[29] Prayerfulness does not mean prayer alongside preparation for preaching, or prayer over and above preparation. Prayer is the heart and center of sermon preparation, starting with our study of Scripture. The intention of praying as sermon preparation is that the word of God in the Scriptures is "interiorized."[30] It is written on the preacher's heart. Whatever our exegetical method or way of studying Scripture, in sermon preparation, we open the Bible and undertake that work prayerfully. We approach every part of sermon preparation as a form of prayer.

We ask God, by the power of the Holy Spirit, to reveal Jesus to us in the word. Preachers pray over the readings, asking for the fire of the Holy Spirit to kindle "the now meaning,"[31] the good news Jesus brings, in our hearts. Since the "now meaning" is for the assembly that will receive the sermon, we ask the Holy Spirit to open the heart of the assembly, so God's Word falls on receptive ears. We pray for the world, for those who will hear the message from members of the assembly or overhear the message in some other way. This prayer keeps the assembly near us as we study. For, as *Fulfilled in Your Hearing* observes, "The homily is not so much *on* the Scriptures as *from* and *through* them."[32]

Prayer requires that preachers make study and sermon preparation both deliberate and leisurely to afford the preacher time, after asking questions of the readings and of God through the readings, to pause, wait, and listen. I find it helpful to have established checkpoints during the week: initial reading of Scripture Sunday evening, prayerful contemplation on Monday, having a hunch of the good news and direction Monday evening, studying Tuesday, selecting the good news Wednesday, writing the sermon by Friday, taking time away until 9:00 p.m. Saturday, memorizing the sermon Saturday night, and preaching Sunday morning.

Preachers listen for the Holy Spirit *breathing* in and through the readings. While we may occasionally hear the Holy Spirit as "a sound like the rush of a violent wind" in Acts 2, most often we hear the Holy Spirit like the sound of breathing in John 20. I experience hearing the Holy Spirit like a parent lying awake, listening to their child breathing as she sleeps in the next room, and finding meaning in the sound. I also hear the Holy Spirit breathing in the readings as I spend the week memorizing aloud one of the readings—for me, usually the appointed gospel—as I "interiorize" the reading and match its words to my breathing and my breathing to its words.

Study

Biblical scholarship blesses preachers with a host of exegetical methods for studying Scripture. Historical criticism, canon criticism, structuralism, literary-critical studies, and performance criticism are but a few. While I would not presume to describe and assess these methods, I offer seven suggestions on how to use exegetical methods to study Scripture to preach Jesus.

First, *use a method that requires you to spend time with the text or reading before turning to the commentaries.* Set aside what you think the reading is about, at least for a while, and invite it to speak to you anew. Look at words and word choices, as well as how the reading holds together. Plot out the story using the elements of story—actor, action, object, time, place, and props. When we do, we find, for example, the innocents King Herod slaughtered in Bethlehem function in the story as props; sermons are not about the plight of those innocent children.[33] Noting the stages of the transformation in the story may help to specify relationships in the text. I think, for example, of how the woman at the well addresses Jesus—Jew, prophet, Messiah—reveals her coming to faith.[34]

Spend enough time with the text or reading that it makes you curious and stimulates thinking. When you do, the purpose of study becomes finding answers to your questions and testing your hunches, as opposed to indiscriminately soaking up information like a sponge. To spend time with the text or reading gives Scripture the first word and guarantees that sermons come from the Bible and not a commentary.

Second, *focus on Christ—or God or the Holy Spirit.* Consciously resist the temptation to focus on the human characters in the story to determine what we are—or are not—to do or to be. As God's family stories, the texts or readings are primarily about God. In preaching, we study Scripture to proclaim Christ. Ask *What is God, Jesus, or the Holy Spirit doing that is good news from God to God's people and the world?*

Third, *employ a method that assumes Scripture is true.* Preaching is not the occasion to deconstruct or demythologize the

Bible in a way that undermines preaching Jesus. For example, Christmas Eve is not the time to question the historical reality of the incarnation. Use a method that affirms the Bible's normative status as God's word in and for the church. It is certainly appropriate to question and challenge the Bible. However, the sermon is not the place to raise questions and leave them either unresolved or resolved in a way that undermines God's promise in Jesus Christ. As I tell students and remind myself, "Don't lead the congregation into the woods if you don't know the way out."

Fourth, *use a method that takes you into the world of the Bible.* Although Scripture speaks *to* us, Scripture was not written *for* us. The Bible exhibits an existential "otherness" that demands interpretation. This "otherness" affirms the place of sound exegesis because these texts were written, and these stories told, in another time and place. In addition to understanding the differences, noting the correspondence or connection between the biblical world and our own can help us grasp the "now" meaning of the text.

Fifth, *consider the reading or text in its various contexts.* I most often consider a reading's biblical, lectionary, seasonal, and pastoral contexts. A reading's biblical context is its place in any relation to the book of the Bible in which it is found. The lectionary context considers how the appointed readings for a given Sunday speak to and relate to one another. I am particularly interested in the relationship between the Old Testament reading and the Gospel. Together, these two contexts remind us that the text or reading has integrity. We need to be cautious about how we color readings through our use of other readings.

The seasonal (church year) context takes seriously that festivals and seasons help us to hear the same reading from different perspectives and with different emphases. Depending on the season, a reading demands a different interpretation. To consider the seasonal context requires knowing what the seasons are about. For example, Holy Week is always about Jesus; if we could do what Jesus does for us during Holy Week, we would not need Jesus as our Savior.

Likewise, the pastoral context shapes interpretation, depending on our own relationship to the text or reading. Preachers cannot interpret Scripture objectively as surely as congregations cannot receive Scripture objectively. We all bring questions, perceptions, and experiences that influence our relationship with Scripture. Preachers might ask themselves: What promise, and demand, has God made on my life through this reading? How will preaching a sermon on this reading affect me? Turning to the congregation, preachers consider how it will be for the congregation to receive a sermon on this reading from this preacher. For example, I eventually learned that my being legally blind influences how some people receive sermons on stories of Jesus healing from me. More important, most preachers come to believe over time that they and their parishioners are more similar than different, and so share—or should share—the same questions and concerns. We need to check that.

Sixth, *become proficient enough at your method of study that you trust yourself*—your insights and your conclusions—enough that the commentaries become colleagues you consult. After writing commentaries for preaching, I realized that, while some commentators certainly possess scholarly knowledge and expertise, the gift of many commentators is the time, energy, and deliberation they devoted to the reading well in advance of preaching. They are colleagues with whom we can check our own insights, hunches, and conclusions. Of course, to approach commentaries as colleagues, we need to know about the commentators: their background, perspectives and biases, method of study, and whether we find them trustworthy. This is especially true with online commentaries. We need to decide whether this is a colleague whose consultation we value and respect.

Finally, *determine how much study you will do and how much of the fruits of your study you will include in the sermon.* When I learned to be a barista, I realized that coffee is like the Bible and the grind is exegesis—the process of analyzing and interpreting the biblical text. Relying too much on biblical commentaries is like using pre-ground coffee. Much of the work is done for you but, like the coffee, the exegesis is dated. The best sermons, like the best espresso, require freshness.

Preachers, then, are like coffee grinders. Some grind very finely; their exegesis is thorough and detailed, even scholarly, and they are eager to share it in the sermon. The risk is that the living water of the gospel can get clogged up in the exegesis. Some preachers grind very coarsely; they rely more on their response to Scripture than on research, and there is little if any biblical background in the sermon. The risk here is that the living water of the gospel flows so quickly and easily through the sermon that it lacks substance, depth, and flavor. Of course, the proper amount of exegesis varies, depending on the discipline of the preacher and the expectations of the congregation.

So how much studying should we do? When making espresso, we adjust the time and the grind until we find the "sweet spot." That can vary, depending on the coffee and the atmospheric conditions. Our study depends on the reading and what is happening in the congregation and in the world. No one may ever see the fruit of our labor; however, they are likely to notice if we have not done the work. Using another image, study and exegesis is a rudder. We need to do enough to stay on course. Like a rudder on a ship, we do not need to see evidence of study in the sermon to know that it is there. Even without seeing it, though, the congregation will know when the rudder is not there or is not working.

Holy Imagination

After studying a text or reading, preachers can spend time exercising their "holy imagination." Holy imagination attempts to recreate the event contained in the reading as faithfully and multidimensionally as possible. Holy imagination is different from both free association and turning off the internal editor or filter while allowing the imagination to run free. Holy imagination is informed, grounded, bounded by study and prayer, and accountable to the church. Its purpose is, as much as possible, to reconvert the written text or spoken story back into the event of God from which it emerged. Preachers exercise holy imagination so that, in addition to reading words on a page, preachers can draw on sounds, smells, and scenery to bring the event of God to life for their hearers.

I periodically recall a sermon on Jesus's encounter with the widow of Nain,[35] in which the preacher, using holy imagination, proclaimed the good news that Jesus raised the widow's son. The preacher vividly described the widow walking slowly, slumped over, following her dead son, carried on the bier, in the funeral procession. The widow stopped suddenly and looked up in shock and anger when Jesus told her not to weep. She stood up straight when Jesus told her dead son to rise and opened her arms wide when Jesus gave him to her. The good news, communicated in the widow's posture, is Jesus raises us from grief, isolation, and poverty, as well as death.

To exercise holy imagination is to look beyond the text to what the text points to. Like a play script, the text is the written word; then there is the play, the event, concept or idea the text points to. To exercise holy imagination is like directing a play. We consider those elements the text may not provide. For example, we might ask how something was said. We have the words, but what was the tone? We can read direct quotes aloud with different emphases, moods, and intonation. We can ask why something was said. What was the context and intent of these words?

We can explore the setting. For example, that Jesus went to Nain is significant. Nain is small and out of the way; why did Jesus decide or feel compelled to go there? We can consider where people are positioned. With Jesus and his crowd heading into town and the widow and her crowd heading out of town, the gate becomes the point of collusion between death and life. We imaginatively exercise all our senses. How would we visualize the story? What sounds do we hear? What smells do we smell?

We can imagine the perspectives of different characters in the story. How do their perceptions differ? For example, how would someone in the crowd accompanying Jesus experience Jesus stopping the funeral procession compared to someone who is in the funeral procession? It is helpful not to confine ourselves to the perspective of a single character. I advise preachers to never imagine themselves as Jesus since, in the example we are using, we cannot command anyone to rise from physical death to life.

Speak the Bible

We develop a panoramic view of the Bible and cultivate holy imagination by speaking the Bible the way people speak in slang, jargon, and pop culture references. With practice, speaking the Bible becomes second nature. When we speak the Bible, we learn to connect scriptural characters, stories, images, and phrases with one another and with our lives and the world. In time, stories, characters, images, and phrases become our frame of reference. They come to us in our minds and memories; then we turn to the book to locate and confirm them. Speaking the Bible is one way God writes the word on our hearts.[36]

Speaking the Bible is not using the Bible to justify, defend, and reinforce other worldviews or operating assumptions. Instead, speaking the Bible invites us to reflect on everything using biblical images, narratives, and frames of reference. For example, I rejoice when lay leaders caution against burying our talents in the ground and storing up too much wheat in our barns. Speaking the Bible teaches us to understand ourselves—church and world—in biblical terms and see the church as a continuation of God's saving work recorded in the Bible.

Church Check-In

Preachers hold themselves accountable to the church, through its creeds and doctrines, to check that both their interpretation and their holy imagination are in keeping with the church's teaching, since they preach on behalf of the Christian church. To preach according to the church's creeds and confessions, preachers must know the creeds and confessions.

To know the creeds and confessions is to be clear about the questions the creeds and confessions are meant to address and the ones they are not. For example, the first article of the Apostles' Creed names God the Creator "Father." Yet, this name for God does not define God the Creator's gender. Those who use the creed to "prove" God's maleness answer a question the creed was never intended to address. On the other hand, the Lutheran explanation of the Third Article found in Luther's Small Catechism, "that by my own understanding or strength I cannot believe in Jesus Christ my Lord or come to him,"[37] has direct implications for Lutheran preaching, including the inappropriateness of using the words *shall*, *ought*, and *must* to name the human response to the gospel.

To know the creeds and confessions is to understand our relationship to these church documents. Many pastors promise to preach and teach in accordance with the creeds and confessions of the church. I invite preachers to notice that we promise to preach and teach and not to believe. We will have doubts and dark nights of the soul; we do not work these things out in the pulpit. These conversations are had with a colleague, pastor, mentor, spiritual director, or confessor.

Preachers also check how the church uses a given passage of Scripture to proclaim Jesus Christ. Preachers exhibit a respect for the interpretations that have shaped the church's use of a text. These are passages that have given the church insight in the past and to which it returns again and again. Even when preachers depart from the church's use of a text, they acknowledge the church's use before moving in a new direction, if only to help the congregation to follow along.

Typology

Typology invites us to find Christ in the Old Testament by considering how the realities of the Old Testament are figures of Jesus's person and actions in the New Testament. I previously considered typology as a way Christ is present in the Scriptures. Now, I present typology as a tool for interpretation. To do this, we must embrace the paradox that the "original" meaning of a given passage of Scripture can have nothing to do with Jesus and everything to do with Jesus because of its "type," and we do not need to decide which interpretation is correct because both are true. While Moses did not regard crossing the Red Sea as a figure of Christian baptism, I suspect Moses would not have been surprised that God would find a way to use that crossing to save more than the people of Israel who actually passed through the sea on that day. Scripture overflows with layers of meaning.

The word *type* may be used for any "model" or "pattern" or "parable" foreshadowing its fulfillment, whether an event or a repeated ritual. For Christian preaching, typological interpretation involves discerning meaning by consciously or unconsciously reading Scripture to discover correspondence with the person or actions of Jesus as described in the New Testament. Preachers identify the details in the type and in Jesus that demonstrate their correspondence. The preacher then identifies how, together, Jesus and the type disclose God's saving activity. Typological interpretation depends on the preacher possessing familiarity with the details of the stories of Scripture or having access to the types the church has historically used to proclaim Jesus.

Modern scholars distinguish between typology or "historical" events that foreshadow later events and allegory, textual elements that are taken as referring to other, usually spiritual, realities. Allegory is rightly regarded with skepticism. Typology is an accepted tool of interpretation, perhaps because to employ typology is to preach biblically.

The Gospel of Matthew, for example, portrays Jesus as a type of Moses even greater than Moses. God delivered both Moses and Jesus from the king who sought to kill them.[38] God called both Moses and Jesus out of Egypt.[39] Both Moses and Jesus ascended a mountain in relation to God's law. Moses received the law; Jesus reinterpreted the law.[40] On Mount Sinai, Moses saw the glory of God. On another mountain, Moses saw Jesus transfigured into the glory of God.[41] In this and other instances, typological interpretation is true to Matthew's intent.

Law and Gospel

Lutheran Christians turn to and even treasure the categories of "Law" and "Gospel" to understand and explain the proclamation of God's Word, Jesus Christ: "Jesus Christ is the Word of God incarnate. The proclamation of God's message to us is both Law and Gospel."[42] Lutheran Christians consider the distinction between Law and Gospel a central key to interpreting the Scriptures in a way that proclaims Christ. Lutheran theologian Herman Stuempfle writes: "As preachers we will actively 'listen' for many things in the text—its form, its linguistic structure, its referents to a history outside itself—but we will listen for nothing more intently than for the dominant accent with which it speaks, whether of Law or Gospel."[43]

Law refers to God's law. God's law is first a gift from God. The law is God's gracious pattern for creation and for human relationships that offers life and peace in community.[44] Martin Luther drew upon the insights of the apostle Paul to identify another use of the law. The law convicts people of sin and at the same time reflects the broken nature of human existence. Thus, the law drives us to look for help from someone who can deliver us from the depths of our human predicament.[45] Glenn Monson encapsulates Law in the declaration, "You need Christ!" More universally, Paul Scott Wilson calls Law "trouble."[46] The preaching of the law brings a word of judgment to our estrangement from God, ourselves, one another, and creation and diagnoses the depth of human need.

The *gospel* is God's promise of forgiveness and gracious reconciliation. God loves us and all creation with an everlasting love. We are reconciled to God through Jesus Christ, crucified and risen. The Holy Spirit continues to form our lives with gifts of grace and to empower us in bearing witness to the good news.[47] Glenn Monson encapsulates Gospel in the proclamation, "Here is Christ!" Paul Scott Wilson calls Gospel "grace."[48] The preaching of the gospel conveys to us God's forgiveness and new life with a word of hope that answers our deepest need.

Stuempfle encourages preachers to ask, "Does this text utter a judgment which throws our life and that of our culture under radical question? Does it evoke some poignant aspect of our alienated humanity—loneliness, anxiety, hopelessness?" Alternatively, "Does it resound with some liberating word of affirmation and promise? Does it lay upon us some inexorable demand growing out of God's own unconditional and indescribable generosity?"[49]

Some readings demonstrate our need of God. Other readings proclaim God's loving response in Jesus Christ and how Jesus meets our need. Still other readings reveal the movement from our need to God's response in Jesus to the new life that results. Stuempfle writes, "Some texts will bid us answer 'Yes' to all of those questions. Others will speak more loudly with only one accent. As preachers we will pray for sensitivity to hear the characteristic Word of each text, and for integrity and skill to allow that Word to dominate the sermon we preach."[50]

Law and Gospel in a reading is contextual. Preachers will certainly consider a reading's original or historical context. Preachers also take seriously the congregation—as a community and as an assembly of individuals—in determining whether a reading is Law, Gospel, or both. The question is whether a reading is Law or Gospel for this faith community in its current situation.

For example, Mary said of the Lord God: "He has brought down the powerful from their thrones, and lifted up the lowly; he has filled the hungry with good things, and sent the rich away empty."[51] Whether these words are Law or Gospel depends on whether those hearing them are rich and powerful or lowly and hungry. Rather than categorizing a reading as either Law or Gospel, we might better ask: What is the law, trouble, or bad news in this passage? What is the corresponding law, trouble, or bad news today? What is the gospel, grace, or good news in this passage? What is the corresponding gospel, grace, or good news today?[52]

Even when a reading appears to be in itself wholly Law or Gospel, the actual sermon will not be without its counter dimension. Stuempfle instructs, "In living proclamation, we are always concerned about Law *and* Gospel. These categories live within the sermon in a dialectical relationship manifesting the same dynamic interchange as inhaling and exhaling or the coursing of blood outward from the heart through the arteries and its return through the veins."[53]

The inseparability of Law and Gospel is true because the total biblical witness is the wider context of each individual reading and cannot be ignored when we preach. On the one hand, the gospel is the promise of John 3:16, and this promise is our hermeneutic. Preaching is the place where promises are spoken and not where Scripture is explained. On the other hand, we cannot make the Gospel credible in our preaching without at least some indication of our awareness of those aspects of the human situation to which it speaks.

Herman Stuempfle says, "The proclamation of God's word is Law, Gospel, and the call to obedience"[54]—what I call the invitation to participate in what God is doing. This paradigm invites preachers to consider what is different at the end of a biblical narrative than at the beginning, what God, Jesus, or the Holy Spirit did to bring about this change, and how we can be part of the difference the triune God accomplishes in our lives in the world. Law is about God's purpose for and relationship with a creation God calls good and a humanity created in God's image. We preach good news and not legalism. Gospel is the good news that God in Christ is restoring creation to goodness and accomplishing God's purpose among us.

Return to Prayer

I return to prayer as a reminder to "pray without ceasing,"[55] to be prayerful in everything we do to understand and interpret Scripture. After I have done this work, returning to prayer calls for creating space in my mind and being in a place where insights, thoughts, glimpses, connections, and revelations come to me. I never hear the Holy Spirit breathing through the readings when I tell God it is time to write the sermon. God makes the "now meaning" of Scripture known to me when I allow time to wait on God and space to be open to God.

Finally, a regular routine of sermon preparation can be a form of prayer. While we can neither verify it nor point to Scripture to guarantee it, many preachers find the Holy Spirit works through a sound and faithful homiletic method. A homiletic method can be (and is for me) a form of prayer that is sacramental. In the next chapter, I share the homiletic method I use to help you consider your own.

6

The Walk to the Pulpit

"What's the Good News?"

When I taught preaching, I met with every student a day or two before they preached for what we called "logjam" sessions, a practice I learned from my mentor. Preachers are more interested in input before they preach than in feedback afterward. It is also much easier to learn good habits than to unlearn bad habits. In preaching, it is more fruitful to emphasize preparation than evaluation.

When I met with a student and the sermon was progressing well, I worked through the student's manuscript and offered suggestions. When it truly was a "logjam" session, I worked to get the student "unstuck." My question after greeting the student was always the same: "What's the good news?" If a student stated the good news of the sermon in a single sentence, we were in great shape. If the student answered with several sentences or a paragraph, I knew we had more than one sermon percolating, and I needed to help the student focus or choose which sermon to preach. If the student told me there was no good news or said they could not find any good news, I knew I was in trouble.

"What's the good news?" To preach Jesus is to pursue, discover, and proclaim good news. "The kingdom of heaven is like treasure hidden in a field, which someone found and hid; then in his joy he goes and sells all that he has and buys that field."[1] I am convinced that, when we find God's good news, Jesus is never far away. As much as we want to stumble upon this treasure, finding good news takes time, commitment, and work. The preacher's "walk to the pulpit" is long and frequently arduous. How this weekly journey unfolds depends on how we prepare sermons.

I regard sermon preparation as a *pilgrimage*, a journey of spiritual significance into the very presence of Jesus as Savior. I compare my sermon pilgrimage to that of Nicodemus, questioning at the start and bearing witness at the finish. To make this pilgrimage is to be guided by a map, a recipe, a routine, a route, or a method—a weekly walk to the pulpit we follow because we trust it to bring us to Jesus, so we return with good news to share.

In this chapter, I lay out the method of sermon preparation I teach. It is also the map I follow on my weekly walk to the pulpit. I trust this route and routine to bring me to Jesus and good news. This method is one of many from which preachers can choose. I offer this method to help you examine and evaluate your own walk to the pulpit and discover aspects of your route and routine where you want to stay the course and perhaps other aspects where you might want to change direction and come to Jesus by another way. I present this method in six sections: (1) build, (2) ponder, (3) order, (4) create, (5) proclaim, and, optionally, (6) memorize, to spiritually prepare to preach. For this homiletic method and my presentation of it, as for so much of my homiletic pedagogy, I am indebted to John Allyn Melloh.[2]

Build

All homiletic methods are built on foundations. Before appraising their methods, preachers identify the foundations on which their routine of sermon preparation are built. This homiletic method is built on three: (1) the goal is to preach Jesus, (2) method is a way of welcoming the Holy Spirit, and (3) Scripture is a record of God's saving events.

First, the goal is to preach Jesus, to proclaim Christ, crucified and risen, as the power and wisdom of God.[3] To preach Jesus is to raise the dead, to move people from death to new life. To preach Christ crucified and risen, then, it is not enough to get the gospel *said*. Preachers are responsible to God and their congregations to get the gospel *heard*. So, sermon form and delivery are as important as the message. A homiletic method is effective when preachers get the gospel heard so people move from death to new life.

Second, we embrace a homiletic method as a friend, rather than as a constraint. A method, an orderly way of proceeding, guarantees some result. Surgeons, chefs, musicians, and pilots all use methods; they do not just "try something." Having a method, knowing what to do, creates confidence. A method releases and governs creativity in liberating ways. A method also helps preachers do what we need to do during weeks we would rather not, because, regardless of how we feel, Sunday is coming.

Whether they know it or not, whether they can name it or not, every preacher has a method of sermon preparation. Preachers who do not plan for getting to the pulpit eventually realize their walk is unnecessarily stressful; some Sundays, they arrive unprepared. Most preachers map out their walk to the pulpit by building on others' methods, particularly methods they find welcome and work with the Holy Spirit. A homiletic method should convince the preacher that, as the Holy Spirit works through means—word, water, bread, and wine—the Holy Spirit works through a sound homiletic method followed faithfully. Developing a method of sermon preparation we trust and rely on empowers preachers to *expect* the Holy Spirit to act in all the ways Jesus promises.

Third, the Bible is the written record of the scripted stories of God's saving events. God reveals Godself in events in time and space, which always give rise to a story. These stories are "slanted" and "scripted" by the community for whom they are significant. Eventually these scripted stories get written down. In sermon preparation, we study Scripture so we can tell the story and uncover or recover God's saving event proclaimed in the Bible and continuing today. We move from how God reveals Godself to us in the events of the Bible to how God reveals Godself to us here and now in the events of the world in which we live. We do this because we understand Scripture not as presenting things that happened long ago and far away but as presenting models or paradigms or prototypes of how God has dealt with God's people and is dealing with God's people. We make this claim because we are confident God is faithful in dealing with God's people. Thus, we identify the event that is taking place in biblical time and the event that is taking place in our world.

On these foundations we build a four-step process of sermon preparation: (1) ponder, (2) order, (3) create, and (4) proclaim. Most weeks, I ponder Sunday evening, Monday, and Tuesday. I order on Wednesday. I create Thursday and Friday. I proclaim Saturday night when I memorize and Sunday morning when I preach. During the pandemic, the pattern shifted so that Sunday morning became Wednesday morning, when I recorded my sermon for the following Sunday. Regardless of when my preaching week begins and ends, I am most aware of being yoked to Jesus in the fourth leg of my walk to the pulpit when, like Nicodemus, I come to Jesus by night.

Ponder

In sermon preparation, we ponder Scripture as a story. To *ponder* Scripture is to think about the readings carefully and prayerfully, especially before making a decision or reaching a conclusion about their meaning. To ponder is to read, pray over, and study Scripture. Paul advises, "Let the word of Christ dwell in you richly."[4]

To ponder Scripture is to read the readings not once but over and over; to ponder is to let Scripture work on us before we run to the commentaries. Pondering includes reading Scripture in different ways: aloud as well as silently, alone and with others, at different places and different times. To ponder Scripture is to return to the readings again and again throughout the week, during every phase of our walk to the pulpit, even after we have decided what the readings mean and what the sermon is about. My best way of pondering Scripture is to memorize it.

To ponder is to read Scripture in "uncluttered space." These are places of peace, quiet, solitude, and intentional conversation with others about the reading. Uncluttered space is not a place of interruption, commotion, or multitasking. To ponder Scripture in an uncluttered space is to join Mary, seated at the Lord's feet and listening to what he is saying. When someone tells us or we tell ourselves to abandon our uncluttered space because we should be about more pressing or important work, we hear Jesus speaking to us as he says, "Martha, Martha, you are worried and distracted by many things; there is need of only one thing. Mary has chosen the better part, which will not be taken away from her."[5]

Pondering includes converting the reading back into the story from whence it came. We do this by telling the story as if to a six-year-old. We stay as close to the language of Scripture as possible but translate biblical and theological concepts into the language of experience. Preachers become practiced doing this by reading stories to children.

Once we have done the work necessary to "interiorize"[6] the reading, we are prepared to study the reading. Whatever tools we use, it is important to do our own work before turning to others. Congregations send their preachers to study Scripture on their behalf, but they desire the fruits of their preacher's direct encounter with God's word and not a report on a commentator's encounter with God's word. Regardless of how expert the commentator, no one knows and cares about the congregation like their preacher; no one is better able to bring them to God's word and to bring God's word to them.

We do not rush too quickly to arrive at a conclusion about what a reading means. Instead, we try out possibilities. We might ask: How is the event present to us in our time? What is going on in the liturgy, congregation, community, and world that impacts hearing and understanding this reading? Before making a final decision on what the reading means, we intentionally wait on the Holy Spirit. We allow time for incubation. "Sermons are prepared in slow-cookers and not microwave ovens," we caution preachers. Cooking them too quickly may result in their being half-baked.

Especially during times of incubation, we recognize and attend to "aha" moments, times when and places where insights bubble up unexpectedly, and are prepared for them. Once we have given the readings and the Holy Spirit their say, we check the commentaries as a "conversation partner" and a colleague.

Order

Pondering results in lots of insights, lots of information, lots of images, and lots of good news, often too much for any single sermon. Pondering leads to ordering, to determining the central idea or focus or message of the sermon. I was taught the helpful adage: "Light mist in the pulpit equals heavy fog in the pew." If the preacher is not crystal clear about the message of the sermon, the congregation will likely be completely lost.

In determining the central message of the sermon, decide on one and only one insight. Preachers cannot talk about everything, the entire mystery of faith, in every sermon. For preachers and congregations that follow a lectionary and liturgical calendar, different parts of the *kerygma*, or apostolic proclamation of salvation through Jesus Christ, are emphasized at different seasons or times of the year. We allow the festival and liturgical season to contribute to the central message.

The goal when determining the message of the sermon is to formulate a "focus statement." A *focus statement* is a "single sentence that summarizes the thrust of the sermon."[7] The focus statement is good news from God concerning God's love for the world and God's will for justice in the world. It is a simple sentence that includes a subject, action verb, and predicate. The subject is normally God, Jesus, or the Holy Spirit. The action verb is usually an activity of God: loving, healing, saving, freeing. The predicate is usually a benefit or consequence of God's love and justice. The tone of the focus statement is ordinarily positive, hopeful, and encouraging. "Jesus loves us to the end"[8] is a good focus statement; "Let us do better" is not.

The focus statement is appropriate to the congregation. The preacher's task is to decide what about the Gospel is new and good for the congregation in its situation. To speak to the community of faith, the preacher considers all who make up the congregation. Some congregations may need to hear more about the freedom of the gospel; other congregations may need to hear more about the responsibility of living under the gospel. But the preacher's task is always to discover and proclaim the gospel. Even when the congregation falls under the indictment of the law, the focus statement seeks to show how the gospel empowers the congregation to move beyond its limitations.

I like to think of the focus statement as a beacon or light-house that shines on everything—content, form, and style of delivery—the preacher considers including in the sermon. As a general rule, if the beacon is enhanced or reflected by what-ever the preacher is considering, it is appropriate to the ser-mon; if the beacon is diminished or obscured, it is not. Things that diminish the light in this sermon might enhance the light in another; therefore, they are best saved and included where they fit rather than wasted by being forced into a ser-mon where they do not belong.

At this point in the walk to the pulpit, many preachers are given to pause or even find themselves stalled because they are not positive what to say. They want a burning bush or a voice from a cloud to tell them. While God may occasionally speak miraculously or so loudly and clearly that the preacher has no doubt about what needs to be said and heard, most often determining the central message of the sermon is a matter of consideration and choice. Preachers must decide "the now meaning,"[9] the good news Jesus brings, in our hearts. Deciding is easier when our goal is to preach Jesus.

Create

Creating the sermon is giving form to focus. The goal is not only to get the gospel *said* but to get the gospel *heard*. Creat-ing the sermon takes seriously the point of contact where the message meets the listener. Therefore, the shape or form of the sermon is based on the message or content of the sermon but, more than that, the shape or form of the sermon is a way of getting the message heard. Fred Craddock writes, "The form of a sermon is active, contributing to what the speaker wishes to say and do, sometimes no less persuasive than the content itself."[10]

The impact of how sermons are created becomes evident when we compare Peter's and Stephen's first sermons as recorded in Acts.[11] When Peter addressed the people concerning Jesus on Pentecost, "those who welcomed his message were baptized, and that day about three thousand persons were added.[12] Yet, when Stephen preaches, Stephen is stoned to death.

Both preachers were filled with the Holy Spirit. Neither was looking for trouble. Both preached about how God is fulfilling God's promises. Both preached from the Scriptures. Peter used Joel and the Psalms. Stephen chose Genesis and Exodus. Both Peter and Stephen preached as most important what God has done and is doing in Jesus. Peter preached, "This Jesus God raised up, and of that all of us are witnesses." Stephen's message is even more vivid. "Look," he said, "I see the heavens opened and the Son of Humanity standing at the right hand of God!"

But the sermons they created are different. First, Stephen's sermon is much longer than Peter's; perhaps that is why they stoned Stephen. Second, their audience analysis differs. Peter addresses the Pentecost crowd as "fellow Israelites," what we might call "siblings, members of the people of God." But Stephen calls the high priest and council "stiff-necked, uncircumcised in heart and ears, oppressors of the Holy Spirit, and murderers and betrayers of the Righteous One." Though Peter's and Stephen's message is the same, the reaction to their sermons is completely opposite. This difference is partially explained by the language and construction of their sermons. Creating the sermon matters.

Creating the sermon includes developing or choosing a sermon form, structure, or design and enriching that structure with word choice, description, illustration, and tone. I believe the best way to create a sermon is to write a manuscript.

Writing is a means to arrive at good organization, clarity of expression, and concreteness. A manuscript provides the necessary distance we need to examine, evaluate, and edit the sermon; this is more difficult when the sermon never leaves the preacher's mind and heart during the creative process and when the sermon remains imprecise in an outline. I write the manuscript by speaking the sermon out loud, often using a dictation application, so the sermon is an oral rather than a literary form. For example, long, clause-lead sentences that are beautiful in books are difficult for the preacher to speak and the congregation to receive and comprehend. The manuscript must reflect the way the preacher speaks and facilitate the congregation's listening.

Designing the Sermon

Once the focus or good news statement is determined, the first step in creating the sermon is to decide on or develop the sermon design. The sermon design is the sermon's frame, structure, or skeleton. No single, established form is suitable for all sermons. There are distinct forms or structures that work best for creating a sermon on a particular text for a particular context. Designs include central image, story or narrative, binary oppositions, siding against the text, and moving from our problem to God's solution; these designs can all produce effective proclamation of the gospel. The preacher's task is to select or develop a sermon design that is hospitable not only to the gospel encapsulated in the focus statement, but also to the congregation receiving, experiencing, understanding, and appropriating the good news.

The sermon design is biblical. The sermon is constructed to connect the biblical world of "there and then" to our world of "here and now." In creating the sermon, preachers allow both the authority of the sermon and the way it is crafted to flow from the features of the reading. For example, the design respects the reading's genre; it treats a parable like a parable and not an object lesson with an obvious moral. The sermon design goes with (or at least acknowledges) "the grain"—the genre and church's interpretation of the reading. For example, neither Mark nor Luke brings their account of the resurrection to an airtight conclusion. Sermons on these readings ought not be created to tie up the message neatly with a bow.

The sermon design is appropriate to the congregation. In most congregations, inspiring works better than directing; exploring is better than defining. The preacher considers the forms of sermons the congregation is accustomed to and appreciates. While preachers do not automatically create sermons using these forms, they recognize that a new or unfamiliar sermon design might influence how the congregation receives—or does not receive—the message.

The preacher also anticipates how the congregation will likely feel about the message and respond to the sermon. Telling a story or moving from the particular to the general is a better approach when the sermon must change minds and hearts or move people to a different response. Laying out a theme and building on it works best when the congregation agrees with the premise. In addition to creating a sermon for the congregation, preachers remain aware of all who may overhear the message by speaking to as diverse a community as possible. There is no *them* in God's reign; in Christ, all have a place.

To preach Jesus, sermons are structured to proclaim good news. These sermons name with equal vigor sin and grace, law and gospel, cross and resurrection, judgment and mercy, then they fall on the side of grace. I taught students to include a shovel of grace for every shovel of dirt they buried the congregation with and then add an extra shovel of grace to get the congregation out of the grave. The concreteness and intensity of judgment and mercy must match. Convict the hearers of their sin but then convince them of God's grace; we need both sides of the coin. We also need a moment of deliverance when the congregation experiences being saved from sin by God's grace in Jesus Christ. This moment of deliverance includes a clear and unambiguous statement of the gospel. More than mouthing the gospel in a doctrinal or formulaic manner, the sermon must mean the gospel; that is, the sermon proclaims the gospel as good news that means something to these hearers.

To preach Jesus, sermons are structured so invitation or exhortation to remember, believe, give, serve, change, grow, or do follows and flows from the proclamation of the gospel. The sermon is crafted so any explicit call for faithful response does not overshadow, undermine, obscure, or equivocate the gospel in a way that people feel coerced by the erroneous notion that God's love depends upon their actions.

When the gospel proclamation is big and bold, the invitation or exhortation can be simple, straightforward, and, in fact, feels natural and fun. On the other hand, I have learned to regard the need to insist, cajole, and convince in any given sermon as an indication that the gospel proclamation is weak or small. Expanding the gospel proclamation diminishes the need to tell people to respond. It is best to create a sermon to preach Jesus, describe what God is doing, lift up possibilities for our participation, and then invite people to remember, believe, give, grow, and serve.

Turning to the invitation or exhortation itself, to preach Jesus is to recognize the congregation's first response is to experience Jesus in worship by singing Jesus's praise, confessing faith in Jesus as part of the creed, turning to Jesus in prayer, and receiving Jesus in the Lord's Supper. Sermons are crafted to inspire and empower the congregation to do these things. Sermons leave the congregation with a *eucha-ristic attitude*: "I want to give God thanks and praise." This is distinct from "I want to feel good." We can be aware of our brokenness and the ways we have failed to live as God's people and still thank and praise God for Jesus Christ.

Sermons that preach Jesus avoid language that makes God's mission dependent upon us, because it is not. These sermons are realistic in their call for response. Since sermons have a life span of one week, if we are lucky, preachers craft sermons to lead the congregation to *do* something *in the coming week*. Preachers recognize that, sometimes, asking people to con-tinue to have faith, despite everything they see happening around them, is the most difficult thing they can be asked to do. When these responses seem small and insignificant, preachers can console themselves by recalling preaching's "cumulative effect."

Sermons that invite people to respond to the gospel are created to identify the obstacles that prevent the congrega-tion from responding and show how Jesus overcomes them, freeing us to respond in faith and love. They are designed to appeal to people's best selves, entreating them as God's children, claimed by Christ, filled with the Holy Spirit, and empowered for service by God's grace. We use Peter's "fellow Israelites," and not Stephen's "stiff-necked, uncircumcised in heart and ears, oppressors of the Holy Spirit, and murderers and betrayers of the Righteous One."

Enriching the Structure

Once the sermon design is determined, the next step in cre-ating the sermon is to enrich the structure with word choice, description, illustration, and tone. Recalling Ezekiel's vision of the valley of the dry bones,[18] we are attaching sinews, flesh, and skin on our way to God breathing life into the sermon.

Preaching to show up in people's fear and speak a word of peace in Jesus's name demands language that creates an experience of Jesus and not merely provides information about Jesus.

In creating these sermons, the amount of experiential language far surpasses the amount of informational language. In fact, informational language is used in service to the experiential. Informational language is provided to assist the hearers in exploring, clarifying, understanding, and appreciating their experience of Jesus. So, preachers explain theological language. Better yet, they do not use it. Instead, they translate theological concepts into the language of experience using stories and examples.

Exclusive language of any kind (language used singularly and habitually) limits rather than expands experience, especially of God. Preachers do well to expand and use a variety of names and images for God, Jesus, and the church. Preachers are also sensitive to language that, when used consistently and exclusively, "splits consciousness" as it takes the hearer somewhere other than where the sermon is going. For example, just as I am expected to become increasingly sensitive to language surrounding race, class, gender, and sexual orientation, I find myself increasingly distracted by sermons that use the language of disability to communicate negative and undesirable characteristics.

Description creates experience in the hearers. Description is strengthened by study and holy imagination as preachers consider elements of the story and event that Scripture does not provide. So, preachers start with the reading as they look to describe the good news. Characters, actions, and settings all receive attention. Preachers can then draw on biblical themes and imagery generally. Descriptions are made with an economy of words and are therefore incomplete. In preaching, description is more akin to radio than television and movies.

For a long time, I taught preachers to draw upon three kinds of illustrations: biblical, cultural, and natural illustrations. I am now concerned that, as our culture becomes more divided and tribal, cultural illustrations are also becoming divisive and difficult to use. I increasingly employ biblical illustrations, especially Old Testament types and stories from Jesus's life, since Scripture is the story the church shares. Especially when they are not biblical, illustrations should not overshadow the message, or the temptation will be to abandon the reading and even escort Jesus to the rear of the pulpit and preach from the illustration.

Finally, in creating the sermon, preachers attend to tone. I find a trustworthy guide in the question, "Did you taste the gospel?" It is possible to preach grace as content while crafting a sermon that communicates guilt. Ask yourself what emotional flavor or taste the sermon leaves in your mouth. To create an appropriate tone, explore the message, the preacher's feelings about the message, the congregation's anticipated response, and the occasion.

I rarely write a sermon in a single setting. I determine the good news, rough out the sermon structure, fill in the pieces, then review and revise several times. When the manuscript is written and I am satisfied with it, no later than Friday night, I set the sermon aside and spend Saturday sleeping late and doing things unrelated to preaching. This renews and readies me for the work I have yet to do. Then, when the clock chimes nine at night, I make my way to the manuscript and to Jesus in the last leg of my journey to the pulpit, proclaiming.

Proclaim

The Lord speaks to us as to the prophet Ezekiel: "Eat this scroll, and go, speak to the house of Israel."[14] To *proclaim* is to "eat this scroll" or internalize our sermon manuscript. When we do the work to eat it, we agree with Ezekiel that "in my mouth it was as sweet as honey."[15] God sends us to God's people to "speak my very words to them."[16]

Some preachers seem unaware of the importance of practicing their proclamation. I continue to be surprised when preachers plop their laptop in the pulpit, raise the screen as a barrier between themselves and the congregation, and never look up as they read their sermon to us from the screen. I continue to be dismayed by preachers who hit print a few minutes before worship, carry their manuscript from the printer to the pulpit, and make clear to the congregation they are reading the sermon cold. Both preachers would be better off distributing the manuscript to the congregation as they enter worship and then giving them time to read.

Poor proclamation completely undercuts what might be an otherwise excellent message. God knows this. Proclamation or sermon delivery is essential to preaching Jesus because God knows *how* one communicates is as important as *what* one says. In the fullness of time, Paul tells us, God came in the person of the Son.[17] We believe Jesus continues to come to us when the gospel is preached. Sermons, then, are not mere words. Sermons are themselves God's saving events, moments when we experience God's presence, grace, wisdom, and power in Jesus Christ.[18] In these events, the preacher is the incarnation of the good news as well as the bearer of it. To neglect preparing to proclaim reduces preaching to words in a manuscript.

Effective proclamation enhances the preacher's authority. Preachers cannot rely on authority that comes from rank, power, superior knowledge, and greater Christian experience.[19] Our authority comes from seeing and hearing something of God; we are witnesses to what we have seen and heard God doing in Jesus Christ. While some of our hearers seek answers they agree with, more want to know whether we know, love, and trust Jesus—not do we know about Jesus, but do we know the crucified and risen Christ? Our authority as preachers grows out of our seeing and hearing Jesus and how we bring this experience to others and others into the experience. Witnessing to Jesus involves how we herald as well as what we say.

Preachers must decide how they will proclaim the gospel, whether they will deliver their sermons extemporaneously, from memory, from notes or an outline, or from a manuscript. All of these can be effective; all are skills that need to be cultivated and so require practice. Making value judgments about the use or nonuse of manuscripts or other notes may be more harmful than helpful. Preachers should instead determine which way of proclaiming their sermon most effectively frees both themselves and the listeners so that the good news will be received.

My emphasis on the importance of writing a manuscript does not in any way imply that sermons should normally be read. Out of necessity, I normally preach from a memorized manuscript. While I am resigned to lecturing with a paper close to my face so I can read it, preaching deserves more from me.

Regardless of which style of proclamation they select, preachers practice the sermon so that it goes from being a written document to a proclaimed event. Preachers practice the sermon enough that their proclamation is natural and authentic and not wooden and rehearsed. Preachers are familiar enough with the sermon that they can look at the congregation and respond to their reactions and participation. As one who has encountered Christ and is witness to that experience, the preacher cultivates the urgency that the gospel deserves. Ultimately, the preacher practices enough that they are free to preach with the power of the Holy Spirit. Practice welcomes the Holy Spirit; poor proclamation can constrain the Holy Spirit.

Preachers practice their sermons with their whole selves. They say their sermons out loud to develop clear articulation, determine how the voice will respond to their words, and incorporate both pauses and vocal variation. They develop movement, gesture, eye contact, and facial expression so their nonverbal communication supports and does not undermine the message, especially by their bodies not being involved in preaching.

Ideally, preachers have the opportunity to practice in the worship space to account for acoustics, the pulpit, and especially the sound system. As I preach in a different church building every Sunday, I find standing in the pulpit or on the platform and saying even a few words, usually the gospel reading, helps me get my bearings and adjust my delivery to the space.

Memorization

Memorizing sermons is for me a holy, prayerful, and precious practice. After forty years, I memorize the gospel reading and a twelve-paragraph sermon from 9:00 p.m. to 1:00 a.m. the night before I preach. Of course, I have spent the previous few days immersed in the gospel reading and revising the manuscript, so I begin with a good foundation.

When I return to the manuscript after spending a day away, my heart often sinks, and I utter an expletive because of my disappointment in the sermon I have written. In the early years, I would panic and start over; with experience came the wisdom that my heart sinking is simply an indication that I cannot do this alone, that I need Jesus and the Holy Spirit to spin this straw into gold. This is when, like Nicodemus, I come to Jesus by night and memorizing becomes prayer.

I memorize the manuscript like a play script: word for word, sentence by sentence, one paragraph after another. I repeat it out loud. When my mouth says something one way and the manuscript has it written another, my mouth wins. I build paragraphs one upon another in my memory, preaching first one, then two, then three, until I am preaching the gospel and all twelve. Then I repeat the entire sermon one or two times more. Along the way, I determine voice, movement, and gesture. Because I do not see well, I cannot make eye contact with my listeners, but through practice, I have learned to focus on the congregation in a way that makes people say they would swear I am looking right into their eyes. The process is interspersed with prayers and pacing. In the morning, I practice the sermon a few times more in the shower and on the way to church.

Barbara Brown Taylor compares preaching to walking a tightrope.[20] Memorizing is how I prepare to step out without a net. My adrenaline rushes. All distractions disappear. I am singularly focused. I am yoked closely and securely to Jesus. I hope Jesus and I won't fall during the sermon, and I know Jesus will be with me and will raise me up if we do.

For a while during the pandemic, I missed this holy, precious, and prayerful time with Jesus. Preaching to a camera is different from preaching to a congregation. I can pause the camera and decide to start over, and the video can be edited. I did all these things; my preaching felt flat, and Jesus seemed more the subject of than a participant in my sermons. Then I learned the phrase "live on tape." Now that is what I do; I preach the sermon as a live event being recorded and prepare for it as I always have. I once again feel yoked closely and securely to Jesus.

Understanding my routine of sermon preparation as my "walk to the pulpit," I examined the route I was following and found parts I needed to change to bring me back to Jesus. Comparing our method of sermon preparation to other methods can bring grace, energy, and renewal. It might also help us discover maps that expand our route to include preaching Jesus to and for the world and preaching Jesus to lead the congregation out into the world to encounter Jesus. I examine these "maps" to the pulpit in chapters 7 and 8.

7

Empty Pew

How Do You Preach for the "Least of These"?

Since becoming a bishop, I choose to wear a purple clergy shirt. Some think I wear this royal color because I fancy myself a prince of the church. I do appreciate vestments as a perk of the office. However, I wear purple to remind myself that Jesus told a story about "a rich man who was clothed in purple" and neglected a poor man named Lazarus.[1] The Gospel of John reports that Jesus wore purple when he was crucified.[2] I wear purple as a daily reminder of the bishop's and church's responsibility to care for, advocate on behalf of, and be in solidarity with the poor and suffering.

Empty pews remind me of these children of God. They are not in worship because Sunday morning finds them working their third job, unable to attend because of the absence of mass transit, waking up in a park or a homeless shelter, spending another day in a jail cell, searching for food or to satisfy their addiction, fleeing their home country to save their children, or unwelcome in worship because of their race, class, gender, sexual orientation, or physical or mental impairment. Jesus names the "least of these" and asserts that we care for Jesus as we care for them.[3] Wearing purple reminds me each day of my responsibility as a bishop to lead the church to care for the "least of these" as Jesus did.

Yet, advocating for and being in solidarity with the "least of these" is more than a responsibility, especially in preaching. People want preaching to help them understand the word of God and to connect it to their lives, to guide and encourage them in living their faith every day. People hunger for the meaning, purpose, and direction that will make their lives whole and their communities and the world better. This desire makes Christians gathered to worship and hear the word of God the most important setting for sharing the gospel's call to justice and peace and the church's social teachings. The sermon is where most Christians will hear—or not hear—the connection between the good news of Jesus proclaimed through the Scriptures to the church's participation, as "salt, light, and leaven,"[4] in Jesus's own work of reconciling the world to God's very self.

Sharing the social dimensions of the gospel is one of the privileges and joys of preaching Jesus. Proclaiming the ways Christ and his church are at work in the world today, and inviting the congregation to participate in this work, can bring life, substance, and energy to preaching. "If preachers do not reflect the biblical call to 'choose life' (Deuteronomy 30:19), to care for the 'least of these' (Matthew 25:34–46), to 'hunger and thirst for justice,' and to become 'peacemakers' (Matthew 5:1–12), then the preaching is not truly and fully [the gospel]."[5]

We preach *for* the "least of these" in two ways. First, we preach so the least of these receive the gospel in ways relevant and meaningful to their lives and circumstances. We preach Jesus in ways that address the realities of suffering, injustice, deprivation, and oppression experienced by billions of people around the world and creation itself.

We also preach *for* or on behalf of the "least of these," so their voice is heard, and their reality named, inspiring the church to caring, advocacy, and solidarity as Jesus did. This preaching is more complex than taking stands on issues from the pulpit. It begins with (1) preaching Jesus, (2) reinforcing values for our world today based on the gospel, and (3) explicitly connecting the particular concern to Jesus. The purpose of this preaching is to (4) form faithful, wise, and active citizens. As they undertake preaching for the "least of these," preachers (5) know the preaching context, (6) gain credibility with the congregation, and (7) count the cost. When preparing sermons that speak for the "least of these," preachers (8) enlist the lectionary and (9) carefully craft the sermon.

Preach Jesus

Our calling is to preach the gospel and not any issue. We do not preach *for* the "least of these" by preaching *about* the "least of these." We preach to and on behalf of those who hunger, thirst, are naked, sick, imprisoned, and everyone experiencing suffering and oppression by preaching Jesus. In fact, preaching social justice that is not anchored in the broader purpose of preaching is likely to be ineffectual and counterproductive.[6]

Preaching for the "least of these" cannot feel like the preacher is imposing an agenda on the assembly and its worship. Rather than preaching the "least of these" in place of Jesus or by forcing the "least of these" into the sermon, preachers connect Jesus and the "least of these" in terms of God's intention, Jesus's ministry, and our participation and response. This is not difficult because Jesus declares that what we do or fail to do for the "least of these" we do or fail to do for Jesus.

Our approach, then, is to integrate the "least of these" in sermons about Jesus rather than isolate them in sermons about themselves. Preachers integrate the "least of these" as we preach Jesus by reinforcing gospel values, explicitly demonstrating how an issue is appropriate for preaching Jesus, and connecting our response to the way the "least of these" connects to and flows from the ministry of Jesus.

Reinforce Gospel Values

Congregations respond more positively to gospel values than stands on issues. When a preacher takes a stand on an issue, the congregation either agrees or disagrees; then their consideration of the issue likely stops. Preaching Jesus and reinforcing values and commitments that flow from the gospel invites and encourages deliberation and dialogue about how to respond. These values belong to the church; while preachers may share them, reinforcing gospel values is distinct from reinforcing the preacher's own values. Examples of values that flow from preaching Jesus and are held by the church include the nearness of God's reign and tenets summarized in Catholic social teaching and *Church in Society: A Lutheran Perspective*, a social teaching statement of the Evangelical Lutheran Church in America.

The Nearness of God's Reign

"Now after John was arrested, Jesus came to Galilee, proclaiming the good news of God, and saying, 'The time is fulfilled, and the kingdom of God has come near; repent, and believe in the good news.'"[7] Jesus announced the Reign of God is here and now. Liberation theology describes the reign of God proclaimed by Jesus as a kingdom of love and justice that is God's plan for human history. This kingdom is both gift and demand. It is the gift of a gracious God because it is the result of God's unmerited love for all human beings and all creation. Jesus's proclamation of God's reign also includes a call to repentance, to accept the demands of the reign of God.[8]

Gustavo Gutiérrez points out that nothing makes more demands on us than the experience of gracious love. Acceptance of the reign of God entails a particular concern for the poor. It means "refusing to accept a world that instigates or tolerates the premature and unjust deaths of the poor."[9] Jesus's proclamation of the kingdom is also characterized by universality and preference. No one is excluded from either the gift or the demand of the kingdom. At the same time, Jesus's proclamation of the Reign of God is marked by preference for the "least of these." Gutiérrez is convinced that the gospel accounts of Jesus's ministry make it clear that the despised of the world are those whom God prefers.[10]

Catholic Social Teaching

I appreciate Catholic social teaching, in part because it teaches me that Christians can hold the same values and arrive in different places when considering an issue. The Roman Catholic Church succinctly presents its social values in *Seven Themes of Catholic Social Teaching*.[11] These themes or values are summarized as follows.

1. Life and dignity of the human person proclaims that human life is sacred and the dignity of the human person is the foundation of a moral vision for society.
2. The call to family, community, and participation affirms that how we organize our society directly affects human dignity and the capacity of individuals to participate in community.
3. Human dignity can be protected and healthy community achieved only if human rights are protected and human responsibilities met.
4. An option for the poor and vulnerable considers how well a society's most vulnerable members are faring to be the basic test of its morality.

5. The dignity of work and the rights of workers directs that the economy is to serve people rather than people serving the economy.
6. Solidarity affirms that we are one human family, whatever our national, racial, ethnic, economic, or ideological differences.
7. We show respect for our Creator by our care of God's creation.

A Lutheran Perspective

As a preacher in the Evangelical Lutheran Church in America (ELCA), I turn to the values of my Christian denomination. In the social teaching statement *The Church in Society: A Lutheran Perspective*,[12] the ELCA affirms nine dimensions of its life as a church relating to the world, and commits itself to engage society in three ways as it witnesses to the living God who in love creates, judges, and preserves the world and redeems, sanctifies, and brings it to fulfillment in God's reign.

The ELCA affirms (1) care of the neighbor and the earth is our grateful response to the gospel. God's good news of salvation, given in the life, death, and resurrection of Jesus, liberates the church from sin, death, and evil and motivates the church to care for neighbor and the earth. The witness of this church in society therefore flows from its identity as a community that lives from and for the gospel. In gratitude for God's grace in Jesus Christ, this church carries out its responsibility for the well-being of society and the environment.

(2) The ELCA's witness in society is informed by the history and the various theological traditions of the one church of Jesus Christ. The church (3) is *in* but not *from* the world; the gospel does not take the church out of the world but calls it to enter more deeply into the world, since the church and the

world share a common destiny in the reign of God. (4) The gospel does not allow the church to accommodate the ways of the world. Instead, (5) the church advocates for the sake of the world in hope and in prayer. Thus, (6) the church's responsibility in society is to announce that the God who saves expects all people to do justice, which addresses both the obligations of our relationships and the challenges of the world, as God preserves creation, orders society, and promotes justice in a broken world.

The ELCA affirms that (7) God works through the family, education, the economy, the state, and other structures necessary for life in the present age. Simultaneously, since they are also marked by sin, the church must participate critically in these structures. As an institution through which God is at work, (8) the church ministers to human need with compassion and imagination, strives to pioneer new ways of addressing emerging social problems and environmental degradation, mediates conflict and advocates just and peaceful resolution to the world's divisions, supports institutions and policies that serve the common good, and works with and learns from others in caring for and changing global society. As a prophetic presence, this church has the obligation to name and denounce the idols before which people bow, to identify the power of sin present in social structures, and to advocate in hope with poor and powerless people.

One way the church participates in society is through its members, who serve God and neighbor in ordinary life, including family, marriage, work, and community service. Christians also function as wise and active citizens by defending human rights and working for freedom, justice, peace, environmental well-being, and good order in society. Christians exercise their responsibility to vote and may even serve in public office. (9) Christians often passionately disagree about how to respond to social questions. United to Christ and to all believers in baptism, Christians are obligated to deliberate together on the challenges they face in the world.

In response to these affirmations, the Evangelical Lutheran Church in America commits itself to (1) sustain and support its members in their baptismal vocation to serve God and neighbor in daily life and as wise and active citizens. The ELCA further commits itself to (2) serve God and neighbor in its life and work as an institution; this service may be distinct from serving itself. The ELCA commits itself to (3) foster moral deliberation on social questions. All three of these commitments appropriately find expression in preaching.

Preachers do not reinforce social values by quoting social statements in sermons. Rather, preachers become so familiar with these values that they serve as lenses through which we interpret Scripture, warrants that empower the messages we preach, and when appropriate, catechesis for the baptized.

Show How the Issue Flows from the Gospel

In sermons that name the experience of the "least of these," preachers explicitly name the connection between individuals, situations, issues, and systems that make them appropriate topics for preaching. In other words, preachers demonstrate how the "least of these" flow from Jesus and the gospel. Naming this connection is necessary because many Christians individualize and spiritualize the gospel and accept an understanding of the separation of church and state that holds the church has no place in the public square. They believe "politics has no place in the pulpit" and sermons addressing social issues are inappropriate. To presume or assume the connection between social justice and the gospel gives people a reason to dismiss the sermon, deny an aspect of faith they find difficult and challenging, and ignore any social issue in which they are complicit.

Showing how a social concern flows from the gospel can be different from the way it flows from the Bible. Throughout the Covid-19 pandemic, when in-person worship was suspended, people repeatedly quoted to me Deuteronomy 5:12: "Observe the Sabbath day and keep it holy, as the Lord your God commanded you." They used this quote as part of an accusation that by advising against in-person worship, and not forcing people to attend in person, I was causing the church to sin. Some even recalled God protecting the three men in the fiery furnace as "proof" God would protect people in church buildings from Covid-19.[13] When I grew impatient reminding people that Jesus said, "The Sabbath was made for humankind, and not humankind for the Sabbath" and "Again it is written, 'Do not put the Lord your God to the test,'"[14] I needed to explicitly connect the precautions the church was taking during the pandemic to Jesus and the gospel.

In letters, videos, and sermons, I told the people of the synod (diocese) I serve that, when I grow weary of sacrificing, I hear words of Jesus, which reduce me to a puddle. On the night before he was crucified, Jesus prayed, "While I was with them, I protected them in your name that you have given me. I guarded them, and not one of them was lost."[15] In the garden, Jesus fulfilled these words by insisting that his disciples go on their way before those who came for Jesus could take him; not one was lost, including Judas.[16] Lifted up from the earth on the cross, Jesus drew all people to himself, so that no one would be lost.[17]

Mindful that I will one day stand before God and give an account of my ministry as bishop, I do not want to have to explain why I made decisions that resulted in even one whom Jesus protected with his life being lost. I suspect many pastors, deacons, and faithful Christians feel the same way. In gratitude to Jesus that we were not lost, and to participate in

Jesus's own work of making certain not one is lost, we sacrifice and take actions to protect our neighbors. During the Covid-19 pandemic, we did this by staying home, keeping social distance, and wearing masks. While we are hopeful the pandemic is waning, we are also mindful that we may need to continue making these sacrifices for Jesus's sake, so no one is lost.

While many (but not all) who heard this message resonated with it, I was the true beneficiary. Explicitly articulating my understanding of the connection between the precautions we were taking and Jesus and the gospel guided my decision-making, emboldened my leadership, and enlivened my proclamation of the good news that, in Christ, not one is lost, even to a pandemic that has claimed hundreds of thousands of lives. More than implying that Jesus is concerned about public health, I needed to say why.

The connection between Jesus and climate change was less obvious to me and required research and reading. Growing up, I learned more about conservation and the environment from the Boy Scouts than from the church. Jesus saved souls, not plants and animals. In fact, I was taught that God bade humankind to "subdue" the earth and "have dominion" over its creatures.[18]

The twenty-first century is a time of unparalleled ecological crisis as the very survival of complex forms of life and beauty, including humankind, are threatened by the decisions and actions of human beings. The ecological damage that modern humanity has inflicted on the planet has reinforced our awareness that the survival and flourishing of humanity are intimately linked with the well-being of the planet. Responding to this concern is a divisive and pressing issue for individuals, communities, companies, and governments.

While addressing climate change is certainly a matter of survival, why is climate change a matter of faith, a concern of the church, and an appropriate topic for preaching? The answer is that the story of salvation in Jesus Christ includes not only the human history of salvation, but also grace bestowed on the cosmos. We show our respect for the Creator and participate in Jesus's saving work by our stewardship of the creation. Created in God's image, we "have dominion" over the earth and its creatures by caring for them as God does.[19]

Jesus embraces all creation in the saving work of his life, death, and resurrection. In Jesus's incarnation, God became one with and transformed not only human nature, but also material creation, so the divine is made present and available to us in and through creation. Traces of the mystery of God, definitively disclosed in Jesus Christ, can be discovered throughout the universe.[20] From this perspective, "the term *sarx* in John 1:14 connotes not just human flesh but all that is finite and perishable, the matter that extends throughout the universe."[21] God became flesh to so connect God and the world that the "stuff" of the cosmos is granted dignity, such that matter mediates God's presence to humanity, and a future for a creation marked by decomposition and suffering becomes possible by the redeeming grace of Christ.

The "earthy" nature of Jesus's public ministry reveals God's concern for the entire cosmos. Jesus attended to people's bodily needs by feeding the hungry, healing the sick, and welcoming the outcast at the table. In his preaching of the reign of God, Jesus often turned to what early and medieval Christians termed the "Book of Nature" as the starting point for his parables. Jesus directed his disciples to "read the signs of the times" in the signs of nature. "He used images of seeds randomly sown, dying fig trees, untended vineyards, and wandering sheep as entry points for speaking about God's providence, fidelity, justice, and compassion."[22] Jesus's concern for physical needs and use of nature images to reveal God indicate that God's reign encompasses the entire planet with all its ecosystems and, in fact, the entire cosmos. Moreover, God's word is disclosed not only through the Scriptures, but also through the Book of Nature, a genuine source of revelation. As two expressions of the word of God, the Bible and the Book of Nature need to be interpreted in light of each other.

Turning to the cross, when Jesus says that, lifted up from the earth, he will draw all *people* to himself,[23] we might hear *creation* or the *cosmos*. On the cross, Jesus draws all creation to God. Jesus's solidarity on the cross extends beyond humanity to all creatures. Paul observes, "We know that all creation is groaning in labor pains even until now."[24] Theologians understand creation's "groaning" as the suffering and death that are intrinsic to evolutionary development. They press us to consider how the groaning of all creation is intertwined with the cries of the human poor.[25] Jesus embraces creation's agony in his agonizing death. While the cross itself remains an unjust act perpetrated by human beings, the divine solidarity revealed in Jesus's participation in death makes the bold claim that no creature, human or nonhuman, is ever alone in its suffering. God is always present in divine compassion.[26]

The church's proclamation of Jesus's resurrection has always included the bodily or corporeal dimension.[27] Jesus has been raised by the Father in every aspect of his personhood. Those who proclaimed Jesus as risen from the dead envisioned his destiny as the hope for all creation. The author of Colossians names Christ "the firstborn of creation" and "the firstborn from the dead."[28] Ambrose of Milan asserted that "the universe rose again in Him, the heaven rose again in Him, the earth rose again in Him."[29] Ambrose even suggested that at the end of time all creation will join human beings in the beatific vision.[30] The risen Christ is the crown of God's new creation.

In both examples, I endeavor to frame the connection between Jesus and social concerns, as well as our response, as good news or as participation in God's good news in Jesus Christ. We took precautions during the pandemic in gratitude to Jesus that we are not lost and to participate in his work of ensuring not one is lost. We combat climate change because the earth and its creatures are encompassed in God's reign and reveal and mediate the divine to us. When possible, it is best to frame the connection between Jesus and "the least of these" as good news for the congregation. For example, in the reign of God, we are not defined or measured by our possessions, and we do not need to spend our lives acquiring and protecting them. This is good news to people regardless of how much they possess. Responding to good news better motivates God's people to be faithful, wise, and active citizens.

Form Faithful, Wise, and Active Citizens

The ultimate purpose of preaching on behalf of the "least of these" is freeing and empowering God's people to be faithful, wise, and active citizens. In grateful response to God's love in Jesus Christ, the baptized embrace their twofold vocation by standing in solidarity with and advocating on behalf of the "least of these." Solidarity includes faithfully providing food, drink, clothing, housing, healthcare, and visitation. Advocacy involves faithfully, wisely, and actively participating in society as citizens, so systems and institutions more fully reflect and participate in God's coming reign announced and inaugurated by Jesus Christ. As we pray, "your kingdom come, your will be done on earth as in heaven," our faithful, wise, and active citizenship is an answer to our prayer.

As followers of Jesus, our citizenship is faithful. Faithful citizenship means our faith shapes our politics rather than our politics shaping our faith. The citizenship we preach and seek is political, relating the gospel to government and public affairs, but not partisan. "The challenge is to be 'salt of the earth,' 'light of the world' and social 'leaven' in ways large and small."[31] That "our citizenship is in heaven"[32] does not relieve us of our responsibilities as citizens here on earth. Rather, our citizenship in heaven frees and empowers us to fulfill our earthly responsibilities as followers of Jesus.

Because we are followers of Jesus, our citizenship is wise. Wise citizenship is prayerful and discerning rather than pre-determined. It is principled and not ideological, civil without being soft, collaborative and not siloed. Wise citizens understand the separation of church and state is a constitutional and not a Christian doctrine. Its purpose is to prevent the state from regulating or interfering with religion, not to remove religion from public discourse and debate. Wise citizens regard their right and responsibility to vote as sacred and godly and prepare themselves to exercise it.

Because we are followers of Jesus, our citizenship is active. Preaching for the "least of these" helps Christians connect their faith and their roles as parents and siblings, consumers and investors, workers and employers. Preaching helps Christians find ways to practice charity, solidarity, advocacy, and justice in their own lives. Preaching also helps the congregation as a faith community identify and celebrate ways it actively serves the "least of these," including in partnership with other faith communities and by supporting the church beyond the congregation.

Know Your Context

The preaching context or climate can dramatically impact how we preach for the "least of these" and form faithful, wise, and active citizens. I serve the Lower Peninsula of the State of Michigan, excluding metropolitan Detroit, Flint, and Ann

Arbor. In Michigan, Donald Trump beat Hillary Clinton by 0.23 percent of the vote in 2016, and Joe Biden beat Donald Trump by 2.8 percent of the vote in 2020. The division of our state is reflected in our congregations. On the one hand, the synod (diocese) I serve includes Christians and congregations on fire to "do justice, and to love kindness, and to walk humbly with your God." They identify their mission as actively bringing good news to the poor, proclaiming release to the captive and recovery of sight to those who are blind, letting the oppressed go free, and proclaiming the year of the Lord's favor.[33] On the other hand, the synod I serve also includes Christians and congregations convinced that the doctrine of the separation of church and state means the church has no place in the public square and that including social justice in sermons is "political" and therefore inappropriate. Many of the Christians and congregations in our synod (diocese) are somewhere in the middle.

Elected to my first term as bishop in 2013, I was initially surprised that, as a bishop, I was expected to provide a gospel perspective on the issues that we face locally, nationally, and globally to a degree that I was not permitted as pastor and professor. My most politically conservative congregations accepted that, as bishop, I would bring the word of God to bear on what is happening in society, community, state, nation, and world. I routinely addressed subjects that once made me shudder—racism, refugees, same-gender marriage, guns—and no one seemed to flinch, though there are always harsh words and nasty emails afterward. While people certainly disagreed with some of my assertions and perspectives, they did not challenge either my preaching with a public voice or my message taking on a prophetic edge.

Everything changed in 2016. Around the presidential election, I began to be accused of being overtly political, even partisan, in my preaching. I was berated in one congregation for using the image of the new Jerusalem, a city with "a great, high wall with twelve gates [that]. . . will never be shut,"[34] as a not-so-subtle attack on Donald Trump, God's "new Cyrus."[35] I was shouted at in another congregation for "making Jesus political." On the Sunday following President Trump's inauguration, the appointed gospel reading from the Revised Common Lectionary was from the Sermon on the Mount. I received complaints from two people in the same congregation, one criticizing the pastor for selecting readings and preaching sermons to embarrass President Trump and the other complaining that the same pastor was watering down Jesus's teaching to spare President Trump.

The social dimension of the gospel does not change; however, the context or climate of preaching greatly affects how this message is received. Preachers are better able to negotiate a challenging climate by gaining credibility with the congregation and counting the cost, so they are prepared and not surprised.

Gain Credibility

Preachers endeavor to gain credibility with their congregations, so they are in the best possible position to lead the church to advocate for and be in solidarity with the "least of these" and perhaps weather a stormy preaching climate. Preachers with credibility are trusted and looked to by their congregations and are therefore convincing. Establishing and gaining credibility takes time and requires honesty, attention to the pastoral dimensions of the gospel, consistency, willingness to build bridges, and patience.

Beginning with the interview process, *preachers and congregations need to be honest* with themselves and upfront with one another about their level of comfort with the social

dimensions of the gospel and the intensity of their commitment and passion for the "least of these," in the same way
they discuss, for example, worship style. Passion for God's
restorative justice for the world burns in some preachers' and
congregations' bones. For others, this fire needs kindling or
tending. Still others fear the flames or think it wrong to strike
the match. Including this conversation as part of an interview
lessens the chance that either preacher or congregation will
be surprised by the other after they begin serving together.
Even if the preacher and congregation discern not to enter
into ministry together, this conversation helps all involved
to recognize that advocating for and being in solidarity with
the "least of these" is essential to following Jesus and living
according to the Bible.

Preachers gain credibility to preach the social dimensions
of the gospel by *faithfully attending to the pastoral dimensions of
the gospel*. Preachers need to be priests as well as prophets and,
in most faith communities, need to establish themselves as
priests before taking on the mantle of the prophet. Priestly
ministry and prophetic ministry are both important; neither is a matter of choice. Jesus, who in Matthew declares the
nations will be judged by their treatment of the "least of these,"
also commissions the apostles to make disciples, baptize, and
teach. In Luke, Jesus tells the disciples that repentance and forgiveness of sins are to be preached in his name to all nations.
In John, the risen Christ sends the disciples to forgive and
retain sins and commands Peter to "feed my sheep."[36] People
need to experience that their preacher knows Jesus, loves
them, and can name grace, forgiveness, and new life in their
midst. To receive the prophetic word, the congregation needs
to know the preacher is "a servant of Christ sent by God to
serve all people with the gospel of hope and salvation."[37]

In practical terms, congregations are more willing and better able to receive and respond to preaching for the "least of

these" from a pastor or deacon who baptized their children and taught them the faith, stood by them in the emergency room and the police station, visited their parents in assisted living, and held their hands and prayed when a loved one died. People will more readily receive an appraisal of their community from the perspective of God's word from a preacher who is present and actively engaged in that community, loves its people, and is on its side. People are also more likely to receive a prophetic word from preachers who demonstrate they understand people before challenging and criticizing them. Speaking pragmatically, even crassly, I sometimes tell pastors and deacons that they need to "pay the rent" in order to move their congregation in a new direction. As a bishop, I know that I cannot effectively speak to the social dimensions of the gospel when congregations are preoccupied and frustrated with me because they are without a pastor. Similarly, pastors and deacons cannot effectively preach for the "least of these" when the people they serve are themselves feeling unloved and neglected.

Increasingly, tragedies, including hate crimes and gun violence, occur that require preachers to speak a prophetic word; preachers gain (or lose) credibility by the prophetic word they preach at these times. The closer the tragedy is to the community, the more urgent the need for the preacher to offer a word from the Lord. Since the word is from God, it should be what God would say to the people in this moment. God would speak of God's love, solidarity, and promise of a new life. In these moments, assigning blame surely divides. A call to respond is best when the response is short-term and immediate. Preachers might call people to pray, remain calm, reach out to people in need, demonstrate peacefully, and denounce violence. Preachers are mindful that in these moments, believing the gospel can be the hardest thing we ask people to do.

Preachers and congregations gain credibility by *practicing consistency.* For preachers, consistency means doing or striving to do in our own lives what we preach and call others to do or strive to do. In the pulpit, preachers guard against compartmentalizing their ministry by being extremely prophetic when preaching and extremely pastoral when confronted about a sermon and at congregational council meetings. For example, we cannot say "Thus says the Lord" from the relative safety of the pulpit and then completely fold when someone gets in our face.

For congregations and the church as a whole, consistency means practicing in our own community and common life the values we proclaim and press for society and the world. As earnestly as we strive to be perfect as our heavenly Father is perfect,[38] we know that neither the preacher nor the church is. Therefore, when we fall, we gain credibility by acknowledging our failings, asking for forgiveness, amending our ways, and trusting Jesus, beginning anew and trying again.

Preachers gain credibility by *building bridges rather than walls.* Especially when society is divided, people look to Christian preachers to be examples of civil, even gracious, discourse and communities bearing the name of Jesus to manifest commitment to seeking common ground. Speech and actions of some who identify themselves as Christians regularly disappoint this expectation and undermine the church's witness to Jesus. In preaching for "the least of these," the church has the burden of overcoming obstacles that are of our own making. Nevertheless, building bridges does not mean being indecisive and ambiguous. The preacher and the church speak simply and straightforwardly. Obviously, doing this proves difficult and complicated when the church is discerning, or God's people hold more than a single perspective.

In preaching, we build bridges by always talking to, rather than about, people from the pulpit, even when they are not there. We are made one in Christ; from Jesus's perspective, there is no *they* or *them*. Preachers do well to examine how we use these pronouns in sermons. To build bridges is to respectfully engage people who disagree with the sermon. Regrettably, building bridges may also mean assisting people who disagree with the preacher or the church to find a place to stand within the faith community, even if it is a small place. As painful as it can be, sometimes the only way to build bridges is to be honest with people who disagree that there is no place for them to stand within the faith community and help them find a new faith community where there is.

Preachers gain credibility with both themselves and others by *practicing patience*. Early Christians believed that God was in charge of events; they knew they were not. Instead of wringing their hands in despair or raising their fists in outrage, early Christians cultivated and promoted a perspective that they called "patience." They concentrated on developing practices that contributed to a *habitus*—a system of embodied dispositions that organize the ways individuals perceive the world around them and react to it—for both individual Christians and Christian communities. Their theology was unhurried—a theology of patience.[39] Patience comes from trust and confidence in Jesus's proclamation, "The time is fulfilled, and the kingdom of God has come near; repent, and believe in the good news."[40] Patience is especially necessary for the church to remain resilient and not despair as it preaches for the "least of these" and works for justice and peace so society and the world better reflect God's reign.

People sometimes counter that patience is a luxury of the privileged, serves the status quo, and so should not be tolerated, especially when people's rights, dignity, and very lives are at stake. I can only share my experience. Not only have my life and livelihood been threatened, I also have at least a small understanding of the loss of rights and dignity. During the months between my election and installation as bishop, when I visited congregations wearing "civilian clothes," without exception, someone in every congregation received and responded to me as a person who is blind and assumed I was looking for some financial assistance. Many were angry that I came for assistance on Sunday and not during the week. When I was introduced as the new bishop, awkwardness ensued. I was corrected for not identifying myself better and instructed to find a way to do so. To pastorally respond to this request, I chose to wear purple. When church people see me carrying a white cane, they assume I am a beggar looking for a handout, just like the people who are blind in the Bible. When I wear a purple clergy shirt, they do not. Therefore, wearing purple reminds me of my responsibility to the "least of these" because when I am not wearing purple, I am dismissed as one of them.

On the other hand, I once taught a student who asked me how I could possibly know anything of what it means to be disenfranchised by the church. This student perceived me as a white, cisgender male who sat at a seminary professor's desk and held all the cards. The student had learned well that, in our Christian tradition, "disenfranchised" means race, class, gender, and sexual orientation, not disability. The student did not know that I am routinely asked if it might be better for me to step down from my position when, because of my visual impairment, I carry out my responsibilities in ways a few people find unusual or inconvenient.

I serve a denomination whose advocacy for and solidarity with the "least of these" who are disabled is tepid at best. I understand firsthand how difficult it is to be patient. I also understand wringing my hands, raising my fists, or even preaching the perfect sermon will not immediately change things. I need to practice patience, if only for my own sake. I also need to commit to patience as a perspective and practice. Patience is neither acceptance nor passivity.

We practice patience by remembering that, like good ideas, calls to advocate for and be in solidarity with the "least of these" are generally not received the first time they are presented. Remembering Jesus's parable of the mustard seed, we practice patience by taking the long view of the in-breaking of God's reign.[41] We practice patience by humbly recognizing that Jesus names us *salt*, *light*, and *leaven*.[42] While we may at times be powerful ingredients in God's work of creating and redeeming the world, ultimately bringing the reign of God is God's work. We practice patience by calibrating our expectations accordingly and celebrating small but significant steps forward. We practice patience by recognizing that we do not work alone. People of faith in our community, across our country, and throughout the world serve on our behalf and by our side. In preaching, we can share stories of these servants and their ministries. Most important, perhaps, we practice patience by counting the cost of preaching for the "least of these," so that we are neither surprised nor disappointed when we must pay a cost for our preaching.

Count the Cost

To warn those who would follow him to count the cost, Jesus told stories about a man who set out to build a tower and was unable to finish building it and a king who waged war against an enemy and, not having enough troops to defeat him, had to sue for peace.[43] Counting the cost when preaching for the "least of these" does not mean weighing whether or not to do it, as if the social dimension of the gospel is somehow optional. Rather, preachers count the cost to ensure they are adequately informed about an issue before preaching about it, not surprised and undone by negative reactions and consequences, and can assess how willing and ready they are to sacrifice for a particular group, issue, situation, or circumstance.

Counting the cost involves *determining whether we are prepared to preach a particular message for the "least of these."* First, preachers must be confident that the message is "the word of the Lord" and not something they personally want or need to preach. Biblical prophets do not seek that call; if preachers are eager to be prophetic, the message they are eager to speak might be their word rather than God's Word. Once preachers decide the message comes from God, counting the cost means determining whether they have the information necessary to proclaim it and, if not, how they will acquire the information they need. Passion must be grounded in accurate information. Preachers need to formulate the connection between Jesus and the social justice issue or situation. Preachers are also prepared to offer suggestions and opportunities for the congregation to faithfully respond in action. Preachers assess the climate or atmosphere surrounding the issue in the faith community and community at large to craft and deliver the sermon appropriately. Preachers certainly consult with other congregation and community leaders, so the preacher is better informed, and the leaders are not surprised and can be supportive.

Preachers count the cost so that *they are not surprised or undone by negative reactions and consequences.* I am frequently amused by young preachers who speak a prophetic word and are genuinely surprised when the congregation does not thank them and immediately repent and amend their ways. The Bible reveals that most prophets end up dead. "Jerusalem, Jerusalem," Jesus laments, "the city that kills the prophets and stones those who are sent to it!"[44] Preachers cannot expect to

be treated any differently and instead must prepare themselves to suffer the consequences of their proclamation.

In my experience as a bishop, preachers do not end up
dead like the prophets of old. Instead, congregants opposed
to "politics in the pulpit" and the preacher "taking a stand" on
an issue with which they disagree may become angry, critical,
and divisive. They may treat the preacher with frustration
and disaffection. The conflict often escalates as those who are
offended meet clandestinely, garner support, withhold their
offerings, threaten to leave, call for the preacher to resign,
and undertake to have the preacher fired. These voices are
often loud and few in number, as few as two or three. Yet, they
are enough to demoralize the preacher, upset the preacher's
family, and derail the congregation's ministry.

Preaching for the "least of these" requires resilience. Preachers protect their hearts and muster their courage, so they are
neither surprised nor undone by reactivity, negativity, or
resistance. We do this because we are best able to preach for
the "least of these" when we are not afraid. Courage comes
from believing that what we say is deeply rooted in the Word.
Courage also comes from building a relationship in which
the congregation knows the preacher will always be open and
honest with them, naming things for what they are from the
perspective of God's love embodied in Jesus and the church's
call to love God and neighbor, and carry God's creative and
redeeming word in this world. Courage comes from distinguishing between reactivity and response and not allowing
oneself to be sidelined by reactivity. Finally, courage comes
from protecting our hearts and our families, and not allowing people to hurt us.

Assuming they are preaching God's word and not their own
agenda, preachers need to respond to reactivity and opposition by being more prophetic rather than less. For example,

they may need to speak to those withholding their offering about the power of mammon to oppose God, undermine the gospel, and seek to replace Christ as Lord of the church. The only response to people who threaten to leave is to help them go; when people undertake to have a preacher fired, the preacher and the judicatory might call their bluff rather than cower in fear.

Preaching for the "least of these" makes some people so uncomfortable that they leave the congregation or denomination. Preachers and congregations therefore recognize that they will lose a few people as they address social issues over time. When this happens, congregations are honest about who they are and are becoming; they bless those who are more comfortable in a faith community that shares their understanding of the gospel, assisting them to find where they need to be. As they do this, preachers and congregations recognize those who become part of the faith community because of the congregation's commitment to the "least of these."

When people undertake to have a preacher fired, the preacher might, in partnership with the judicatory, outline the conditions under which they will leave. More important, preachers cultivate in themselves the honest peace of knowing that, while a change may be upsetting, even devastating for the preacher and family, God will be with them and bring them to a new place of service and life. Alternatively, if a change is not possible, preachers will take this into account as they preach for the "least of these."

Preaching for the "least of these" brings suffering. Preachers count the cost to prepare themselves to suffer. Counting the cost includes *determining how ready, willing, and able a preacher and congregation are to suffer, and how much suffering they can endure, for a particular group, situation, or circumstance.* I advise preachers and congregations to decide in advance on which hill(s) they are willing to die or be crucified. In other words, for which of the "least of these" are they willing to offer up their lives? The hill might be a social dimension of the gospel to which the preacher or congregation has a personal connection—for me, persons who live with disabilities. The hill might be dominant in the community and the news; unaccompanied minors at the border elicit compassion that other refugees do not. Local hills are often more important than those in the remote distance. In light of the Flint water crisis, clean water is important to people in Michigan. There are simply too many needs and not enough life to offer ourselves up for them all, however.

While this sounds harsh, faith communities are truly liberated and empowered to respond to the "least of these" when they recognize that, as finite beings and limited communities, we cannot fully engage every need and issue. One of the blessings of the body of Christ is that some are passionate about feeding the hungry, others about visiting the prisoner, and still others about providing refugees with safety. Deciding on which hill we are willing to die frees us to delve deeply into one or two areas rather than dabble in many.

Preachers will certainly address many issues in sermons; however, we will not look for individuals and even the congregation as a whole to respond to all of them with the same intensity and in the same way. Preachers recognize that including many issues with the same passion, intensity, and urgency may cause them all to sound the same with the result that none of them is heard. Preachers and congregations that offer themselves up on every hill lose their impact and effectiveness as their sacrifice becomes routine. Without focus, they may find themselves uncertain of the reason their sense of mission is dead and in need of resurrection. Rather than selecting their hills, many preachers and congregations allow the "least of these" to step out of the Scripture or lectionary readings and perhaps choose them.

Enlist the Lectionary

Preachers should not and need not impose an agenda to preach for "the least of these." Instead, whenever possible, preachers allow the "least of these" to step out of the Scriptures selected or appointed to be read in worship. In the sermon, preachers bring these characters' realities, issues, and concerns, which continue in our day, to Jesus through the church. To do otherwise, perhaps by "spiritualizing" or "theologizing" Scripture read in worship, is to ignore the regular opportunities provided by Scripture and preaching to connect our faith and everyday lives in society and the world.

Following a lectionary, the list of the portions of the Bible appointed to be read in worship on a particular day, helps the congregation understand that preaching for the "least of these" grows out of faithfully preaching the Bible and is not an agenda imposed by the preacher. Preaching for the "least of these" from the appointed scripture readings reinforces that placing the social mission and message at the center of preaching and the Christian life is not a diversion from the gospel but a privileged expression of the gospel.[45] Week after week, the lectionary calls the faith community to reflect on Scripture's message of justice and peace. Preaching these biblical values makes clear that the pulpit is not a partisan soapbox, and to try to make it one would be a mistake. Yet ignoring the social dimensions of our faith does not truly reflect the gospel of Jesus Christ.

Preaching from the lectionary helps preachers to stand with their people under God's Word rather than standing with God's Word against their people. Jesus stood with us under God's word when he came to the Jordan and was baptized, chose to heal the daughter of the Canaanite woman, and was condemned for blasphemy. To stand with our people under God's Word is to receive God's message anew ourselves, meet God's people where they are, and discover with them rather than telling them how God is inviting them to respond.

Early in their tenure in a congregation, as they are getting to know a congregation and community, some preachers establish a weekly Bible study that focuses on the Scripture readings for the coming Sunday and is open to everyone who wishes to attend. As the group looks at the readings, they find that the readings always connect to our world today and what is happening in our context and culture. The Bible study is a place to discuss these connections; the preacher allows them to inform and impact the sermon. Through the Bible study, the congregation participates in the message and the way God calls the congregation to respond to that message by living our faith in the world so that the Word truly becomes embodied in us.

Sometimes compelling local, national, or global events must be immediately addressed, and Scripture readings that directly address it must be selected. Inevitability, this approach is better received by the congregation when the preacher and leaders determine in advance who decides whether an event is so compelling that it merits changing worship. Ideally, the preacher and leaders make this decision together. Preachers also exercise wisdom by consulting leaders about the Scripture readings they select and explaining the reasoning behind their choices. In this process, preachers can assess the congregation's reaction to and perspective on the event, which must be considered when crafting the sermon.

Create Sermons for the "Least of These"

Preaching for the "least of these" can be both enhanced and undermined by the way the sermon is created. Preachers craft sermons that enhance the message in several ways. First, sermons for the "least of these" *reflect the Church's teaching* and not the preacher's opinion. Our responsibility as preachers is to communicate the perspectives and statements of the church we serve and not to commandeer the pulpit as our personal soapbox. Preaching for the "least of these" often means that the preacher's personal opinions and feelings about an issue simply do not matter. In fact, expressing political opinions in the pulpit may cause people to dismiss the message as partisan and inappropriate. Relying on the church's teachings rather than the preacher's opinion helps to maintain the pastoral relationship.

Reflecting the church's teaching means that the preacher's personal agendas and most burning issues must find their place in a mosaic that transcends these concerns and that part of the preacher's job is to help others do the same. Preaching for the "least of these" means including the church beyond the congregation in sermons and identifying the ways in which it is the body of Christ for the sake of the world. Preachers therefore find other ways of expressing their political opinions and exercising their right to free speech. Of course, when preachers speak out on public issues and express their opinions, whether in sermons or elsewhere, they will be held accountable for their public voice. This is part of counting the cost.

Second, sermons for "the least of these" are *created with a public and not a private voice.* These are not sermons for a faith community that has gone into its room, shut the door, and is praying to its Father who is in secret. Public sermons create a public voice. People listen and actively respond to sermons for the "least of these" in ways they do not to sermons on other subjects. Preachers need to anticipate how sermons may be heard and overheard, tweeted and retweeted, with comments posted on Facebook that neither the preacher nor the congregation can control. In my experience, word choices and throwaway lines I speak in passing take on a life all their own and overshadow the message.

Third, sermons for the "least of these" are *concerned about people* and not issues or statistics. I intentionally use the phrase the "least of these" rather than "social justice" or "issues" because this preaching is about people, siblings in Christ, God's beloved children, and fellow creatures beloved by our Creator. Jesus makes things very personal when he says, "I was hungry, naked, sick, and in prison."[46] Jesus did not talk about the issues of hunger, poverty, healthcare, and prison reform.

Images and stories are more compelling than concepts and statistics, because they touch the heart as well as the mind. Statistics reinforce people already committed. The purpose of telling stories and showing and describing images is to help the congregation walk in the shoes of the "least of these," empathetically share their experience, and even encounter Jesus. The story can be as simple as one about the fourteen-year-old boy interviewed at a food bank who matter-of-factly explained, "It's not my day to eat." Similarly, specific examples of how changes in climate adversely impact human beings and especially animals, and not statistics and predictions, transform a concept into a reality.

Fourth, sermons for the "least of these" *ask questions more than they give answers*. Open-ended questions that invite the congregation to consider their response to the good news proclaimed in the sermon, and its implications for the "least of these," are most effective. Questions that can be answered "yes" or "no" quickly disappear from human consciousness.

Preachers might ask what it means to be Christ's church and respond in a manner consistent with the ministry of Jesus. How can we best participate and live into God's dream for this world? When considering questions like these, preachers and congregations are aware that the realities of life for the "least of these" are complicated. Our answers, therefore, are not always simple and obvious. The immediate answer might be for the faith community to commit to concretely support the "least of these" as it devotes time, discernment, and prayer to understanding the realities they face.

Fifth, sermons for the "least of these" give permission rather than direction. Sermons are crafted to appeal rather than command, inspire rather than shame. Most importantly, sermons are crafted to give license—some might even say "cover"— for people to say and do the things they want to, except that they are afraid. As an itinerant preacher, I am permitted, even expected, to say what settled preachers wish they could, in part because I leave and am in a different pulpit the next Sunday. Whether the pastor and congregation accept what I say, debate it, or dismiss it outright, they have received permission to include the "least of these" in their common life. The same holds true as people carry their pastor's sermon outside the church and discuss it in their homes and other areas of life. "I am sending you to them," God says to the prophet Ezekiel, "and you shall say to them, 'Thus says the Lord God.' Whether they hear or refuse to hear (for they are a rebellious house), they shall know that there has been a prophet among them."[47]

Sixth, sermons for the "least of these" include *suggestions for realistic ways to respond* in faith. Preachers provide suggestions rather than prescriptions as an acknowledgment that, as the body of Christ with many members, we express our faith and act on our values in different ways. The best suggestions of ways to respond are part of everyday life and not something additional. For example, consider the cumulative impact on the planet of all communities of faith abandoning plastic foam and other disposable cups at coffee hour. Suggestions provided in sermons include opportunities for both solidarity and advocacy.

Seventh, sermons for the "least of these" should be *partnered with opportunities to learn*. Preachers might identify a reality such as climate change in the sermon and then hold learning events that focus on becoming better informed and conversant on the topic, learning the church's or denomination's perspective, and determining the congregation's response as a faith community. Learning events can cultivate partnerships with other faith communities and groups committed to the same issue. Ideally, these events are an inseparable extension of worship and preaching and are not tangential to them.

"And the king will answer them, 'Truly I tell you, just as you did it to one of the least of these who are members of my family, you did it to me.'"[48] Perhaps the best suggestion for crafting sermons for the "least of these" is to remember Jesus says he can be found among these members of Jesus's family and create sermons that place the preacher and congregation with Jesus.

The Empty Pew

I began this reflection on preaching for the "least of these" by recalling Jesus's parable about a rich man dressed in purple who feasted sumptuously, and a poor man named Lazarus who laid at the rich man's gate and longed to satisfy his hunger with what fell from the rich man's table.[49] Jesus warns that the "chasm" that exists between the rich and the poor in this life will continue in the life to come, and the tables will be turned. Lazarus will be seated in the place of blessing with Abraham and the rich man dressed in purple will be in the place of torment. The good news seems to be that we can determine where we will sit in the life to come by determining who we sit with in this life.

That I locate the "least of these" in an empty pew suggests that we are not sitting together in worship. I, at least, still have work to do in preaching for the "least of these" and celebrating the social dimensions of the gospel. Many preachers identify the crux of the problem as being caught between preaching Jesus and radical grace and preaching to maintain or sustain the institutional church. I confront this dilemma as we turn to the church door and preaching so people leave the building.

8

Church Door

How Do You Preach so People Leave the Building?

Our synod (diocesan) staff member responsible for evange-
lism, outreach, and community engagement returned from
a conference very excited about a new interpretation of the
classic picture of Jesus knocking at the door, which you can
easily find on the internet. Jesus says, "Listen! I am standing
at the door, knocking; if you hear my voice and open the
door, I will come in to you and eat with you, and you with
me."[1] The "old interpretation" of the picture based on this
verse is that Jesus is knocking at the door of our hearts and
we have to let him in to be saved. The new interpretation
adds, in essence, "and, after we eat, we will go out into the
neighborhood together." Rather than knocking on the door
of the heart to come in, Jesus is knocking on the door of the
church building to get the congregation to come out.

How do we preach so people hear Jesus knocking, make a
beeline for the church door, and leave the building to minister,
serve, and bear witness in the neighborhood? If I could preach
such sermons, and teach others to do so, and congregations

immediately went out the church door, left and let go of their building, and witnessed to Christ in their neighborhoods, I would retire as bishop, become a full-time preacher, consultant, and conference speaker, and get rich. I have no plans to retire, because preaching so people leave the building is not a quick-fix solution or money-back-guaranteed approach to the church's problems. This preaching is a process requiring time, repetition, and patience; at least it was for Jesus.

In John's Gospel, it takes (at least) three sermons to get the disciples to leave the building where they gathered after the resurrection and even more to persuade them to minister, serve, and witness to Jesus.[2] Mary Magdalene preaches the first Easter sermon to the disciples early on the first day of the week. "Mary Magdalene went and announced to the disciples, 'I have seen the Lord,'" and she told them the things Jesus had said to her.[3] That evening, the disciples met behind locked doors in a house. Jesus himself came to them, showed them his hands and side, sent them as the Father had sent him, breathed the Holy Spirit into them, and commissioned them to forgive sins. "A week later his disciples were again [still?] in the house."[4] John continues, "Now Jesus did many other signs in the presence of his disciples, which are not written in [John's Gospel]."[5] How many of those signs were aimed at getting the disciples to leave the building to carry out Jesus's commission? I wonder because, when the disciples leave the house, they go fishing rather than forgiving. Jesus must come to them one more time by the Sea of Tiberias.[6]

Preaching at the church door is a process. A sermon is sometimes compared to an iceberg. Like an iceberg, most of the process of sermon preparation remains "underwater"; the congregation never sees it. This "iceberg work" is particularly important for sermons aimed at moving the congregation out the church door. It involves prayerful and honest consideration about the building, the church, the reason for going out the door, the neighborhood, Jesus, and being holy or sanctified. This iceberg work lays a foundation for and yields hunches about how to preach so the congregation follows Jesus into the neighborhood. Ideally, pastor and congregational leaders engage in this work together and its fruits find their way into preaching.

Commend the Building to God

Preaching to move the congregation to the church door helps the congregation release their beloved church building as their personal possession by commending it to God's care. Just as we cannot leave a young child or an aging parent until we know they are cared for, so congregations cannot leave their buildings until they commend them to God's care. To help the congregation entrust their building to God, preachers acknowledge, accept, and appreciate congregations' deep attachment to their buildings rather than dismissing or disparaging the building as an obstacle to mission. Then, preachers might better pastorally assist the congregation in commending their church building to God and approaching it as a partner with them in God's mission in the neighborhood.

The Covid-19 pandemic revealed just how beloved our church buildings are to us and how attached we are to them. Congregations demanded to return to their buildings. After all, they believe Jesus is in the building in a special way he is not anywhere else. In a sense, this is true. Christians, especially those who have belonged to the same congregation their entire lives or for much of their lives, experience Jesus on significant occasions—baptisms, confirmations, weddings, funerals, and feast days, for example—in that one particular space in profound ways they have not experienced anywhere else. Less obvious, the space where people worship forms and reflects them in ways more influential than what the preacher says in a sermon.[7] For example, when people can see each other during the sermon, they experience the church as a community. Worshippers' experience is compounded by what the church has taught them about church buildings.

For generations, the church in the United States taught that church buildings are tangible expressions of the faith and devotion of people personally and directly involved in the worship of God at a particular time and in a particular place. A church building proclaims how a faith community conceives of and experiences God, relates to its neighbors, and understands the church's mission. Church buildings attract people and show how this congregation is different from (and superior to) other congregations. Church buildings are the location of community and service, as well as worship.

The emphasis on buildings, and the amount of money congregations raise for and invest in buildings, are so great that, in the United States, *church* is a building; church is the place where one goes or where others go to church. Only secondarily is the church a body of people that gathers for worship and fellowship. Despite the best efforts of bishops, theologians, and ministers, the word *church* rarely means something beyond the local congregation, such as the denomination or "holy catholic and apostolic church."

Increasingly, church buildings may need to give their lives for the sake of mission and even for the sake of the congregation. Congregations with large, historic edifices may find that they are no longer able to maintain or heat the building. Many congregations that took on loans to expand or improve their facilities, trusting that the building would attract more people, are finding that their overriding purpose for existing is to pay off the mortgage. Some congregations find their neighborhoods change significantly, and they are not willing or able to change accordingly, with the result that the only thing the congregation shares with the neighborhood is that the building is located there.

As is true in many sectors of society, the Covid-19 pandemic caused some members of congregations to quietly question the necessity and purpose of church buildings. In fact, many new mission congregations are not building elaborate new church buildings, which are expensive and draining on resources. Instead, new congregations use existing structures and repurpose them for mission or choose not to own or even rent a structure at all. Rather than following the strategy that a church building attracts people, some denominations require mission congregations to become viable before they can own property.

Congregations discerning their relationship with their church building are often helped by conceiving of congregations as consisting of (1) the building, (2) the people or community, and (3) the mission or service. Congregations can ask themselves, if the congregation can have only two of these three, which two would we choose? Their answer usually charts the path toward deciding about the building. For example, occasionally, congregations choose "building" and "mission" because of the ministry to the neighborhood that happens in the building. They regularly end up giving the building to a faith community more connected to the neighborhood on the condition that the ministry of the congregation that gave away its building continues.

Preaching can help the congregation commend the building to God and enlist the building as a partner in leading worshippers into the neighborhood. Preachers can give the church building a "voice" in sermons as a wise and beloved member of the congregation and a leader in its mission. Asking what the walls and furnishings would say if they could talk, whether as part of sermon preparation or rhetorically in the sermon, can help preacher and people consider together what the space indicates about the congregation's priorities, practices, and participation. Speaking the building's memories can help the congregation reclaim its mission or purpose. For example, if the walls could talk, would they tell of a time in the congregation's history when the community used the building? In the future, what will the walls say about what this generation did and how they felt about the building, and the reason they either stayed inside or went out into the neighborhood? Preachers can allow the building to provide a lens to see Jesus in the neighborhood. We might, for example, consider where Jesus is when we preach and then consider what the corresponding place is in the neighborhood. Preaching can also help the congregation reimagine their building from a spiritual home for members of the congregation to a center for the community and even an expression of Jesus's presence and God's reign in the neighborhood.

Scripture provides some guiding images of what church buildings can be. The psalmist declares, "There is a river whose streams make glad the city of God, the holy habitation of the Most High. God is in the midst of the city; it shall not be moved; God will help it when the morning dawns."[8] The author of Revelation offers another image: "The city has a great, high wall with twelve gates, and at the gates twelve angels, and on the gates are inscribed the names of the twelve tribes of the Israelites; on the east three gates, on the north three gates, on the south three gates, and on the west three gates... The city's gates will never be shut by day—and there will be no night there. People will bring into it the glory and the honor of the nations."[9] First Peter offers a third image of what church buildings might be: "You, as living stones, are being made into a house of the spirit, a holy order of priests, making those offerings of the spirit which are pleasing to God through Jesus Christ."[10]

Accept the Nature of the Church

Preaching that moves the congregation through the church door helps the congregation accept that the church's nature is not endless expansion and continuous growth. To celebrate its two-hundredth anniversary, a congregation established a timeline on the walls of the sanctuary. Significant events appeared steadily from its founding until the time period labeled "1950–1970." Then there was an explosion of events and activity. Continuing along the timeline, significant events returned to the frequency before the fifties, sixties, and seventies, and, in fact, slowed. As the congregation continues to age, events and activities will eventually cease because few people are joining the church. The timeline illustrates that, looking at the big picture, the church's "golden age" of fifty years ago, to which so many love to point and harken, is the exception rather than the rule.

We can identify several reasons that 1950 to 1970 was exceptional. Looking back through rose-colored glasses, we see the church enjoyed and came to expect society's center stage. Society expected and rewarded church attendance and involvement. Salvation and faith in Jesus Christ were understood as a personal, private matter that prepared one for heaven, rendering it acceptable to pursue success, power, affluence, and the American dream here on earth. In many places, Christianity was reinforced by the culture as other faiths existed at the margins. Institutions, including government, were considered good and trustworthy; the church assisted them by supporting those who "fell through the cracks." Stable and growing congregations were expected unless something unfortunate and unforeseen happened. It never occurred to church leaders that, like all living things, congregations have lifespans.

Whatever else we might say about the institutional church generally and our own context in particular, we can say the church has changed and is changing. Today, many leaders of and commentators on the mainline institutional church frame the changes the church faces negatively and express them urgently. "The church as we know it is dying." Many Christians feel this death in their bones. They forecast the unthinkable, inevitable demise of their beloved congregation. Worse than the loss of their church, these saints who served faithfully for so long fear their labor has been in vain, the congregation will die on their watch, and they will be blamed because the death of their church will be their fault. Having tried unsuccessfully to save and grow their congregation, these saints retreat to the safety and stability of their church building.

The psalmist declares, "God is our refuge and strength,"[11] which Martin Luther translated, "A mighty Fortress is our God." Faced with a changing, dying church, it does not take long for scared saints to go from "A mighty fortress is our God" to "A mighty fortress is our church" and take refuge in the closest thing they have to a fortress, their church building. When we experience our faith under siege, our church under siege, even our God under siege, we draw the bridge, lock the gates, and settle in safely behind beloved stained-glass walls. To keep our fear at bay, we sing, "A mighty fortress is our God," as if this is how God intended it to be, and our mission becomes maintaining the fortress.

Preaching to move the congregation out the church door speaks honestly about the state of the church in a manner that proclaims the promise of the gospel without giving cause for false security or illusory hope. We do this by speaking of the church as the body of Christ. As Jesus was on the cross, so the church as we know it is dying. But as surely as Jesus rose from the grave, Jesus is raising the church to new life.

The church will rise; the church is rising. Jesus is raising his church to new life.

We can say this because Jesus is. We can also say that, if we want to see resurrection, if we want to experience the new life Jesus is bringing, we need to get out of our building and into the neighborhood, because the chances are good that is where Jesus is raising the church to new life while we remain locked away in our fortress.

One problem with locking ourselves away in a fortress is that eventually we starve to death. The bread of God's Word grows stale, and the fount of living water runs dry. Another problem with locking ourselves away in a fortress is we miss when the siege is over. Our enemies are defeated, or perhaps they grow bored or indifferent and move on. There we sit, locked away, defending ourselves from an enemy who no longer exists. Yet, the main problem with locking ourselves in a fortress, clinging to absolute safety, stability, and security, is that we reduce Easter to little more than an anniversary of the past and the hope for after we die. Locked away in a fortress that has become a safe and comfortable tomb, we miss out on Christ's resurrection today. We miss out on the new thing God is doing and the new life Jesus is bringing.

The church is certainly smaller than it was, and it is living on the margins rather than taking center stage. But this "dying" has characterized the church for much of its life. I cannot help but wonder whether this change means Jesus is getting his body back in shape, getting his body down to fighting weight. For I also see instances of the church rising in new commitments to take up our cross and follow Jesus, new energy to participate in the in-breaking of God's reign here on earth, and new openness to sharing God's unconditional love, revealed in Jesus Christ, with *all* people.

Decide Why the Congregation Should Leave the Building

Why should a congregation leave their spiritual home, their beautiful building, to follow Jesus out the church door to engage the neighborhood? Why not wait expectantly to share our friendliness and God's love with anyone who comes to our door? What is our reason or motivation for leaving the building? Preachers get to decide what they will say in their sermons. Preachers and congregation leaders cite several reasons for leaving the building.

The first reason to leave the building is eminently practical: our need for *numerical growth*. The question I am most frequently asked as a bishop is, "What can we do to grow?" What can we do to attract young families? My answer is always a question: Why do you want to grow? I am forever grateful to a leader who answered honestly: "Butts and bucks. We want to grow to pay our bills, provide volunteers, and secure our future and legacy. We want to be here forever."

We go out into the neighborhood to acquire more members for our church. To survive forever, which many congregations are convinced is what they are supposed to do, we need a never-ending supply of members to do the work, pay the bills, and keep the church stable by keeping things the same. So, we push the congregation out the church door in an urgent search for new members, especially young families, because they will provide years of service and income.

The problem with this reason is that we turn people into a commodity, a resource to maintain the institutional church. How often I hear sermons that suggest Jesus saved us so we can volunteer in the congregation. Visitors show up and, if they are someone we can use, we smell fresh meat. And if not, we ignore them altogether at coffee hour or, in worship, tell them they are sitting in our pew.

Engaging the neighborhood for numerical growth presents several problems. First, it does not work; people can tell when they are being received as fresh meat, and they turn away and run. Second, our work in the neighborhood becomes transactional; we give to get. If they do not receive, congregations tend to return to their buildings, complaining about the neighbors, and lock the door tighter than ever. Jesus directs, "But when you give a banquet, invite the poor, the crippled, the lame, and the blind. And you will be blessed, because they cannot repay you, for you will be repaid at the resurrection of the righteous."[12] Jesus never received people as fresh meat for the work of the kingdom.

Yet, the real problem, of course, is that God did not give us Jesus to make us worker bees for the congregation, cogs serving an ecclesiastical machine. Jesus died on the cross because God loves us that much, because Jesus is with us always, no matter what. We preach to and about people as God's beloved, for whom Jesus died, and this is how we are to treat them. We start by renouncing preaching, even implicitly, that Jesus died on the cross for us so we can serve the church, save the world, or accomplish whatever our cause is.

Discipleship, growing into the fullness of Christ, participating in Jesus's own work of reconciling the world to God's very self, is so much bigger than volunteering in a congregation. Joining us to Jesus's death and resurrection, God "claims us as daughters and sons, making us heirs of God's promise and servants of all."[13] We are "sealed by the Holy Spirit and marked with the cross of Christ forever."[14] We are God's beloved children. Recruiting more members to serve our congregation is not an appropriate reason to push people out the church door.

Back in the 1990s, I was taught to encourage the congregation to go out into the neighborhood to demonstrate and advertise that they are the "best" church in the neighborhood. While being best always includes "quality" and "user-friend-liness," congregations have defined their best by determining a "target audience" and their needs, then ministering, pro-gramming, and marketing to them. People outside the target audience have been gently encouraged to worship elsewhere. In a certain sense, this approach is nothing new. In the United States, beginning with the earliest immigrants, denomina-tions have been formed based on theological distinction, ethnic heritage, and socioeconomic status and have grown by ministering to that target audience.

Ideally, according to this model, preaching, along with the congregation's entire life, so appeals to the target audience that the congregation excitedly enters the neighborhood to invite neighbors who fit within the specified parameters to "come and see."[15] Congregations continue to do this by high-lighting, for example, music, social justice, children, or their family feeling as qualities that distinguish them from other congregations.

Today, some pastors and congregations continue to embrace striving to be the best. Yet, the intervening years since pastors were first taught this approach have revealed its problems. First, striving to be the best presumes a Christian culture in which church affiliation is a given and people look for the "best church," the church that best meets their needs. This approach may very well work for churchgoing Christians, but the pool is shrinking. Today, people are increasingly dis-interested in becoming part of any church, no matter how outstanding it is.

Second, striving to be the best turns Christianity and the church into a product, a consumable. The goal becomes meet-ing people's needs. In the process, the church may adopt a consumer mentality as it strives to give people what they want or to package the gospel the way people want, sometimes forgetting the packaging affects the content. This approach contributes to Christians bearing witness to their congregation rather than Jesus. The goal of being the best experienced a resurgence during the pandemic in congregations that prioritized meeting people's needs over keeping people safe. In the coming years, the church will discover how the way it packaged worship, preaching, and sacrament during the pandemic shaped what we will come to believe and how we will practice our faith.

Third, target audiences, competition, and free-standing, like-minded congregations reflect neither the reign of God nor the church as the body of Christ. Jesus's encounter with the Canaanite woman, his commission to the apostles to be his witnesses from Jerusalem to the ends of the earth, and Paul's ministry to the gentiles make clear that the gospel's target audience is ever-expanding rather than limiting.[16] Also, Paul's image of the church as the body of Christ, which is as relevant to congregations in a neighborhood as it is to individuals within a congregation, makes clear that we are meant to cooperate for the good of all rather than compete to be the best.[17]

Some preachers appeal to Jesus's Great Commission as the reason for congregations to exit the church building to engage the neighborhood. "Go therefore and make disciples of all nations."[18] We go obediently because Jesus commands us to—or at least this is how this rationale is supposed to work. We can imagine our church filled with people who have come to be baptized and taught to observe all that Jesus commanded. If we do not go, we are not observing all that Jesus commanded.

In chapter 3, I reported church historian Alan Kreider's observation that early Christian preachers did not appeal to the Great Commission to inspire their members to "make disciples of all nations," because they assumed Jesus's eleven apostles plus Paul had accomplished this in the church's earliest years; the Great Commission had already been fulfilled in the church's global expansion. These early preachers would be puzzled, even shocked, by the way church consultants pair the Great Commission with statistical graphs showing declines in church membership and worship attendance to create panic and a sense of failure, and to imply congregations' unfaithfulness in responding to Jesus's command. While decline is certainly a concern for the institutional church, appealing to decline and somehow threatening our relationship with Jesus is inconsistent with the risen Lord's assurance that he is always with his apostles, to the close of the age.

For this approach to succeed, preachers will need to explain *why* congregations should enter the neighborhood to make disciples. For most people, saying that Jesus told us to does not suffice. In an interreligious world, where all faiths are valued and respected, they wonder, why is it important to make disciples of Jesus? Many feel the church lost its rationale for making disciples when we stopped condemning people to hell and started espousing ecumenical and interreligious relationships.

Preachers will also need to teach their congregations *how* to make disciples. This is very challenging. Many people regard their faith as precious, personal, and private—a treasure buried in a field.[19] Large sections of our culture reinforce this perspective. Jesus said, "By this everyone will know that you are my disciples, if you have love for one another."[20] Many, if not most, Christians want to so trust that people will know they are Christians by their love that they never have to utter a word about Jesus. Perhaps this is because most Christians feel unqualified and uncomfortable telling others how they should be disciples and teaching others what Jesus commands. On the other hand, Christians eager to make disciples can be off-putting if they fail to convey to others the love with which Jesus loves them or do so in an overwhelming manner. Perhaps Christians who observe that "making disciples" is a charism or spiritual gift given to some but not all are correct.

Personally, I am excited about preaching that sends people through the church door and into the neighborhood to *share the good news.* Matthew's snapshot of Jesus in the neighborhood is inspiring. "Jesus went throughout Galilee, teaching in their synagogues and proclaiming the good news of the kingdom and curing every disease and every sickness among the people."[21] I experience "proclaiming the good news of the kingdom" as more gracious than making disciples. I am pleased that Matthew pairs teaching with healing. In this snapshot, Jesus is a herald who cannot contain the good news he has to share. Jesus asks nothing of the neighbors except that they receive it.

Preaching that sends the congregation through the church door to proclaim the good news must give them news so good they cannot contain it, news so good they are excited to share it. This good news must be from God and not depend on us or circumstance. It would be great if the announcement of this good news was accompanied by signs verifying its truthfulness, such as healing. Such good news is hard to find. Yet, when people receive this kind of good news—for example, the undeniably Christian message that Black Lives Matter—they go out into their neighborhoods to proclaim it.

Preaching that sends people out the church door to share the good news in the neighborhood names that good news explicitly, even repeatedly, rendering the good news easy for the congregation to grab onto and repeat. Preachers remain vigilant to frame the good news as a proclamation or pronouncement and not as a task, obligation, or conditional proposition. For example, preachers do not tell people to *remember* Jesus loves them, but instead simply tell people that Jesus loves them.

The good news is not a *call*, something God wants, expects, or needs us to do. The good news is God's promise. Most important, preachers never present good news as something we—the preacher, the congregation, the church—possess and the neighborhood does not, and even implicitly suggest the neighborhood needs to come to the church to get it. People may come to the church not to receive the good news but because they have already received it.

We can guarantee God's good news is not perceived as the church's possession by entering the neighborhood to *announce that the reign of God has come near to you or the reign of God is here.* Matthew describes the beginning of Jesus's ministry by saying, "From that time Jesus began to proclaim, 'Repent, for the kingdom of heaven has come near.'" Later in his ministry, Jesus sends the disciples out with instructions to "proclaim the good news, 'The kingdom of heaven has come near.'"[22] The kingdom of God is not something the church possesses or does. God's reign is God's activity, which the church points to and announces and people receive and enter.

Like the preaching of Jesus, our preaching so the congregation exits the church building to proclaim the nearness of God's reign announces and points to this thing God is doing and names the new reality Jesus brings into our world. The preacher points to the nearness of God's reign *in the neighborhood.* Sermons offer an image or description of God's new reality, as Jesus's parables do.

In Luke's Gospel, Jesus sends his disciples as vulnerable guests: "Go on your way. See, I am sending you out like lambs into the midst of wolves. Carry no purse, no bag, no sandals; and greet no one on the road. . . . Remain in the same house, eating and drinking whatever they provide."[23] When the church enters the neighborhood vulnerably as guests, and maintains a position of vulnerability, we are best able to perceive the inbreaking of God's reign and to authentically proclaim its nearness because we are in the best place to meet Jesus and receive God's reign ourselves.

People want to meet Jesus and experience God's reign for themselves. *To meet Jesus*, therefore, is the best reason for congregations to burst through the church door and engage the neighborhood. Rather than providing congregations with a biblical justification never to close their church, Jesus's words, "For where two or three are gathered in my name, I am there among them,"[24] open us to all the places Jesus is and might be.

Preaching that leads the congregation to meet Jesus in the neighborhood pastorally sets Jesus free from our expectations of who and where Jesus is. This preaching discovers and acknowledges Jesus out there—Jesus in the neighborhood, Jesus in the other, Jesus in the stranger, Jesus in the vulnerable. Alternatively, this preaching acknowledges Jesus in powerful people like Zacchaeus and the Roman centurion who sent Jewish elders to ask Jesus to heal his slave.[25] Thus, to preach in a manner that invites the congregation to meet Jesus in the neighborhood, preachers must set aside their own assumptions of where Jesus is and is not, allowing themselves to be surprised when they encounter Jesus anew. Preaching that inspires the congregation to meet Jesus in the neighborhood proclaims Jesus in an inspiring way so the congregation is excited to meet him.

Prepare Sermons in the Neighborhood

To get congregations out of the building and into the neighborhood, preachers need as part of sermon preparation to get out of the church building or home office and into the neighborhood. I am concerned that, for many preachers, getting out of the office means surfing the internet and communicating on social media. Even while respecting public health guidelines related to the Covid-19 pandemic, preachers need to commit to being physically present in the neighborhood as part of weekly sermon preparation.

To lead the congregation out of the building, preachers bring the neighborhood into the pulpit. One way to do this is to prepare sermons in a public place such as the coffee shop, Main Street Café, or YMCA. Wear a clerical collar, bring your laptop, and spread out your books and notes, so the neighbors see you. Invite people like the young adult we met in the imaginary coffee shop into conversation about the sermon you are preparing. Getting out of the office to work in the neighborhood is a rewarding addition to sermon preparation that requires courage, patience, commitment, and time.

Second, preachers can lead Bible studies on the readings in the neighborhood. To the degree possible, the preacher does not inform and teach as much as listen and learn. Our neighbors will be present in the sermon through their reactions to, questions about, and insights from the readings.

Third, the preacher can visit and spend time at places in the neighborhood similar to the location or context of the scripture readings from which the sermon will be preached. I vividly recall the power and emotion experienced in Jesus's words about the temple, "Do you see these great buildings? Not one stone will be left here upon another; all will be thrown down,"[26] when, gathered with Notre Dame preaching students, we heard and considered Jesus's words just outside the Golden Dome on campus. In addition to giving the neighborhood a voice in the sermon, preparing sermons in the neighborhood helps preachers to meet Jesus themselves and help the congregation learn to expect to encounter Jesus in the neighborhood.

Preach Jesus

The goal of sermons that move people out the church door and into the neighborhood is to preach Jesus so that the congregation wants to meet Jesus, recognizes Jesus in the neighborhood, and learns how to talk about Jesus. The challenge, of course, is that churchgoers know Jesus, or think they do. Often, they know Jesus in church, in their homes, and in prayer. The opportunity is to introduce the congregation to Jesus in the neighborhood in ways that they want to meet him there. To do this, preachers make a practice of encountering Jesus in the neighborhood, recording those encounters in vivid detail, and sharing them in sermons.

The gospels tell us that, when people hear about Jesus, Zacchaeus climbs a tree to see him and the woman with the hemorrhage fights through the crowds to touch him. When the congregation hears about Jesus anew, in concrete, accessible, and unexpected ways, they may be led out of the church building. We trust that hearing about Jesus in the neighborhood leads us to get out into the community, not to take Jesus there but because that is where Jesus is. Might we start by imagining the gospel stories occurring in our neighborhoods?

As much as they might want to, people may be reluctant to pass through the church door into the neighborhood to meet Jesus because they do not know how to talk to or about Jesus, and they are afraid. Preachers therefore speak of Jesus to teach the congregation how to do it. In this way, preachers serve as "language teachers"[27] who offer the "vocabulary" of Christian tradition to their congregations to use to make meaning of God, self, and the world. In this instance, the preacher shows the congregation how to use the language of the Christian tradition to effectively speak of Jesus. At the same time, the preacher will show the congregation how to use the everyday language of a witness who encounters Jesus and reports on the experience. In so doing, the pulpit models for the congregation how to speak of Jesus. Preachers learn to teach people how to talk about Jesus by remaining cognizant of this responsibility and reviewing their sermons to examine what they are teaching in the language they choose.

Name Sanctification

Preaching to move the congregation into the neighborhood names *sanctification*. *Sanctification* is God making us—or God working with us to make us—holy. *Sanctification* is holiness in living on the quest to the unity of the faith and of the knowledge of the Son of God, maturity, the measure of the full stature of Christ.[28] Preachers name sanctification because what our neighbors see today is not so much the church's preaching and teaching but our behavior, our way of being in the world. Or, perhaps, what our neighbors need to see is how our behavior counters and even contradicts perceptions and experiences of what some parts of the church preach. By naming sanctification, this preaching makes disciples of our congregants, not the neighbors.

In the early church, outsiders noticed how Christians lived and behaved in the world. According to Tertullian, the outsiders looked at the Christians and saw them energetically feeding poor people, caring for boys and girls who lacked property and parents, being attentive to aged slaves and prisoners, and burying the dead who had no one else to care for them. Alan Kreider observes:

> They interpreted these actions as a "work of love." And they said, "*Vide*, look! How they love one another." They did not say, "*Aude*, listen to the Christians' message"; they did not say, "*Lege*, read what they write." Hearing and reading were important, and some early Christians

worked to communicate in these ways too. But we must not miss the reality: the pagans said *look!* Christianity's truth was visible; it was embodied and enacted by its members.[29]

I have long resisted including sanctification in sermons because I have heard far too much preaching that moved directly from our sinful state to how God would have us live and serve. Assumed or presumed, Jesus has almost disappeared from the sermon. These sermons remind me of an hourglass lying on its side. In the first chamber of the hourglass, we get six or seven minutes of how bad we are, how bad things are, how bad the world is. Then, in the narrow part of the hourglass, we get a minute or two about Jesus. Finally, in the second chamber of the hourglass, we get six or seven minutes of what we should, ought, need to, and must do—concluding with, "Let us." In my own preaching, I do not tell people how to respond to the gospel, and I taught students not to as well.

In retrospect, I realize I was blessed to serve a seminary of people who made responding to the gospel the purpose of their lives. In the office of bishop, I have learned that pastors and parishioners alike need to be taught, reminded, and reinforced to live as followers of Jesus in a public way. In a world divided over everything from politics to the pandemic, I certainly do. Perhaps I naïvely assumed people knew what it means to live as a Christian or would learn by osmosis.

Now I advise preachers, once they make proclaiming Jesus as Savior the goal of preaching, to dare to name the behavior the Christian church expects—worship, Bible study, prayer, generosity, service, advocacy, justice. Make clear that this is a response to God's love in Jesus Christ and not a precondition for receiving it. It turns out the best way to preach sanctification is to make Jesus really big, so people have some gospel to respond to. Remind people we commit to Christian behaviors at baptism. Outline the expectation, the church's and God's, that people will grow in grace. Do not tell people what they should, must, or ought to do. Describe what God is doing, particularly in the neighborhood, and invite us to be part of it. Teach us to explicitly connect public Christian behavior and speaking of Jesus so others know for certain that, more than being nice people, we are Jesus's disciples.

Trust that some people in your congregation, a few at least, are looking for an encounter with Jesus that changes their lives. You are telling them how to put themselves in the best place for a life-changing encounter with Jesus. At the same time, expect some people to resist. I have noticed that many Lutheran Christians, for example, are allergic to embodied practices, of behaving in an overtly Christian manner, lest someone confuse our behavior for works righteousness. For Lutheran Christians, faith is all about right understanding—we are justified by grace through faith apart from works of law. Except this is not how people live out their faith or, in Lutheran parlance, their baptism. Dying and rising with Christ is more than an intellectual exercise.

Alan Kreider observes, "In Christianity's early centuries, conversion involved changes in belief, belonging, and behavior—in the context of an experience of God." The church reached out to people who needed to belong—widows, orphans, and the poor. It expected people to behave a certain way, to act their way into who we are in Christ. The church was convinced that believing comes from doing and that truth becomes real to us only when it touches the skin. Being converted to a community's convictions involved "becoming the kind of person who belonged to that kind of community." And this meant that conversion in the ancient church was at least as much about changing one's loyalties and one's lifestyle as it was about changing one's creed.[30] Christian faith is more than intellectual assent to doctrine; the Christian faith is embarking on a chosen way of life that includes behaving differently. In the church building, we train for the journey of faith we will take in the neighborhood.

Jesus Stands Knocking

Jesus stands knocking at the door of our church, bidding us to come out and join him in the neighborhood. When we commend our building to God and head out the church door, the Spirit remodels both the building and its congregation to make them more a part of Jesus's work in the neighborhood. Jesus knocks because the neighborhood needs the church, not a mighty fortress. Jesus knocks because the neighborhood needs the church to lower the bridge and open the gate. The neighborhood needs the church to build more gates. The neighborhood needs the Spirit to remodel the church into a place where all God's people experience God through their synergy as the Holy Spirit gathers us and we act as the body of Christ for and in the neighborhood. Jesus knocks at the door because we need the neighborhood so we can encounter Jesus anew.

When congregations stay inside their buildings and keep their doors closed, Jesus will not stop knocking on the door of our hearts. However, I suspect Jesus will eventually stop knocking at the door of our church. Jesus is not punishing us or abandoning us. Jesus simply has too much to do in the neighborhood and he needs to be on his way from our building. "'Let us go on to the neighboring towns, so that I may proclaim the message there also,' Jesus said to Simon and his companions, 'for that is what I came out to do.' And he went throughout Galilee. . . ."[81] Sometimes, preaching at the church door means pastorally naming what may happen now that we have decided to stay inside and keep our door closed. Preachers can do this only when they are yoked so closely and securely to Jesus that they trust Christ's presence in them and in their preaching.

9

The Preacher

Does Jesus *Really* Leave the Building?

The rite of ordination for the Evangelical Lutheran Church in America includes this instruction: "Receive this stole as a sign of your work, and walk in obedience to the Lord Jesus, serving his people and remembering his promise."[1] The church identifies the stole as a yoke and recalls Matthew 11:28-30—"Come to me, all who labor and are carrying heavy burdens, and I will give you rest. Take my yoke upon you, and learn from me; for I am gentle and lowly in heart, and you will find rest for your souls. For my yoke is easy, and my burden is light"[2]—when newly ordained ministers receive it. Even as I am inspired by William Willimon's image of being yoked so securely and joyously to the word that in the preaching of the word, we become the word and the word dwells in us richly,[3] I continue to wonder how preachers become and remain yoked so securely and joyously to Jesus.

Jesus yokes us to his death and resurrection in baptism. The Holy Spirit yokes us to the Word in preaching. Nevertheless, all preachers know difficult and challenging times when being yoked to Jesus feels more like belief and hope than experience and reality. Too often, I am so challenged to trust Jesus's promise that I need to be convinced and assured that "Jesus's yoke is easy and Jesus's burden is light." So, my silent prayer, as a red stole is laid on a new pastor's or deacon's shoulders, is always: "Lord Jesus, keep them closely and securely yoked to you."

Frequently, other words from Scripture better fit my experience of public ministry. For example, Jesus says, "If any want to become my followers, let them deny themselves and take up their cross and follow me."[4] When I was elected bishop, my predecessor identified words Jesus spoke to Ananias about Paul as the words Jesus was now saying about me: "I myself will show him how much he must suffer for the sake of my name."[5] At the bishop formation event I attended, we were repeatedly reminded of words from Isaiah that I return to again and again: "Do not fear, for I have redeemed you; I have called you by name, you are mine. When you pass through the waters, I will be with you; and through the rivers, they shall not overwhelm you; when you walk through fire you shall not be burned, and the flame shall not consume you."[6] I wonder what Bible verse pastors and deacons would select to describe their experience of public ministry and what verse they return to again and again. I also wonder how many pastors and deacons choose and return to, "For my yoke is easy, and my burden is light."

In this chapter, I respond to seasons when preachers feel Jesus has left the building of their own hearts and their preaching. These seasons can feel like our yoke to Jesus has broken, Jesus is far away, and we are completely untethered and alone; or, if we are still attached to it, Jesus's yoke is hard, and his burden is heavy.

In a particular way, preachers can trust Jesus's promise. Jesus says, "Come to me, all who labor and are carrying heavy burdens, and I will give you rest."[7] This is not the invitation of one who intends to abandon our hearts, lives, and preaching. Still, how do we actively remember Jesus's promise? What does Jesus's invitation and promise mean? Hans Dieter Betz writes: "It is remarkable that the logion of the 'easy yoke and of rest,' which is known to everyone in the ecclesiastical tradition and the content of which is always assumed to be known, belongs nevertheless among the unresolved problems of NT research. In reality the meaning of the passage is unclarified."[8]

Matthew 11 employs wisdom themes; therefore, in this chapter, I contemplate Jesus's promise for wisdom so that, when we toil in our preaching and bringing the word is a burden rather than a joy, we actively engage rather than passively recollect Jesus's promise. These reflections are best approached as an invitation to introspection.

Together, coming to Jesus, taking on Jesus's yoke, learning from Jesus, and finding rest in Jesus are the relational dynamics of remembering Jesus's promise and being yoked to Jesus as preachers. These dynamics are cyclical and continuous. We arrive at finding rest in Jesus and remain there until something changes in us, the congregation, the church, the world, or our preaching. Then we come to Jesus and begin the process again. I believe that as long as preachers are coming to Jesus, taking on Jesus's yoke, learning from Jesus, or finding rest in Jesus, they can assure themselves they are yoked closely and securely to Jesus and trust Jesus is with and in them when they preach.

In Matthew, Jesus invites us to be yoked to Jesus; in John, Jesus compares himself to a vine and us to branches and tells us, "Abide in me as I abide in you."[9] Yoked closely and securely to Jesus, we abide in him and he in us. We bear fruit, become Jesus's disciples, and God is glorified. Regardless of how we feel or what is happening, we can trust Jesus is with us when we preach.

Come to Jesus

Jesus says, "Come to me, all who labor and are carrying heavy burdens." Baptized into Christ Jesus and committing their lives to public ministry, preachers have certainly come to Jesus. Yet, the invitation to come to Jesus is ongoing. Preachers can consider whether we are currently yoked to Jesus as we preach and minister or need to come to Jesus. We might need to come to Jesus if we regard ministry as our own possession rather than as an extension of Jesus's or the church's ministry. When this happens, preaching becomes something preachers do by relying on their own abilities and inner resources. Preachers may even believe themselves responsible for every outcome, success, and failure in preaching. Even as preachers witness on Jesus's behalf and in Jesus's name, they may forget they are yoked to Jesus in a subordinate role. Instead of relying on Jesus, preachers might develop ways of denying the level of their fatigue and the weight of the burdens they carry, become frozen by the yoke of their ministry in Jesus's name, or end up crushed when something unanticipated and terrible happens.

To come to Jesus as preachers is to acknowledge when we are weary and carrying heavy burdens, to hear the gospel, and genuinely, even penetratingly, receive the Word for ourselves and those we love. To come to Jesus is to honestly acknowledge to ourselves, and perhaps also to a pastor or confessor, our feelings about our call to preach. Preachers ask themselves: What is your attitude toward preaching, your call, the people you serve, and the message you preach?

Over time, faithful yet frustrated preachers sometimes empty their homiletic "bag of tricks" or run out of things to say. Many of us begin our preaching ministry "with our hearts burning within us while [Jesus] was . . . opening the scriptures to us."[10] Our minds burst with creative ways to preach the gospel. Then our innovation grows old, and our hearts grow weary. The well that nourishes our preaching seems to run dry. We can seek a new pulpit, where people have not seen our bag of tricks or heard what we have to say. We can determine that, for all sorts of reasons, preaching really does not matter and devote ourselves to more "important" aspects of ministry. Or we can come to Jesus and perhaps discover that, with empty bag and open heart, we are at last prepared to preach. After all, Jesus sent the twelve to proclaim the good news with no bag or anything else.[11] Their proclamation came from a place of vulnerability and dependence.

Preaching from a place of vulnerability and dependence can be challenging for preachers, especially when they are tired and burdened. Preachers can forget God intends the good news of the gospel for them and those they love, as well as the people they serve. I regularly remind pastors and deacons that Jesus said, "I came that they may have life, and have it abundantly."[12] I then ask them to describe Jesus's "abundant life" for them personally and for the people they love most. Rather than focusing on *abundant life*, most pastors and deacons instead respond to the word *they*—"that *they* may have life"—and readily tell me what abundant life would mean for the congregations or communities they serve. They are reticent to name and claim abundant life for themselves, as if Jesus's promise is not meant for us who proclaim it.

Preachers need to be reminded that Jesus's promise is for them and for the ones they love. So, as a bishop, I am thankful to preach to pastors and deacons during the weeks before Christmas and tell them that Christ was born for them and the ones they consider their families, and during Holy Week when I get to tell pastors and deacons Jesus died and rose for them and those they love most. To come to Jesus is to receive and not resist this good news for ourselves. Hear the gospel for you. Read it out loud or invite someone to read it to you:

You are created in God's image.[13] You are baptized into Christ's death and resurrection.[14] Nothing can separate you from the love of Christ.[15]

Jesus says, "Destroy this temple, and in three days I will raise it up." Jesus "was speaking of the temple of his body."[16] Paul asks, "Do you not know that your body is a temple of the Holy Spirit within you, which you have from God?"[17] Jesus speaks of the temple of your body as well. Jesus raises you as surely as Jesus rose himself.

Jesus cries with you when you cry, "My God, my God, why have you forsaken me?"[18] Jesus does not abandon you in God-forsakenness. Jesus suffers with you and brings you to abundant life. Jesus never really leaves the building of your heart, life, and preaching!

When preachers cannot receive the gospel in one way—written in this book, for example—we come to Jesus by going to places where we can receive it. We allow; we do not resist but allow the gospel-for-us to free us to take Jesus's yoke upon us and learn from him.

Take on Jesus's Yoke

Jesus says, "Take my yoke upon you." We take on Jesus's yoke because it is *Jesus's* yoke, which makes this yoke different. We do not take on Jesus's yoke in response to the demands laid upon us, but in response to the good news Jesus brings that is for us. We take on Jesus's yoke by taking off other yokes, submitting, even surrendering to Jesus, and returning to our rightful place as Jesus's disciples.

When as preachers we are not yoked closely and securely to Jesus, we might *consider what yoke we need to remove.* We determine what exhausting burden we are joined to, what hard work causes us to toil, labor, and grow weary. We invite Jesus to free us from it and take what initially may seem small and insignificant steps to remove it, as we increasingly take on Jesus's yoke in its place.

New Testament professor Raymond Pickett suggests one way to explore the meaning and force of Jesus's statement that his "yoke is easy, and my burden is light" is to ask, "Compared to what?"[19] Assuming Matthew is written to a community of Jewish followers of Jesus, "yoke" would refer to the latter rabbinic notion of the "yoke of Torah." Jesus would be saying that his interpretation and embodiment of Torah is easier than that of the Pharisees referred to in Matthew 23:4: "They tie up heavy burdens, hard to bear, and lay them on the shoulders of others." In the Hebrew Bible, especially the prophets, the term "yoke" always refers to the yoke of empire. Jesus's followers live under Roman rule shortly after the destruction of Jerusalem. Pickett maintains that Jesus is referring to a way of life that is characterized by the Sermon on the Mount, Matthew's emphasis on mercy, compassion and righteousness, and justice. This is an easier way or path than legalistic religious observance or living according to the conventions of society, especially authoritarian rule.

If "yoke" is whatever controls people's lives,[20] perhaps everything we are asking pastors and deacons to do, and all the expectations and metrics they internalize, are the yokes that burden preachers. The church needs to consider whether these responsibilities, expectations, and metrics are really in accordance with the way of Jesus. Perhaps this is the yoke preachers should be taking off to take on Jesus's yoke. Preachers might ask whether they are exhausting themselves propping up the ecclesial institution rather than following Jesus. If we claim to be following Jesus and are burning out, perhaps we need to question our patterns of living and being church.

I have long worried that the contemporary church asks preachers to do two competing, even conflicting, things: proclaim God's unconditional love for all people in Jesus Christ and maintain the institutional church. During the pandemic, we added a third expectation: Preachers are to reinforce everyone's perspective and meet everyone's particular needs. The result is many preachers spend themselves trying not to offend as if doing so renders them unrighteous and even unclean. These yokes undermine the proclamation of the gospel; therefore, preachers need to find ways to remove them and receive support when they do.

Taking on Jesus's yoke means *submitting to Jesus, even surrendering to Jesus, as preachers.* Preachers submit themselves in the manner of Jesus who emptied himself, humbled himself, and became obedient.[21] Preaching is unique in that, if its overall effect is to draw attention to the preacher, preaching has missed the mark. As John the Baptist said of Jesus, so preachers say, "He must increase, but I must decrease."[22] Taking Jesus's yoke upon us means accepting both the grace and the humility that, when preaching is at its best, the preacher becomes transparent as the congregation experiences the sermon as an encounter with Jesus, not an encounter with the preacher. In Jesus's words, the act of preaching is a way that preachers "lose their life for my sake."[23]

Taking on Jesus's yoke means surrendering our preaching to Jesus. Preachers regularly revisit the goal of their preaching and either affirm it is Jesus or reclaim it as Jesus. We ensure that what may have initially been included in preaching as an expression or an extension of Jesus's ministry has not replaced Jesus as the subject or purpose of sermons. Recognizing that all blessings are mixed, preachers guard against their greatest strengths becoming either a crutch or an idol as those strengths cease to be tools in service to the gospel.

Taking on Jesus's yoke means submitting to Jesus's way of being in the world. We preach that Jesus "must go to Jerusalem and undergo great suffering at the hands of the elders and chief priests and scribes, and be killed, and on the third day be raised." We preach that Jesus says, "if any want to become my followers, let them deny themselves and take up their cross and follow me."[24] Nevertheless, part of every preacher hopes good and effective preaching will yield blessing, growing congregation, a better world, recognition, and reward. To submit to Jesus's way of being is to challenge this desire and hold it in check. Jesus names this, setting our mind on divine things rather than human things.[25]

To submit to Jesus's way of being in the world is to reject what Jesus rejected and to embrace what Jesus embraced. Jesus rejected satisfying his own needs, putting God to the test, and compromising with the powers of this world.[26] What does this mean for preaching? Jesus embraced being despised and rejected, suffering, and infirmity.[27] Jesus did not deny death or avoid death; Jesus embraced death to bring new life. To submit to Jesus is to ask how Jesus calls us to do this in our preaching.

Preachers submit to Jesus's way of being in the world by coming to terms with their willingness to suffer for Jesus's sake and for the sake of the gospel. This is different from suffering for the sake of the institutional church. How can I as a preacher submit to Jesus's way of being, in the church and in the world, when I preach? To take on Jesus's yoke is to consider this question in a practical and not merely theoretical manner, contemplation that leads to action. Seriously asking ourselves about our willingness to suffer for the sake of the gospel eventually results in our taking Jesus's yoke upon us.

Walter Burghardt, SJ, observes that preachers are most strongly yoked to the Word and, therefore, preach best when they are suffering servants.[28] Suffering charges our words with fresh power because in that suffering, we are uncommonly aware that of ourselves, apart from Jesus, we can do nothing.[29] Burghardt contends suffering reveals that, if these words are to strike fire, it is the Lord who must light the flame. Suffering servants, then, do the most difficult thing Christ asks of us, entrusting our whole selves to the Lord who alone can change hearts through our tongues. Burghardt argues preachers come across to their congregations more effectively, more passionately, because we are sharing more intimately in the passion of our Lord and of our sisters and brothers.

Submitting to Jesus leads preachers to *take our rightful place*. The New Testament variously names this place by describing those who preach Jesus and proclaim the good news as disciples, witnesses, ambassadors, stewards, servants, and friends.[30] Preachers take on Jesus's yoke and find grounding for their preaching by contemplating how these New Testament images of those Jesus sent to proclaim the gospel shape our preaching. How would your preaching change, for example, if you prepare a sermon as an ambassador for Christ?

I find these images assist me in setting and resetting my expectations of both myself as a preacher and others as they respond to my preaching. In John, Jesus says, "Very truly, I tell you, servants are not greater than their master, nor are messengers greater than the one who sent them." Jesus is even stronger in Matthew: "The student is not above the teacher, nor a servant above his master. It is enough for students to be like their teachers, and servants like their masters. If the head of the house has been called Beelzebub, how much more the members of his household!"[31] Preachers are not celebrities, headliners, or social media stars. We can expect to fare no better than Jesus.

I find Jesus's words about servants, appreciation, and reward especially graceful: "So you also, when you have done all that you were ordered to do, say, 'We are worthless slaves; we have done only what we ought to have done!'"[32] I find comfort in these words when I am not feeling appreciated as a preacher and my words elicit more penalties than praise. If I have faithfully preached Jesus, I have done only what I was to have done, and that is enough. I am increasingly liberated from disappointment, second guessing, and regret.

Taking on Jesus's yoke as a preacher is a lifelong journey of sanctification. I smile as I recall how, in my first years as a pastor, I struggled to balance sermon preparation and other activities on Saturday evenings until I learned to surrender Saturday evenings to solitude and, as one of my teachers described, "being haunted by the Word." Learning from Jesus is essential to taking on Jesus's yoke. Thus, Jesus pairs, "Take my yoke upon you and learn from me."[33]

Learn from Jesus

"Learn from me," Jesus says. To take the yoke of Jesus means taking the yoke of discipleship; to learn from Jesus is to be his disciple. Thus, some scholars understand "learn from me" as a restatement of "take my yoke." I find it helpful to consider Jesus's invitation to "learn from me" on its own. As our representative to God—one aspect of a model of salvation—Jesus, as our "teacher," demonstrates, empowers, affirms, forgives, strengthens, and challenges us to become the persons whom God intends.

Jesus says, "for I am gentle and humble in heart." Ulrich Luz argues convincingly that the word commonly translated as "for" is better translated as "that," giving the sense that Jesus is not only making a statement about himself; Jesus is also outlining what disciples are to learn from him. Disciples are themselves to be "gentle and humble in heart."[34] We learn to be *gentle*—not overly impressed by a sense of our own self-importance—from Jesus, who identifies himself as "gentle and humble," and enters Jerusalem as a humble king, symbolized by his riding on a donkey.[35] Looking to the cross, *humble* becomes *humiliated*. We learn to consciously choose a lower place in relationship to Jesus, the Word, and the people to whom we bring the gospel. The key to Jesus's "humility" is not "the pious personality of Jesus but . . . his voluntary identification with the lowly."[36]

Jesus invites preachers to learn more than the skills necessary to preach. Jesus invites them to receive individualized instruction within a community rather than to follow a set curriculum. After reflecting on what I as a preacher learned or am (re)learning from Jesus, I can list seven "lessons." I also learned that Jesus has many ways of teaching.

First, I learned from Jesus *the truth about being called to preach*. Whatever else we say about it, preaching the gospel is a privilege, because God in Christ through the church calls us to this task and the Holy Spirit empowers us to do it. God might call some of us through experiences like Moses's burning bush, the disciples' net full of fish, or Paul's disorienting, disabling encounter on the road to Damascus.[37] More often, God uses a nag on our heart, an itch we cannot scratch.

God calls preachers continuously. When preaching is difficult and burdensome, and we would just as soon not mention God or speak any more in God's name, God uses that nag or itch to reignite what Jeremiah describes as fire burning within our bones that we grow weary of holding in.[38] As he did with Peter, Jesus frequently uses something like a charcoal fire to renew and restore us as preachers.[39]

God calls preachers as God called Jesus in the synoptic Gospels, from the baptismal river to the wilderness of temptation to a place of proclamation to the cross. Like Jesus, preachers hear God, generally in the voices of others, declare them beloved and someone in whom God is well pleased as they begin seminary and are ordained and installed. In what often feels like an immediate shift, preachers find themselves alone in a spiritual wilderness as they sort out what God's call to preach means. Preachers then find themselves in a place God sent them to proclaim the good news and, sooner or later, find preaching Jesus brings them to the cross. Along the way, preachers struggle with God as Mark reports Jesus did at Gethsemane.[40]

Even as we know ourselves called by God to preach, our relationship with God may not always or ever be intimate and comfortable. The gospels indicate Jesus had a more intimate relationship with Peter, James, and John than with the other nine.[41] Although Jesus names me his friend, I am prone to stand in awe at the Word-made-flesh through whom all things were made than I am to sing, "What a friend we have in Jesus," and hang out with Jesus, my buddy. Since Jesus wants us to grow into the full humanity God intends for us, our relationship will have an edge as Jesus challenges as well as affirms. I struggle with sermons that tell us God loves us just the way we are and leave it there. I frequently think God loves us in spite of the way we are, and God wants more and better for and from us. God relates to Jonah in this way as Jonah sits under his broom tree, and also to Elijah hiding in a cave. Jesus's interaction with both disciples and Pharisees is frequently marked by tension. Moved by love, Jesus calls for repentance, change, and growth, which brings with it reverent distance and holy friction. The true grace in Jesus calling us friends is that our friend Jesus does not cease to be our Savior, teacher, and Lord.

God in Christ calls preachers through the church. I often describe this call as a three-legged stool. All three legs are necessary or the stool—the call—collapses. The first leg is the *internal call,* the "burning bush" experience or the spiritual "itch" that cannot be scratched, which convinces someone God is calling them to preach. The second leg is *the church's call,* which affirms someone possesses the gifts and quality of life necessary to preach the gospel with the authority of the church. The third leg is the *specific call* in which a congregation or faith community affirms that God is calling someone to preach the gospel to them. When the internal call is strong, the other two legs can seem unnecessary and even obstacles. However, when in the course of preaching God's internal call is faint or weak, the other two legs of the stool obligate and sustain the preacher. The church's call and specific call vest preachers with authority and hold preachers accountable. God uses both to support the call to preach when it is easy to doubt one's internal call.

The last thing to say about the call to preach is that God through the church calls preachers to proclaim the gospel, to preach Jesus. For Christians, jobs, careers, and vocations with our families, communities, and pastimes present opportunities and calls to proclaim God's unending love in Jesus Christ through word and deed. Preaching is the proclamation of the gospel primarily to God's people to sustain them in faith and empower them to bear witness to Jesus in their lives and in the world. All proclamation of the gospel is valid and necessary. Sometimes Christians other than preachers are better able to bring the gospel to people outside the church who desperately need it. For the sake of those who will receive the gospel from those who hear our sermons, it is essential that preachers proclaim Jesus before anything else. Should preachers feel God calling them to proclaim the gospel in another way, they need to respond to that call with a different vocation and not convert the pulpit to another purpose.

Second, since the call is to preach the gospel, I learned from Jesus to *prioritize preaching as much as the gospel.* It did not take long for me to realize that people do not understand the time and energy required to prepare and preach a sermon. In fact, people think preachers get up on Sunday morning and preach. If I did not make preaching a priority by spending time on the sermon each day, my time would be filled with everything else people wanted and needed me to do.

Preachers often find it easier to make preaching a priority when they can point to something external to verify preaching is a priority. For example, at the top of my list of duties as bishop, my first constitutional responsibility is to "preach, teach, and administer the sacraments" and "to have primary responsibility for the ministry of Word and sacrament in this synod and its congregations."[42] I receive this as life-giving good news because, for me, without this priority graciously imposed upon me, I would become, in the words of Ephesians, like "children, tossed to and fro and blown about by every wind of doctrine, by people's trickery, by their craftiness in deceitful scheming."[43] I would be distracted and misdirected by people's momentary expectations and demands.

More than as a matter of will, preachers put structures in place to maintain preaching as a priority. In my ministry as bishop, I record a video podcast for release on Tuesdays that includes reflections on the readings from the Revised Common Lectionary for the coming Sunday; I need to ponder Sunday and Monday, so I have something to say. Prior to the onset of the pandemic, our staff celebrated the Eucharist on Wednesday; my assistants and I took turns preaching on the readings for the coming Sunday, so at least one of us had spent time deep in God's word early in the week and the rest of us benefitted from that work by receiving the gospel and, sometimes, borrowing from the sermon. During the pandemic, we took turns recording a sermon, so each of us preached every third week. The effect of these structures is that we take more time to prepare than we would without them.

Preachers are best able to make preaching a priority when they understand themselves as God's priority. Regardless of what is happening around them or what they do or fail to do, in Jesus Christ, preachers—all of us—are precious and important to God. Jesus, seated at God's right hand, is praying for us. Jesus intercedes for us because he loves us. Jesus prays for *you* because you are God's beloved child, created in God's image, and Jesus's sibling, for whom he suffered and died. Jesus intercedes for you, asking that you be yoked closely and securely to him.

Third, I learned from Jesus to *pray*. "Lord, teach us to pray," one of Jesus's disciples asked.[44] When my prayer grows dry or goes adrift, so do I. In addition to praying in sermon preparation, I pray for myself as preacher. The first thing Jesus taught me about this prayer is, since in love Jesus prays for us, for our own sake, it is neither selfish nor self-centered to pray for ourselves for our own sake. Some preachers confidently pray with the psalmist: "Guard me as the apple of the eye; hide me in the shadow of your wings."[45] I prefer hearing Jesus pray, "Holy Father, protect them in your name that you have given me."[46] I pray, "Our Father," mindful that, because of Jesus, I am addressing Jesus's Abba and mine.

As the apostles said to Jesus, so we can pray, "Increase our faith!"[47] Then, for the sake of our preaching, we can and should tell Jesus what we need. When personal needs and concerns occupy my heart and mind to the degree that they interfere with sermon preparation and preaching, I find it helpful to commend them to God. No need or concern is too small, selfish, or insignificant. If a matter becomes a distraction or an obstacle to my work as a preacher, it is worthy of prayer. While I cannot completely hand things over to God, I can entrust them to God for the time necessary to faithfully prepare sermons and preach. I also distinguish between things I can influence and things that I can only pray for and commend to God. Prayer should certainly lead to action; however, sometimes praying is the only or the best action we can take.

Since I became a bishop, Jesus has so blessed me with the grace and sustenance that comes from others praying for and with me that I regret not explicitly requesting prayer for myself, my family, and my work earlier in ministry. I am moved when I worship with congregations and a petition "for our bishop, Craig" is included in the intercessions. I learned the significance of praying with people over the phone because, during a time of personal need, a colleague bishop phoned to pray with me. My relationship to preaching changed significantly when homebound members told me they pray for me during the hour they know I am preaching; it is great to not be alone in the pulpit. I cannot adequately express the gift of people praying for and with the preacher; I can only encourage preachers to ask people to pray for and with them and experience the gift for themselves.

Praying as I vest (dress) to lead worship is a holy time. Since I studied medieval vesting prayers, I approach putting on an alb (robe), stole, cross, and, when appropriate, other vestments (chasuble, cope, miter) as centering prayer that prepares me to preach. I appreciate Paul's admonition, "Put on the full armor of God so that you can take your stand against the devil's schemes."[48]

My prayers are simpler than those of the medieval church. Putting on the alb, I remember I am baptized. Putting on the stole, I pray to be yoked to Christ. As the chain goes over my head and the pectoral cross rests on my chest, I pray that the cross will be the heart of the sermon. Putting on a chasuble invites me to pray for grace, a cope to pray the world will have a voice in the sermon, a miter that I be anointed with the Holy Spirit, and the crozier that I faithfully preach both law and gospel as I speak to and for Christ's church. Knowing I will pray these prayers before I preach, I act to be God's answer to my prayers in my preparation.

When I am dressed and gather those who will lead worship, my prayer is pretty much the same:

> O God, thank you for the privilege of leading your people in worship. Take from us all those things that would distract us so that, in this time, we may be wholly yours. Send now, we pray, your Holy Spirit to bless the preaching of the Word and administration of the sacraments, the prayers we offer and the songs we sing, that all who gather behold your glory, experience Christ risen and among us, and be strengthened to serve as your people in the world. We ask this through Jesus Christ, our Savior and Lord.

This prayerful preparation takes discipline and practice. Prior to worship, people can press the preacher with chaos and complaints that can undermine the sermon. Once when I was serving as a pastor and pre-worship complaining became particularly distracting, a council president shut me in the sacristy and positioned himself outside the door. When people came to complain to the pastor, he offered to receive their concerns. Within a few weeks, complaining before worship stopped. The president reminded me that, while individuals may have needs before worship, the congregation as a whole needs the pastor (or deacon or bishop) to be spiritually prepared to lead worship and preach. I long for every preacher to have someone to watch over them on Sunday morning the way that council president watched over me.

Fourth, I learned from Jesus the importance of *practicing my faith in ways that actually nourish my faith*. Precisely, I experienced Jesus giving me permission not to do what is expected. People expect preachers to practice the Christian faith in established and specific ways, and preachers faithfully and dutifully do so. During the pandemic, as I "worshiped" with a congregation via Zoom, the pastor shared his screen, which I could not see, so the congregation could read an original litany that I did not know. The litany was followed by a montage of photographs, which I could not see, set to music. I realized that, though I was attending church as a bishop, I needed to do something different that Sunday to nourish my faith. Within a few months, I acknowledged that, after a week of Zoom meetings, Zoom worship doesn't work for me, even when Zoom worship is exceptional. That way of practicing our faith does not nourish mine.

Preachers do not have the right to bend worship, piety, and faith practices to their will or change them only to align with their preferences. Preachers do have the right and responsibility to practice their faith in ways that nourish their faith. It is even appropriate for preachers to acknowledge to themselves, God, and carefully to others they trust that, except for the call of God through the church, they might not belong to the congregation they serve. The question then becomes how and where preachers will practice their faith in ways that nourish, sustain, and help them so they grow into the fullness of Christ. The danger in preachers not doing this is they may attempt to compartmentalize their personal lives from their pastoral lives, a false distinction in public ministry. Or they may so "professionalize" their vocation that expertly fulfilling responsibilities replaces the relationship indispensable to the care of souls.

The Christian tradition provides ways Christians can practice the faith independent of a specific congregation. These practices include asceticism, prayer, Bible study, daily devotions, fasting, confession, almsgiving, spiritual direction, acts of charity, and advocacy. Preachers can experiment and discover whether these or other practices, such as journaling, art, and music, nourish and sustain them in ways that increase their faith. Preachers engage in faith practices for as long as they are helpful; when a practice stops contributing to faith and wholeness, preachers grant themselves grace to stop and try something new. This approach to practicing our faith is not unique to preachers. Sometimes preachers simply need more explicit permission.

Fifth, I learned from Jesus that part of practicing our faith in ways that nourish our faith is *claiming or reclaiming something independent of preaching and the church that brings us closer to God by inspiring our passion.* I rejoice when I experience myself and witness in others how Jesus yokes us closely and securely to himself as God works in these activities. I rediscovered the importance of preachers engaging in "outside activities" by reflecting on Jesus's ministry, watching my pastor, and returning to writing.

Reading the Gospels, I imagine Jesus, cooking and gathering all sorts of people around his table to enjoy the food he prepares. Jesus was known and even criticized for his table fellowship. Jesus says, "The Son of [Humanity] came eating and drinking, and they say, 'Look, a glutton and a drunkard, a friend of tax collectors and sinners!'"[49] Jesus told parables about banquets and feasts. I once heard a chef describe his vocation as giving people joy. I expect cooking provided Jesus with an unconventional way of proclaiming the nearness of God's reign. My faith was certainly impacted by the Covid-19 pandemic and my choice not to receive the Eucharist until all the congregations in my synod (diocese) could come to the Lord's table. While refraining from the Eucharist, I appreciated the grace of my wife's cinnamon rolls as a bread of heaven. Although not a sacrament, I know God is at work when she makes them.

My pastor works with wood. I asked him to make me a crozier, the staff a bishop carries. As beautiful as the crozier is, the real gift was accompanying my pastor via photograph, text, and conversation as he made it. I witnessed God at work in Gary's reverence for the wood, precision in design, patience in crafting, and quest for beauty. My pastor tells me he takes what God has created, beautiful wood, and creates something useful and artistic. In doing so, he has a sense of becoming a cocreator with God.

Making espresso is prayer for me. My coffee bar is the closest thing I have to a home altar. Book-writing is also a passion where I experience God at work. After being called to the office of bishop and experiencing difficulty with my eyesight, I resigned myself to never writing books again. I felt as if a friend died. My editor's query in 2019 about what I was mulling over and her subsequent invitation to submit a book proposal resurrected a part of me I thought was gone. I accepted the contract unsure of whether I could and how I would write the book. In these years of the pandemic, when I could not visit congregations, writing this book became church. I am immersed in Scripture, reflecting on my experience, considering the gospel, creating something new, and knowingly relating to those reviewing the manuscript and you who are reading the book. When Jesus feels far away, I make coffee, write, and find Jesus nearby. Preachers need a passion apart from preaching and the church.

Sixth, I am still learning from Jesus to *practice balance*. I know preaching requires equilibrium—physical, mental, emotional, spiritual, and relational. Preachers need to carve out time to step away from and gain perspective on a calling that is physically, emotionally, spiritually, and intellectually challenging. I know that God's commandment to keep the Sabbath, however preachers define *Sabbath*, is sage advice. I know that seeking balance alerts us to attend to all the areas of our lives, as well as to the lives of those we cherish. I know I admire preachers who maintain balance without complaining about or making themselves the responsibility of the congregation.

I hear Jesus saying, "If you know these things, you are blessed if you do them."[50] I am still learning to do what I know. A full day off does not work for me; I love my work and want to do it. Rather than taking a full day off, I learned during the pandemic to designate hours each day when I do not work and to respect them. I know trouble occurs when I work too long or too hard, leaving me tired and testy; before this happens, I put myself in time out to regain equilibrium. I seek balance in ways that work.

Sometimes people have needs that simply will not keep until tomorrow. I take satisfaction that, after taking the disciples away in a boat to a deserted place by themselves to rest, "as [Jesus] went ashore, he saw a great crowd; and he had compassion for them, because they were like sheep without a shepherd; and he began to teach them many things."[51] Jesus sought balance *after* feeding and dismissing the crowd.

Perhaps most important to my achieving balance, I finally arrived at the place of acknowledging to myself that being legally blind presents obstacles that require me to work harder and biases in others that require me to excel, making balance elusive. For me, balance is always a work in progress. I believe most preachers can name legitimate reasons that it is for them as well. Naming them as reality rather than making excuses is a step toward balance.

Achieving and maintaining balance is easier when preachers have identities beyond preaching and do not take them for granted. Many preachers ground themselves in their families, making their home life, family outings, and activities important to their significant others, partners, spouse, and children their explicit priorities. Others become involved in hobbies that help them cultivate relationships outside the congregation and church. These are all ways of saying that the balance required to preach demands that preachers have identities and activities beyond preaching.

Seventh, I am still learning from Jesus to *practice preaching* as my art and my craft. I have long practiced preaching as a craft as I strive to be the most skilled and effective preacher I can be. I revisit the basics of my preaching—goal, ponder, order, create, and proclaim—to address any gaps that exist between the preacher I have become and the preacher I want to be. I also continue to learn from the field of homiletics by reading books or attending conferences and incorporating the learnings into my preaching.

Yet, at this stage in my preaching, I am more interested in preaching as art. I strive to make certain that I am yoked to Jesus and that the assembly experiences the risen Christ in the room when I preach. Of course, when we are yoked to Jesus, we preach at our best. Thus, preaching as art involves the intangibles that transcend skills, including preachers allowing themselves to become vulnerable about our preaching. Preachers do not become vulnerable by including inappropriate self-disclosure in sermons but, alongside mastering skills and striving for excellence, by intentionally cultivating dependence on Jesus. While attending to preaching as craft builds self-confidence, approaching preaching as art leads preachers to place themselves in God's hands. Both self-confidence and dependence are necessary and call for equal attention and energy.

We become dependent on Jesus by putting ourselves in positions of powerlessness. We expose ourselves to situations in which people need saving and we are utterly helpless to save them. We bring those people and situations with us to sermon preparation and preaching. We ask what our sermons would say to them. During the pandemic, I learned to put myself in these situations without ever leaving the house. Studying systemic racism with cohorts from my synod (diocese) left me feeling heartbroken and helpless. I committed to being present when people who died of Covid-19 were remembered individually on television. I translated those statistics into my reality, frequently calculating the number of deaths in terms of capacity crowds at Notre Dame Stadium. I listened to interviews with families at food banks and homeless shelters, and I was especially undone by the stories children tell. I returned the phone calls of people who needed me to know that I was the devil because I would not order people to return to in-person worship. As we continue to live through the different stages of the pandemic and the new realities of our world, I regularly feel powerless to change anything. As a preacher, I am more dependent on Jesus because I know we need a Savior.

Preachers also become more dependent on Jesus by taking an occasional risk in the pulpit. We try something new; we do something different. For many preachers, the ultimate risk is setting aside the manuscript and stepping out of the pulpit without losing focus, clarity, and beauty. One preacher told me they felt like Peter coming to Jesus on the sea. After placing themselves in God's hands by taking a risk, many preachers are reticent to return to the safety of the boat. Some caution my preaching is riskier because it seems more "political." Indeed, it is always risky to proclaim the gospel into society and not confine Jesus to the church. In these instances, the choice is whether or not to be risk averse.

Of course, preachers become more dependent on Jesus by internalizing the message we preach. As Lent approached during the year I prepared for doctoral candidacy examinations, the director of graduate studies instructed me *not* to give up anything for Lent or take on any Lenten disciplines, since preparing for exams was my Lenten discipline. I should feel free to eat whatever I wanted and do whatever I needed to do to help me prepare. When I protested that I had to give up something or do something for Lent, the director of graduate studies responded in Lutheran fashion, saying, while I preach justification by grace through faith particularly well, I also work very hard to justify myself. Receiving grace as I prepared for exams would be a transforming spiritual experience for me. He was correct on both counts. I needed to internalize my message.

We are yoked to Jesus when we practice the message we preach in our own lives. While the message we preach is influenced by the message we live by, the message we preach can influence how we live, assuming the message we preach is the good news that Jesus saves. Preachers can begin practicing this good news by spending time with their gospel in fifty words and asking themselves how this is good news for them and for those they love, and then what invitation or opportunity God is extending to them through this good news.

Practicing our message continues as we make ourselves the first hearers of our own sermons. Preachers can certainly hear God speaking promise into and making a claim upon their lives through their own words. This happens when preachers consciously become the first and sometimes primary hearer of our sermons. We become one of God's people receiving God's word, which saves us from using God's word against the people. In sermon preparation, we create and proclaim our sermons, so they preach to us. Hearing the gospel in our own sermons is another good reason for reading them aloud as part of preparation.

Finally, we practice our message by recognizing that Jesus's care is different from self-care. Jesus's care is a gift we receive and neither a demand we make nor a task we must complete. Receiving Jesus's care facilitates our caring for ourselves because we regard ourselves as God's beloved children, practicing our faith, exercising our passion, and seeking balance in healthy ways. Perhaps this is the beginning of finding rest in Jesus.

Rest in Jesus

Jesus says those who "take my yoke upon you and learn from me . . . will find rest for your souls." Preachers often describe Jesus's rest by clarifying what Jesus's rest is not. For example, Jesus does not give physical rest. Jesus gives rest *for our souls*. Preachers distinguish *rest* from *laziness*. In Jesus, we find "*rest from work*, or . . . 'cessation from wearisome activity for the sake of rest, *relief*.'"[52] Rest comes before and after work; there is no rest without work. Rest in Jesus, then, is not stopping, taking a day off, or going on vacation, as beneficial as these are. Resting in Jesus is not something we do. Resting in Jesus begins with the experience and admission that, when we "are weary and are carrying heavy burdens," we are able to go on not because of our commitment, endurance, inner strength, piety, or hard work but because of the one yoked to and standing in front of us.

The rest Jesus gives is *serenity*, the state of being calm, peaceful, and untroubled in and because of Jesus. The rest Jesus gives is not removed from the world, discipleship, ministry, and preaching. The rest Jesus speaks of includes the future of the kingdom or reign of God when we will rest from our labors; it also includes what New Testament professor Walter F. Taylor Jr. calls "rest in the midst." That is, Jesus gives rest in the midst of the ongoing labor of taking Jesus's yoke and learning from Jesus.[53] Jesus's rest, which is only attainable through this labor, can be described as the gift of moments when, in the midst of our work, God raises us above the obligations of the work and the cares of the world, so we might dwell in God's presence and soak it in.

The rest Jesus gives is the serenity of belonging to Jesus. Rest is often where God reminds us that we are God's beloved children quite apart from pastoral tasks and preaching. Rest allows us to perceive ourselves, and the world, more fully.

Being rested also informs and provides perspective on the task of preaching when we return to it. We can find rest as God's beloved children by tangibly and habitually remembering we are baptized.

The rest we find from taking on Jesus's yoke and learning from him comes from our freedom as God's children to learn to be like Jesus, who lived faithfully and obediently to God, aware that, at his baptism, a voice from heaven declared, "This is my Son, whom I love; with him I am well pleased."[54] Becoming like Jesus includes learning to be humble by living in ways that the culture and even the church do not affirm. We find rest because Jesus, our teacher, lived this way until and beyond the cross. As our risen Lord, Jesus is present now as the one who promises rest and in a real sense, is our rest. The yoke is easy, and the burden is light, because Jesus bears it with us. We have the serenity that comes from not needing to please God to receive God's love and secure God's favor. Certainty of Jesus's presence raises us above the uncertainty of securing God's presence by our merit.

The rest Jesus gives is the serenity of knowing the church we serve belongs to Jesus and not to us. The tasks and expectations imposed on preachers by others, and that we impose on ourselves, can be a yoke as weighty, difficult, and burdensome as the interpretation of Torah imposed on Jesus's first followers by the Pharisees. We can think of this yoke as a single yoke, the burden born by the preacher alone. Trying to bear this yoke alone, the burdens will eventually crush us. We can think of this yoke as the double yoke intended by Jesus; when we do, we "realize that the other 'beast of burden' in the team matters greatly. When that partner is congregational demands, cultural expectations, what the bishop wants, the dictates of the church, the yoke becomes an enslavement to the ungracious masters of life."[55]

When we are yoked to Jesus, the gifts Jesus gives—acceptance, forgiveness, peace, and the indelible worth that comes from being a child of God—make the burden light and the yoke easy. "The plowing may still be hard going and bring suffering, but 'if God is for us, who can stand against us?'"[56] In our partnership with a suffering God, we find rest in the shared burden and the presence of Christ.

The rest Jesus gives is manifested when we are relieved from trying to do something we cannot do or be someone we cannot be. Jesus's rest is relief from the burden of saving the church or saving the world, which is not ours but Jesus's to bear. Our work, while important, is not, at the end of the day, salvific. Jesus relieves us from fretting and being anxious and frees us to serve faithfully and then rest peacefully. We can release our grip on the church, our ministries, and our responsibilities by remembering that they ultimately belong to God, who is quite capable of sustaining them.

As Jesus left behind the demanding crowds to spend time with his Father,[57] preachers find rest by stepping away from our demands to spend time with the one who nourishes and renews us. We make space in the rhythm of our daily lives to not be responsible for anything but ourselves and our relationship with God. Preachers who find rest in this way understand themselves as dwelling in God as opposed to the Holy Spirit dwelling in them. They know they are not in control and cannot manifest the Spirit on demand.

Some preachers go to a safe space to "be still and know that I am God."[58] They return to a specific place, even at a specific time. That place is often in nature; for example, a pastor might go to the beach to stare at the water on Tuesday morning. While sunshine and calm bring comfort, storms and waves elicit awe of God's power. Other preachers find rest using their mind differently than they do when carrying out pastoral work, including sermon preparation and preaching. Still others lose themselves in physical activity, especially physical work. A growing number of preachers name the importance of entering rest in Jesus as they work pastorally by breathing deeply, physically, and spiritually.

The rest Jesus gives is the serenity that comes from confidence in Jesus strong enough that preachers face death in its myriad forms and proclaim the gospel, Jesus, the Word of life. Standing outside Lazarus's tomb, Jesus said, "Take away the stone." When Martha protested there would be a stench, "Jesus said to her, 'Did I not tell you that if you believed, you would see the glory of God?'"[59] To rest in Jesus is to face death in its innumerable forms, take away the stone that separates us from death, momentarily set aside doubt and fear, and proclaim Jesus who said, "I am the resurrection and the life."[60] To rest in Jesus is to enter tombs of death, defeat, and despair, as the disciple whom Jesus loved did in John's Gospel, and, seeing the grave clothes, trust Jesus to bring resurrection.[61]

To find rest in Jesus is to explore the connection between the rest Jesus gives and Jesus's "Sabbath rest" in the tomb, which the church commemorates on Holy Saturday. Jesus's rest in the tomb, waiting to be saved rather than working to get saved or save himself, is the epitome of humility and gentleness. Contrary to the world's demand to make something happen, Jesus's rest in the tomb is Godly, mirroring the Creator's rest on the seventh day.[62] For us to rest as Jesus rested, to learn from him, is to place complete trust in the one Jesus called Father. These moments are rare. But in those moments when the failure of our own wisdom and strength leaves us no other viable option, we find perfect joy in rest such as this. We cannot work to achieve this rest; it only comes, as a gift, *in extremis*.[63]

Preach Yoked Closely and Securely to Jesus

We conclude our game of hide-and-seek with Jesus by kneeling before the altar, hearing Jesus's promise as stoles are placed on our shoulders: "Come to me, all who labor and are carrying heavy burdens, and I will give you rest. Take my yoke upon you, and learn from me; for I am gentle and lowly in heart, and you will find rest for your souls. For my yoke is easy, and my burden is light."[64]

Some bishops shed tears when they say these words, tears for the burden they know will be laid upon the ordinand and the trials ahead, but also out of love for Jesus, who will also bear the burdens as a constant presence. One bishop interprets these words to new pastors and deacons: "You cannot do this work. You do not have the strength or wisdom to do it. In fact, this work will try to kill you nearly every day. But take heart. Jesus has died to redeem the world, and you have only to watch and see and bear witness as he does so."[65] This is preaching yoked closely and securely to Jesus.

When I ordain pastors and deacons, I shed tears while saying the last words of the charge given them: "And be of good courage, for God has called you, and your labor in the Lord is not in vain."[66] I cry because I know both the work of the church and the needs of the world require every deacon, pastor, and bishop to be strong and let their hearts be brave as we wait for the Lord.[67] We can have good courage only by trusting God has called us and that our labor in the Lord is useful to Jesus. This courage and trust grow as we come to Jesus, take Jesus's yoke upon us, learn from Jesus, and find rest in Jesus. Good courage and trust in God's call also grow as we preach Jesus, even as good courage and trust reveal and express themselves in our preaching. We know where Jesus is when we preach, and so does the assembly. Jesus speaks in our sermons, stands front and center in our pulpits, and is undeniably present in our preaching. Yoked closely and securely to Jesus, we preach Jesus, and that is enough. For the preacher, preaching Jesus is everything.

Notes

Preface

1 Ronald A. Heifetz and Marty Linsky, *Leadership on the Line: Staying Alive through the Dangers of Leading* (Boston: Harvard School of Business Press, 2002), 204.
2 Micah 6:8.
3 See Mary Catherine Hilkert, OP, "Naming Grace: A Theology of Proclamation," *Worship* 60 (1986): 434–48, and *Naming Grace: Preaching and the Sacramental Imagination* (New York: Continuum, 1997).

Acknowledgments

1 "Ordination," Evangelical Lutheran Church in America, *Evangelical Lutheran Worship: Occasional Services for the Assembly* (Minneapolis: Augsburg Fortress, 2009), 192.

Chapter 1

1 "Ordination," Evangelical Lutheran Church in America, *Evangelical Lutheran Worship: Occasional Services for the Assembly*, 192; Matthew 11:28–30.

2   I use the word Judeans rather than Jews in recognition of the regrettable anti-Semitism that surrounded the observance of Holy Week and Easter for many centuries. I acknowledge this choice varies from the New Revised Standard Version and is debated in Johannine biblical scholarship.

3   Luke 24:37.

4   "Ordination," Evangelical Lutheran Church in America, *Evangelical Lutheran Worship: Occasional Services for the Assembly*, 191. Cf. Ephesians 4:11–12.

5   Elizabeth Theresa Groppe, "The Contribution of Yves Congar's Theology of the Holy Spirit," *Theological Studies*, 62 (2001): 463.

6   Martin Luther, "Concerning the Ministry (1523)," *Luther's Works, American Edition*, vol. 40, trans. Bergendoff, Conrad (Philadelphia: Fortress Press, 1958), 11.

7   Numbers 11:29.

8   "Ordination," Evangelical Lutheran Church in America, *Evangelical Lutheran Worship: Occasional Services for the Assembly*, 192.

9   John 10:10.

10   John 14:16.

11   John 14:26, 15:26, 16: 12–13.

12   Acts 7:55–56.

13   Ephesians 1:21–23.

14   John 12:32.

15   Cf. Matthew 27:46; Mark 15:34.

16   Acts 7:51.

17   John 1:14.

18   Luke 24:44–47.

19   Luke 24:25–27.

20   LW 52,206; WA 12,259, 8–13; WA 10,I,1,265ff.; WA 12,259; WA 12,275.

21   Pope Francis, *Evangelii Gaudium: The Joy of the Gospel* (Washington DC: United States Conference of Catholic Bishops, 2013), 136.

22   John 15:15.

23   I have written considerably about preaching on the sacraments. See, for example, Craig A. Satterlee and Lester Ruth, *Creative Preaching on the Sacraments* (Nashville: Discipleship Resources, 2001); Craig Alan Satterlee, *Ambrose of Milan's Method of Mystagogical Preaching* (Collegeville, MN: Liturgical Press, 2002).

24   Matthew 25:31–32.

25   Matthew 25:37–39.

26   Committee on Priestly Formation, *Fulfilled in Your Hearing: The Homily in the Sunday Assembly* (Washington DC: United States Conference of Catholic Bishops, 1982), 3–4; Evangelical Lutheran Church in America, *The Use of the Means of Grace: A Statement on the Practice of Word and Sacrament* (Minneapolis: Augsburg Fortress, 1997), 8–9.

27   Committee on Priestly Formation, *Fulfilled in Your Hearing*, 19.

28   John 5:1–5; Luke 2:27–38; John 5:4.

29   John 3:14–15.

30   Numbers 21:6–9.

31   1 Corinthians 1:22–24.

32   John 3:1–21.

33   John 19:38–42.

34   1 Corinthians 1:24.

Chapter 2

1   Luke 12:11–12.

2   John 14:16.

3   John 3:8.

4   John 3:3–9. γεννηθῇ ἄνωθεν can mean born again, born anew, or born from above.

5   John 3:9.

6   Killian McDonnell, OSB, "A Trinitarian Theology of the Holy Spirit?" *Theological Studies* 46 (1985): 199.

7   Acts 2:6.

8   McDonnell, "A Trinitarian Theology of the Holy Spirit?": 216.

9   John 1:14; Colossians 1:15; Matthew 1:23.

10   Matthew 3:16; Mark 1:11; Luke 3:22; John 1:32, italics added.

11   Acts 2:2–3, italics added.

12   John 3:5–6.

13   Luke 24:49; John 14:16.

14   Raymond E. Brown, *The Gospel According to John (xiii–xxi)* (Garden City: Doubleday, 1970), 669, 1139.

15   1 Corinthians 15:5–8; Galatians 1:12.

16   Matthew 25:40; 18:20; Luke 24:35, 49.

17   McDonnell, "A Trinitarian Theology of the Holy Spirit?": 215.

18   McDonnell, "A Trinitarian Theology": 204.

19   "The Augsburg Confession," V, *The Book of Concord*, ed. Robert Kolb and Timothy J. Wengert (Minneapolis: Fortress Press, 2000), 40.

20   Yves M-J. Congar, "The Human Spirit and the Spirit of God," *Spirit of God: Short Writings on the Holy Spirit*, ed. Mark E. Ginter, Susan Mader Brown, and Joseph G. Mueller (Washington DC: Catholic University of America Press, 2018), 52. This discussion of Congar's pneumatology is indebted to Adrian J. Brooks, "Breathing Forth the Word: Yves Congar's Articulation of the Activity of The Holy Spirit In The

Life of Christ." *New Blackfriars* 101, no. 1092 (February 6, 2020): 196–205. https://doi.org/10.1111/nbfr.12545. Elizabeth Theresa Groppe, "The Contribution of Yves Congar's Theology of the Holy Spirit," *Theological Studies* 62 (2001): 457–478.

21   Nikos A. Nissiotis, "Pneumatological Christology as a Presupposition of Ecclesiology," *Oecumenka: An Annual Symposium of Ecumenical Research* (Minneapolis: Augsburg, 1967): 239.

22   Yves M-J. Congar, "Pneumatologie dogmatique," in *Initiation a` la pratique de la the´ologie,* ed. Bernard Lauret and Francois Refoule´(Paris: Cerf, 1982), 2.495–96.

23   McDonnell, "A Trinitarian Theology of the Holy Spirit?": 193.

24   McDonnell, "A Trinitarian Theology": 208.

25   Acts 2:14–36.

26   Acts 2:33.

27   McDonnell, "A Trinitarian Theology": 215.

28   McDonnell, "A Trinitarian Theology": 215.

29   Brooks, "Breathing Forth the Word": 200. Congar employs more frequently than other images commonly used by patristic sources. Including: sun, light and warmth; spring, river and sea; the root, the branch, and the fruit. Congar, "The Human Spirit and the Spirit of God," 56.

30   John 20:22.

31   Brooks, "Breathing Forth the Word": 200.

32   Yves M-J. Congar, "A Theology of the Holy Spirit," *Called to Life* (Slough: St Paul Publications, 1985), 79.

33   Congar, "The Human Spirit and the Spirit of God," 33.

34   Brooks, "Breathing Forth the Word": 200.

35   McDonnell, "A Trinitarian Theology of the Holy Spirit?": 222.

36   Congar, "A Theology of the Holy Spirit," 84. See a similar expression in Congar, "Pneumatology Today," *Spirit of God*, 221.

37   Congar, "A Theology of the Holy Spirit," 77.

38   Yves M-J. Congar, *The Word and the Spirit*, trans. David Smith (London: Geoffrey Chapman, 984), 85–100.

39   Yves M-J. Congar, "Third Article of the Creed: The Impact of Pneumatology on the Life of the Church," *Spirit of God*, 250.

40   Congar, "Pneumatology Today," *Spirit of God*, 220. See also Congar, *Called to Life*, 84.

41   Congar, "Pneumatologie dogmatique," 495–96.

42   Luke 24:46–48; John 20:21–22.

43   Congar, "Pneumatologie dogmatique," 495–96.

44   1 Corinthians 12:3.

45   "Augsburg Confession," IV, *Book of Concord*, 39–40.

46   "Augsburg Confession," IV, *Book of Concord*, 40.

47   "Augsburg Confession," IV, *Book of Concord*, 40.

48   "Augsburg Confession," IV, *Book of Concord*, 40.

49   McDonnell, "A Trinitarian Theology of the Holy Spirit?": 220.

50   Martin Luther, "The Small Catechism (1529)," *Book of Concord*, 355.

51   "Augsburg Confession," III, *Book of Concord*, 39.

52   Galatians 5:22.

53   This paragraph is inspired by and indebted to Groppe, "The Contribution of Yves Congar's Theology of the Holy Spirit": 459–460.

54   "Augsburg Confession," VI, *Book of Concord*, 41.

55   Luther, "The Small Catechism," *Book of Concord*, 360.

56   McDonnell, "A Trinitarian Theology," 221.

57   See John 14:16; 1 John 3:24; 4:13. McDonnell, "A Trinitarian Theology of the Holy Spirit?": 222–223.

58   Galatians 4:6; Romans 8:14. McDonnell, "A Trinitarian Theology of the Holy Spirit?": 222–223.

59   1 Corinthians 2:14–16.

60   Mary Catherine Hilkert, OP, "introduction, Words of Spirit and Life: Preaching, Theology, Spirituality," Unpublished Manuscript, February 22, 2019. Cited with permission.

61   For further discussion of how the Holy Spirit works through the liturgy to prepare the assembly to receive and respond to the proclamation of the gospel, see Satterlee, *Ambrose of Milan's Method of Mystagogical Preaching*, 294–299.

62   Cf. Matthew 11:29–30.

63   John 15:15.

64   Jeremiah 31:33.

65   Deuteronomy 30:14.

66   John 13:3435; Matthew 5:44; 22:37–39.

67   Colossians 3:16.

68   Yves M-J. Congar, *I Believe in the Holy Spirit*, trans. David Smith (New York: Seabury, 1983), vol. 2, 92.

69   Groppe, "The Contribution of Yves Congar's Theology of the Holy Spirit": 461–462.

70   Luke 12:11–12.

71   William H. Willimon, "The Preacher as an Extension of the Preaching Moment," in *Preaching on the Brink: The Future of Homiletics*, ed. Martha J. Simmons (Nashville: Abingdon Press, 1997), 170.

72   For an expanded discussion of places of grace, see Craig A. Satterlee, *When God Speaks through Worship: Stories Congregations Live By* (Lanham, MD: Rowman and Littlefield, 2009), 123–126.

73   Hilkert, "Introduction, Words of Spirit and Lifelity," Unpublished Manuscript, February 22, 2019. Cited with permission.

74   John 20:24–25.

75   I first reflected on prayer as part of sermon preparation in Craig Alan Satterlee, "That Intimate Link—Ecumenical Contribution of *Fulfilled in Your Hearing*," in *We Preach Christ Crucified*, ed. Michael E. Connors (Collegeville, MN: Liturgical Press, 2013), 124–138.

76   Committee on Priestly Formation, *Fulfilled in Your Hearing*, 10.

77   Craig A. Satterlee, *When God Speaks through Change: Preaching in Times of Congregational Transition* (Lanham, MD: Rowman and Littlefield, 2005), 51.

78   Committee on Priestly Formation, *Fulfilled in Your Hearing*, 10–11.

79   Committee on Priestly Formation, *Fulfilled in Your Hearing*, 10.

80   Committee on Priestly Formation, *Fulfilled in Your Hearing*, 10.

81   1 Kings 19:11–13.

82   John 14:26.

83   Luke 24:49.

84   Congar, "The Human Spirit and the Spirit of God," 33.

85   Charles L. Campbell, *The Word Before the Powers: An Ethic of Preaching* (Louisville: Westminster John Knox Press, 2002), 2–3.

86   "Holy Baptism," *Evangelical Lutheran Worship: Occasional Services for the Assembly*, 59.

87   1 John 4:1–3.

88   Congar, "Pneumatologie dogmatique," 2.496.

89   John 14:16; 16:7.

90   Romans 5:1–11. Congar, "Pneumatologie dogmatique," 496–97. Emphasis original.

91   Congar, *I Believe in the Holy Spirit*, 2.219 with reference to Ambrose of Milan. Congar believed that the theological principle *extra Ecclesiam, nulla salus* does not limit the activity of the Spirit to the domain of

the Church but rather affirms that the Church has an indispensable role to play in God's plan of salvation. Groppe, "The Contribution of Yves Congar's Theology of the Holy Spirit," 460.

92   1 Corinthians 12:7–10.

Chapter 3

1   Evangelical Lutheran Church in America, *The Use of the Means of Grace*, 9A.
2   2 Timothy 4:3.
3   Ephesians 4:14.
4   Matthew 28: 19–20.
5   Micah 6:8.
6   Isaiah 40:1.
7   Mark 1:15.
8   Revelation 3:20.
9   Deuteronomy 30:19.
10   Evangelical Lutheran Church in America, *The Use of the Means of Grace*, 9A.
11   1 Corinthians 1:24.
12   Committee on Priestly Formation, *Fulfilled in Your Hearing*, 10.
13   Hilkert, *Naming Grace: Preaching and the Sacramental Imagination*, 44.
14   Mark 8:27, 29; cf. Matthew 16:13, 15; Luke 9:18, 20.
15   Matthew 16:16–17.
16   Luther, Martin "A Brief Introduction to What to Look for and Expect in the Gospels (1521)," in *Luther's Works, American Edition*, vol. 35, trans. E. Theodore Bachmann, ed. E. Theodore Bachmann and Helmut Lehmann. (Minneapolis: Fortress Press, 1960), 117–23.

17   1 Peter 2:2.
18   1 Corinthians 1:23.
19   Luke 14:25–34.
20   Jeremiah 20:9.
21   Matthew 5–7.
22   John 12:32.
23   John 8:12.
24   John 14:13.
25   Matthew 16:24.
26   Romans 6:3–4.
27   Luke 4:29; John 6:66.
28   Matthew 16:22; Mark 8:32.
29   Mark 16:8.
30   Campbell, *The Word Before the Powers*, 18.
31   Campbell, *The Word Before the Powers*, 60.
32   O. Wesley Allen, Jr., *The Homiletic of All Believers: A Conversational Approach to Proclamation and Preaching* (Louisville: Westminster John Knox Pres, 2005), 57.
33   John 1:1–2.
34   Matthew 3:15; 5:17–20; 26:54, 56; Mark 14:49; Luke 18:31; 22:37; 24:44; John 13:18; 15:25; 17:12; 19:24, 28, 36.
35   Matthew 16:24–26.
36   Fritz West, *Scripture and Memory: The Ecumenical Hermeneutic of the Three-Year Lectionary* (Collegeville: Liturgical Press, 1997), 7.
37   West, *Scripture and Memory*, 30.
38   Isaiah 53:11.
39   Cf. John 12:32.
40   Mary Alice Mulligan and Ronald J. Allen, *Make the Word Come Alive: Lessons from Laity* (St. Louis: Chalice Press, 2005), 5.
41   Colossians 1:15–18.

42   John 1:18.

43   John 14:19–20.

44   "Holy Communion," Evangelical Lutheran Church
     in America, *Evangelical Lutheran Worship: Leaders Desk
     Edition* (Minneapolis: Augsburg Fortress, 2006), 182.

45   Matthew 11:27.

46   John 14:6.

47   Evangelical Lutheran Church in America, "A Declara-
     tion of Inter-Religious Commitment: A policy state-
     ment of the Evangelical Lutheran Church in America"
     (Chicago: Evangelical Lutheran Church in America,
     2019), 2.

48   1 Peter 5:5.

49   John 12:32.

50   John 3:16.

51   "Augsburg Confession," IV, *Book of Concord*, 40.

52   John 14:6.

53   2 Corinthians 5:19–20.

54   Evangelical Lutheran Church in America, "A Declara-
     tion of Inter-Religious Commitment," 3.

55   Mark 3:19–22; 31–35.

56   Mark 1:21–34, 40–45; 2: 1–12; 3:1–12; 5:1–43; 6:53–56;
     7:31–37; 8:22–26; 9:14–29; 10:46–52.

57   Mark 2:1–12.

58   Mark 2:15–17.

59   Mark 6:30–44.

60   Mark 10:17–22.

61   Mark 9:33–37.

62   Luke 18:9–14.

63   2 Corinthians 4:7.

64   2 Corinthians 4:5.

65   John 3:30.

Chapter 4

1   Colossians 4:3.
2   "Eucharistic Prayer III," Evangelical Lutheran Church in America, *Evangelical Lutheran Worship: Leaders Desk Edition*, 196.
3   Galatians 4:4–5.
4   Robert A. Krieg and Brandon R. Peterson, "Models of the Savior: Toward Ecumenical Mosaics," Unpublished Manuscript (August 2021), 11.
5   John 18:5–8; Mark 14:35–36.
6   Mark 15:34; John 19:30.
7   John 20:18; Mark 16:8.
8   Krieg and Peterson, "Models of the Savior," 4.
9   Romans 5:18–19.
10   Romans 5:12–21; 1 Corinthians 15:45.
11   1 Corinthians 15:21–22.
12   Ephesians 1:9b–10. The Greek verb here, *anakephalaiosasthai*, is sometimes translated as "to recapitulate." The idea of "recapitulation" or "re-heading" appears prominently in the writing of Irenaeus of Lyons. Krieg and Peterson, "Models of the Savior," 41.
13   Krieg and Peterson, 41–42.
14   Ephesians 1:7–10.
15   Irenaeus of Lyons, *Against Heresies*, Book V, 1.1 in *The Ante-Nicene Fathers*, vol. 1, *The Apostolic Fathers with Justin Martyr and Irenaeus*, ed. Alexander Roberts and James Donaldson (Buffalo, NY: Christian Literature Publishing, 1885).
16   Mark 2:23–24, 27.
17   Jesus as Victim/Victor operates in Irenaeus and comes to fuller explication in Origen, Athanasius, and Gregory of Nyssa in the East, and in Tertullian, Augustine of Hippo, and Gregory the Great in the West.

18 See, for example, Galatians 3:13; 1 Peter 1:18–19.

19 Luke 11:21–22: Mark 10:45.

20 Krieg and Peterson, "Models of the Savior," 78–79.

21 Augustine, *The Trinity*, trans. Edmund Hill, OP, ed. John E. Rotelle, OSA. (Hyde Park, NY: New City Press, 1991). Cf. Eugene TeSelle, *Augustine the Theologian* (New York: Herder and Herder, 1970), 165–76.

22 Romans 5:5.

23 Augustine, *The Trinity*, trans. Edmund Hill, OP, ed. John E. Rotelle, OSA. (Hyde Park, NY: New City Press, 1991), Book XIII, Ch. 4, n. 16; Hill, 356.

24 Augustine, *The Trinity*, Book XIII, Ch. 4, n. 17; Hill, 356.

25 Augustine, *The Trinity*, Book XIII, Ch. 4, n. 18; Hill, 357.

26 Augustine, *The Trinity*, Book XIII, Ch. 5, n. 19; Hill, 358.

27 Romans 5:10; cf. 2 Corinthians 5:18–20.

28 Philippians 2:7b–8.

29 Anselm of Canterbury, *Why God Became Man*, trans. Janet Fairweather, ed. Brian Davies and G. R. Evans, *Anselm of Canterbury: The Major Works* (New York: Oxford University Press, 2008).

30 Krieg and Peterson, "Models of the Savior," 139.

31 Krieg and Peterson, "Models of the Savior," 140.

32 Philippians 2:6–11.

33 Anselm, *Why God Became Man*, Bk I, Ch. 13; Fairweather, 286; Krieg and Peterson, "Models of the Savior," 137.

34 Anselm, *Why God Became Man*, 10.

35 Anselm, *Why God Became Human*, pref.; Fairweather pp. 261–62; Krieg and Peterson, "Models of the Savior," 137.

36 2 Peter 1:4; Anselm, *Why God Became Human*, Bk I, Ch. 4; Fairweather, 269.

37 Anselm, *Why God Became Human*, Bk II, Ch. 7; Fairweather, 321.

38   Thomas Aquinas, *Summa Theologica*, trans. Fathers of the English Dominican Province, 5 vols. (New York: Benziger Brothers, 1947), I–II, q. 87 a. 7 co.; Krieg and Peterson, "Models of the Savior," 140.

39   Mark 14:36.

40   Krieg and Peterson, "Models of the Savior," 178.

41   Romans 8:38–39.

42   Peter Abelard, *Commentary on the Epistle to the Romans*, trans. and intro. Steven R. Cartwright (Washington, DC: The Catholic University of America, 2011), 167; Krieg and Peterson, "Models of the Savior," 178.

43   Abelard, *Commentary on the Epistle to the Romans*, 167; Krieg and Peterson, "Models of the Savior," 196.

44   Romans 5:8.

45   Krieg and Peterson, "Models of the Savior," 180.

46   See Matthew 8:14–17; Acts 8:30–33; 1 Peter 2:22–25; Isaiah 53:5–12.

47   2 Corinthians 5:20b–21.

48   Krieg and Peterson, "Models of the Savior," 226.

49   Hebrews 4:14–10:31.

50   John Calvin, *Institutes of the Christian Religion* (Final edition, 1559), translation of 1845 by Henry Beveridge (Grand Rapids: William B. Eerdmans Publishing, 1989; reprinted, 1997), Book II, 15.6, Beveridge, 425.

51   Calvin, *Institutes of the Christian Religion*, Book II, 16.6, Beveridge, 425 [italics original, as a translation of the preceding Greek].

52   Isaiah 53:5.

53   Calvin, *Institutes of the Christian Religion*, Book II, 15.1, Beveridge, 425.

54   Calvin, *Institutes of the Christian Religion*, Book II, 15.3–6, Beveridge, 428–31.

55 Calvin, *Institutes of the Christian Religion*, Book II, 16.1, Beveridge, 434.

56 Calvin, *Institutes of the Christian Religion*, Book II, 16.5, Beveridge, 439.

57 Calvin, *Institutes of the Christian Religion*, Book II, 16.6, Beveridge, 440.

58 Robin Ryan, *Jesus and Salvation: Soundings in the Christian Tradition and Contemporary Theology* (Concord, MA: Michael Glazier, 2015), 127.

59 Gustavo Gutiérrez, *A Theology of Liberation: History, Politics, and Salvation* (Maryknoll, NY: Orbis Books, 1988), 151.

60 Gutiérrez, *A Theology of Liberation*, 153.

61 Gutiérrez, *A Theology of Liberation*, 36–37.

62 Ryan, *Jesus and Salvation*, 136.

63 Gustavo Gutiérrez, *The God of Life*, trans. Matthew J. O'Connell (Maryknoll, NY: Orbis Books, 1991), 85.

64 Gutiérrez, *The God of Life*, 99.

65 Gustavo Gutiérrez, *The Power of the Poor in History: Selected Writings*, trans. Robert R. Barr (Maryknoll, NY: Orbis Books, 1983), 15.

66 Ryan, *Jesus and Salvation*, 138.

67 Ryan, *Jesus and Salvation*, 139.

68 Gustavo Gutiérrez, *On Job: God-Talk and the Suffering of the Innocent*, trans. Matthew J. O'Connell (Maryknoll, NY: Orbis Books, 1987), 97, 100.

69 Gutiérrez, *On Job: God-Talk*, 97, 100.

70 Gutiérrez, *On Job: God-Talk*, 97, 100.

71 Ryan, *Jesus and Salvation*, 139.

72 James H. Cone, *The Cross and the Lynching Tree* (Maryknoll, NY: Orbis Books, 2013).

73 Cone, *The Cross and the Lynching Tree*, 2.

74   The most fully developed female biblical image for God is in the wisdom literature of ancient Israel. In these, "the wisdom of God" is often personified as a woman. Scholars now commonly refer to this personification as "Sophia," the Greek word for wisdom.

75   Elizabeth A. Johnson, *She Who Is: The Mystery of God in Feminist Theological Discourse* (New York: Crossroads, 1992), 247.

76   Johnson, *She Who Is*, 270.

77   Ryan, *Jesus and Salvation*, 141.

78   Johnson, *She Who Is*, 153.

79   Johnson, *She Who Is*, 168.

80   Elizabeth A. Johnson, "Jesus and Salvation," Proceedings of the Catholic Theological Society of America 49 (1994): 11.

81   Johnson, *She Who Is*, 157.

82   Ryan, *Jesus and Salvation*, 142; Johnson, "Jesus and Salvation," 14.

83   Johnson, *She Who Is*, 158.

84   Johnson, *She Who Is*, 158.

85   Johnson, *She Who Is*, 158.

86   Johnson, "Jesus and Salvation," 10.

87   Ryan, *Jesus and Salvation*, 144; Johnson, "Jesus and Salvation," 13–14.

88   Womanist theology, which derives from the context of Black women's experiences, rejects oppression as it pursues liberation in Jesus Christ through fundamental aspects of womanism: survival, love, community-building, and social change grounded in love. Elaine Crawford, "Womanist Christology: Where have we come from and where are we going," *Review and Expository* (1998): 95. I am especially indebted to Kelsei Watters, "Solidarity and Suffering: Liberation Christology from Black and Womanist Perspectives," *Obscula* 12 1 (2019): 78–107.

89   Delores S. Williams, *Sisters in the Wilderness; The Challenge of Womanist God-Talk* (Maryknoll, New York: Orbis Books, 2013), 40–60, 127.

90   Joanne Marie Terrell, *Power in the Blood?: The Cross in the African American Experience*, The Bishop Henry McNeal Turner/Sojourner Truth Series in Black Religion, vol. 15 (Maryknoll, N.Y.: Orbis Books, 1998), 142.

91   M. Shawn Copeland, "Marking the Body of Jesus, the Body of Christ," in *The Strength of Her Witness: Jesus Christ in the Global Voices of Women*, ed. Elizabeth A. Johnson (Maryknoll, New York: Orbis Books, 2016), 279.

92   Dwight N. Hopkins and Edward P. Antonio, *The Cambridge Companion to Black Theology* (Cambridge: Cambridge University Press, 2012), 163.

93   Thomas Bohache, *Christology from the Margins* (London: SCM Press, 2008), 128–153.

94   M. Shawn Copeland, "'Wading though Many Sorrows': Toward a Theology of Suffering in Womanist Perspective," in *A Troubling in My Soul: Womanist Perspectives on Evil and Suffering*, The Bishop Henry Mcneal Turner Studies in North American Black Religion, vol. 8, ed., Emilie Maureen Townes (Maryknoll, NY: Orbis Books, 1993), 279.

95   M. Shawn Copeland, "The Cross of Christ and Discipleship," *Thinking of Christ: Proclamation, Explanation, Meaning*, ed., Tatha Wiley (New York: Continuum, 2003), 185.

96   Copeland, "Marking the Body of Jesus," 280.

97   Bohache, *Christology From The Margins*, 128–135.

98   Copeland, "Marking the Body of Jesus, the Body of Christ," 274.

99   Williams, *Sisters in the Wilderness*, 130–13.

100 Williams, *Sisters,* 132.

101 Patrick S. Cheng, *From Sin to Amazing Grace* (New York: Seabury Books, 2012).

102 Cheng, *From Sin,* 40.

103 Cheng, *From Sin,* 36.

104 Cheng, *From Sin,* 54.

105 Nancy L. Eiesland, *The Disabled God: Toward a Liberatory Theology of Disability* (Nashville: Abington Press, 1994).

106 Nancy L. Eiesland, "Encountering the Disabled God," *The Other Side* (September/October 2002): 13.

107 Luke 24:36–39

108 Eiesland, "Encountering the Disabled God," 14.

109 John 9:2–3.

110 Eiesland, *The Disabled God,* 11.

111 Genesis 1:31.

112 Mark 9:43–47.

113 Mark 9:42.

114 Matthew 4:24–25.

115 1 Corinthians 15:54; Romans 8:11; Job 19:26.

116 John 12:31.

117 Matthew 25:30.

118 Luke 19:9–10; John 8:1–11; John 4:6, 28–30; John 21:15–19.

119 Luke 12:6–7.

120 Luke 10:20.

121 Mark 13:2.

122 Ecclesiastes 1:14.

123 Luke 12:33.

124 Galatians 3:28.

125 2 Corinthians 5:16–19.

126 Matthew 27:27–31, 38–45.

127 John 15:13; Matthew 26:52; Luke 23:34.

128 1 Thessalonians 4:13.

Chapter 5

1   1 Corinthians 1:23–25.
2   Luke 1:1–3.
3   Justin Martyr, *First Apology*, in *The Ante-Nicene Fathers*, vol. 1, chap. 67 *The Apostolic Fathers with Justin Martyr and Irenaeus*, ed. Alexander Roberts and James Donaldson (Buffalo, NY: Christian Literature Publishing, 1885), 290.
4   Luke 24:447.
5   John 1:1–2.
6   Genesis 1:3, 6, 14.
7   Genesis 9:11.
8   Exodus 14:16.
9   Jeremiah 31:33.
10 John 1:14.
11 John 6:48; 8:12; 10:9, 11; 11:25; 14:6; 15:5; 18:6.8; 19:25.
12 Revelation 22:13.
13 Satterlee and Ruth, *Creative Preaching on the Sacraments*, 17.
14 Martin Luther, "Preface to the Old Testament (1545)," *Luther's Works, American Edition*, vol. 35, trans. Charles M. Jacob, revised E. Theodore Bachmann. Philadelphia: Fortress Press, 1960, 236.
15 John 13:34.
16 Satterlee, *Ambrose of Milan's Method of Mystagogical Preaching*, 225–30.
17 Jean Daniélou, *The Bible and the Liturgy*, (Notre Dame: University of Notre Dame Press, 1956), 4.
18 Isaiah 54:9
19 Isaiah 11:6–12; 43:16–21.
20 Romans 5:16
21 Matthew 24:37–39; Luke 17:26–27.

22   Cf. Mark 9:2–10; Matt 17:1–9; Luke 9:28–36; Exodus 19:16–25; 24.12–18; 33:17—34.8, 34.29–35.

23   1 Peter 3:21.

24   Hebrews 8:5.

25   1 Corinthians 10:11.

26   Leviticus 21:17–24.

27   John 9:2-3.

28   See Matthew 5:17–48.

29   Committee on Priestly Formation, *Fulfilled in Your Hearing*, 10.

30   Committee on Priestly Formation, *Fulfilled in Your Hearing*, 11.

31   Committee on Priestly Formation, *Fulfilled in Your Hearing*, 10.

32   Committee on Priestly Formation, *Fulfilled in Your Hearing*, 20.

33   Matthew 2:16–18.

34   John 4.

35   Luke 7:11–17.

36   Jeremiah 31:33.

37   Jeremiah 31:33.

38   Exodus 1:15-2:10; Matthew 2:13–17.

39   Exodus 3:6–10; Matthew 2:19–21.

40   Exodus 19:16—20:21; Matthew 5:1–2, 17–48.

41   Exodus 33:18–23; Matthew 17:1–5.

42   Evangelical Lutheran Church in America, *The Use of the Means of Grace*, 9 A.

43   Herman G. Stuempfle, Jr., *Preaching Law and Gospel* (Minneapolis: Fortress Press, 1978), 78.

44   "Preaching," Evangelical Lutheran Church in America, *Principles for Worship*, Renewing Worship, vol. 2 (Minneapolis: Augsburg Fortress, 2002), 8A.

45   "Preaching," Evangelical Lutheran Church in America, *Principles for Worship, 8A*.

46   Glenn L. Monson, *Afflicting the Comfortable, Comforting the Afflicted: A Guide to Law and Gospel Preaching* (Eugene, OR: Wipf & Stock, 2015), 10; Paul Scott Wilson, *The Four Pages of the Sermon: A Guide to Biblical Preaching* (Nashville: Abingdon Press, 1999); 16–17, 78–79, 108, 110–117.

47   "Preaching," Evangelical Lutheran Church in America, *Principles for Worship*, 8B.

48   Monson, *Afflicting the Comfortable, Comforting the Afflicted*, 11; Wilson, *The Four Pages of the Sermon*, 16–17, 78–79; 158

49   Stuempfle, *Preaching Law and Gospel*, 78.

50   Stuempfle, *Preaching Law and Gospel*, 78.

51   Luke 1:52–53.

52   Wilson, *The Four Pages of the Sermon*, 261.

53   Stuempfle, *Preaching Law and Gospel*, 77.

54   Stuempfle, *Preaching Law and Gospel*, 76.

55   1 Thessalonians 5:17.

Chapter 6

1   Matthew 13:44.

2   Cf. John Allyn Melloh, SM, "Homily Preparation: A Structural Approach," *Liturgical Ministry* 1 (Winter 1992): 21–26.

3   1 Corinthians 1: 23–24.

4   Colossians 3:16.

5   Luke 10:39, 41–42.

6   Committee on Priestly Formation, *Fulfilled in Your Hearing*, 11.

7   Ronald Allen, *Preaching the Topical Sermon* (Louisville: Westminster/John Knox Press, 1992), 63–64.

8   Cf. John 13:1.
9   Committee on Priestly Formation, *Fulfilled in Your Hearing*, 10.
10   Fred B. Craddock, *Preaching* (Nashville: Abington Press, 1985), 172.
11   Acts 2:14–36; 7:1–53.
12   Acts 2:41.
13   Ezekiel 37:1–14.
14   Ezekiel 3:1.
15   Ezekiel 3:3.
16   Ezekiel 3:4.
17   Galatians 4:4.
18   Hilkert, *Naming Grace*, 46–48.
19   Thomas G. Long, *The Witness of Preaching* (Louisville: Westminster John Knox, 1989), 44.
20   Barbara Brown Taylor, *The Preaching Life* (Lanham, MD: Rowman and Littlefield, 1993), 81.

Chapter 7

1   Luke 16:19.
2   John 19:2–5.
3   Matthew 25:34–46.
4   Matthew 5:13–16; 13:33.
5   John Carr, "Preaching and Catholic Social Teaching," ed. Edward Foley, *A Handbook for Catholic Preaching* (Collegeville: Liturgical Press 2015), 275.
6   Carr, "Preaching and Catholic Social Teaching," 276.
7   Mark 1:14–15.
8   Ryan, *Jesus and Salvation*, 138.
9   Gutiérrez, *The God of Life*, 102.
10   Ryan, *Jesus and Salvation*, 138.

11   Department of Justice, Peace & Human Development, *Seven Themes of Catholic Social Teaching*, Publication No. 5–315 (Washington DC: United States Conference of Catholic Bishops, 2005); Carr, "Preaching and Catholic Social Teaching," 277–79.

12   Evangelical Lutheran Church in America, *The Church in Society: A Lutheran Perspective* (Chicago: Evangelical Lutheran Church in America, 1991).

13   Daniel 3:8–25.

14   Mark 2:27; Matthew 4:7.

15   John 17:12.

16   John 18:8–9.

17   John 12:32.

18   Genesis 1:28.

19   Genesis 1:26.

20   Mary Catherine Hilkert, OP, "Preaching from the Book of Nature," *Worship* 76, no. 4 (July 2002): 291.

21   Ryan, *Jesus and Salvation*, 157.

22   Hilkert, "Preaching from the Book of Nature," 292.

23   John 12:32.

24   Romans 8:22.

25   Hilkert, "Preaching from the Book of Nature," 293.

26   Ryan, *Jesus and Salvation*, 159.

27   See Luke 24:4–14; John 20: 17, 20.

28   Colossians 1:15, 18.

29   Ambrose of Milan, *On the Death of His Brother Satyrus*, Book. 1:102, H. DeRomestin, *Saint Ambrose: Select Works and Letters*. A Select Library of Nicene and Post-Nicene Fathers of the Christian Church, Second Series, vol. 10 (Grand Rapids, MI: Wm. B. Eerdmans Publishing Co., 1978), 191.

30   Ambrose of Milan, Epistle 35:13, Mary Melchoir Beyenka, OP, *Saint Ambrose: Letters*. The Fathers of the

Church, vol. 26 (New York: Fathers of the Church, Inc., 1954), 281–82.

31   Carr, "Preaching and Catholic Social Teaching," 283.

32   Philippians 3:20.

33   Micah 6:8; Luke 4:18–19.

34   Revelation 21:12, 25.

35   Isaiah 45:1.

36   Matthew 25:31–46, 28:16–20; Luke 24:45–48; John 20:21–23, 21:15–19.

37   "Ordination," Evangelical Lutheran Church in America, *Evangelical Lutheran Worship: Occasional Services for the Assembly*, 193.

38   Matthew 5:48.

39   Alan Kreider, *The Patient Ferment of the Early Church: The Improbable Rise of Christianity in the Roman Empire* (Ada, MI: Baker Academic, 2016), 74.

40   Mark 1:15.

41   Matthew 13:31–32.

42   Matthew 5:13–16; 13:33.

43   Luke 4:28–33.

44   Matthew 23:37.

45   Carr, "Preaching and Catholic Social Teaching," 277.

46   Matthew 25:35–40.

47   Ezekiel 2:4–5.

48   Matthew 25:40.

49   Luke 16:19–31.

Chapter 8

1   Revelation 3:20.

2   John 20.

3   John 20:18.

4   John 20:26.

5   John 20:30.
6   John 21:1–14.
7   Craig A. Satterlee, *When God Speaks through You: How Faith Convictions Shape Preaching and Mission* (Lanham, MD: Rowman and Littlefield, 2007), 44–45.
8   Psalm 46:4–5.
9   Revelation 21:12, 25.
10 1 Peter 2:5.
11 Psalm 46:1.
12 Luke 14:12–14.
13 "Thanksgiving for Baptism," Evangelical Lutheran Church in America, *Evangelical Lutheran Worship* (Minneapolis: Augsburg Fortress, 2006), 97.
14 "Holy Baptism," *Evangelical Lutheran Worship*, 231.
15 John 1:39.
16 Matthew 15:21–28; Acts 1:8; Colossians 1:24–29.
17 Corinthians 12.
18 Matthew 28:19.
19 Matthew 13:44–46.
20 John 13:35.
21 Matthew 4:23.
22 Matthew 4:17; 10:7–8.
23 Luke 10:3–7.
24 Matthew 18:20.
25 Luke 19:1–10; 7:1–10.
26 Mark 13:2.
27 Allen, *The Homiletic of All Believer*, 55–56.
28 Cf. Ephesians 4:13.
29 Kreider, *The Patient Ferment of the Early Church*, 61.
30 Alan Kreider, *The Change of Conversion and the Origin of Christendom* (Harrisburg: Trinity Press International, 1999), xv.
31 Mark 1:36–39.

Chapter 9

1   "Ordination," Evangelical Lutheran Church in America, *Evangelical Lutheran Worship: Occasional Services for the Assembly*, 192; Matthew 11:28–30.

2   "Ordination," Evangelical Lutheran Church in America

3   Willimon, "The Preacher as an Extension of the Preaching Moment," *Preaching on the Brink*, 170.

4   Matthew 16:24.

5   Acts 9:16.

6   Isaiah 43:1–2.

7   Matthew 11:28.

8   Hans Dieter Betz, "The Logion of the Easy Yoke and of Rest (Matt 11.28-30);" *Journal of Biblical Literature*, vol. 86, no. 1 (Society of Biblical Literature, 1967), 10. My exegetical commentary on Matthew 11: 28–30 is indebted to Raymond A. Pickett, "Re: Exegetical help?" Email sent to Craig A. Satterlee, March 2, 2021; especially Walter F. Taylor, Jr., "Response to Craig Satterlee on Matthew 11:28-30," Email Exegetical Note, March 6, 2021.

9   John 15:4–11.

10   Luke 24:32.

11   Matthew 10:5–15.

12   John 10:10.

13   Genesis 1:27.

14   Romans 6:3–5.

15   Romans 8:38–39.

16   John 2:19, 21.

17   1 Corinthians 6:19.

18   Matthew 27:46.

19   Pickett, "Re: Exegetical help?"

20   John J. Pilch, *The Cultural World of Jesus: Sunday by Sunday, Cycle A* (Collegeville, MN: The Liturgical Press, 1995), 107.

21   Philippians 2:7–8.

22   John 3:30.

23   Matthew 10:39.

24   Matthew 16:21, 24.

25   Matthew 16:23.

26   Matthew 4:1–11.

27   Matthew 4:1–11; Isaiah 53:3–4.

28   Walter J. Burghardt, SJ, *Preaching: The Art and the Craft* (Mahwah, NJ: Paulist Press, 1987), 117.

29   John 15:5.

30   Matthew 10, 23:11; Luke 24:48; John 15:15–16; 1 Corinthians 4:1; 2 Corinthians 5:20.

31   John 13:16; Matthew 10:24–25.

32   Luke 17:10.

33   Matthew 11:29.

34   Ulrich Luz, *Matthew 8–20*; Trans. James E. Crouch; Hermeneia (Minneapolis: Fortress Press, 2001), 156, n. 3.

35   Matthew 11:29, 21:5.

36   Mark Allan Powell, *God with Us: A Pastoral Theology of Matthew's Gospel* (Minneapolis: Fortress Press, 1995), 126, n. 42.

37   Exodus 3; John 21:1–8; Galatians 1:11–24.

38   Jeremiah 20:9.

39   John 21:9–19.

40   Mark 14:32–42.

41   Matthew 17:1, 26:37; Mark 9:2, 14:33.

42   *Constitutions, Bylaws, and Continuing Resolutions of the Evangelical Lutheran Church in America: Constitution for Synods, †S8.12.a.; †S8.12.b., 2021, Evangelical Lutheran Church in America.*

43   Ephesians 4:14.

44   Luke 11:1.

45   Psalm 17:8.

46   John 17:11.

47   Luke 17:5.

48   Ephesians 6:11.

49   Matthew 11:19.

50   John 13:17.

51   Mark 6:34.

52   Taylor, "Response to Craig Satterlee on Matthew 11: 28–30."

53   Taylor, "Response to Craig Satterlee on Matthew 11: 28–30."

54   Matthew 3:16–17.

55   Timothy V. Olson, email sent to Craig Satterlee, March 11, 2021.

56   Timothy V. Olson, email sent to Craig Satterlee, March 11, 2021; Romans 8:31.

57   Matthew 14:23; Luke 9:18.

58   Psalm 46:10.

59   John 11:38–40.

60   John 11:25.

61   John 20:8.

62   Genesis 2:2.

63   Kurt F. Kusserow, "What is the rest that Jesus promises?" Letter to Craig A. Satterlee, March 9, 2021.

64   Matthew 11:28–30.

65   Kusserow, "What is the rest that Jesus promises?"

66   "Ordination," Evangelical Lutheran Church in America, *Evangelical Lutheran Worship: Occasional Services for the Assembly*, 192.

67   Cf. Psalm 27:14.

Bibliography

Abelard, Peter. *Commentary on the Epistle to the Romans.* Translated by Steven R. Cartwright. Washington, DC: The Catholic University of America, 2011.

Allen, O. Wesley, Jr. *The Homiletic of All Believers: A Conversational Approach to Proclamation and Preaching.* Louisville: Westminster John Knox Press, 2005.

Allen, Ronald. *Preaching the Topical Sermon.* Louisville: Westminster John Knox Press, 1992.

Anselm of Canterbury. *Why God Became Man.* Translated by Janet Fairweather. Edited by Brian Davies and G. R. Evans, *Anselm of Canterbury: The Major Works.* New York: Oxford University Press, 2008.

Aquinas, Thomas. *Summa Theologica.* Translated by Fathers of the English Dominican Province, 5 vols. New York: Benziger Brothers, 1947.

Augustine. *The Trinity.* Translated by Edmund Hill, OP, Edited by John E. Rotelle, OSA. Hyde Park, NY: New City Press, 1991.

Betz, Hans Dieter. "The Logion of the Easy Yoke and of Rest (Matt 11:28–30)." *Journal of Biblical Literature* 86, no. 1, Society of Biblical Literature, 1967, 10–24.

Beyenka, Mary Melchoir, OP. *Saint Ambrose: Letters.* The Fathers of the Church, Vol. 26. New York: Fathers of the Church, Inc., 1954.

Bohache, Thomas. *Christology from the Margins*. London: SCM Press, 2008.

Brooks, Adrian J. "Breathing Forth the Word: Yves Congar's Articulation of the Activity of The Holy Spirit in the Life of Christ." *New Blackfriars* 101, no. 1092 (2020): 196–205.

Brown, Raymond E. *The Gospel According to John (xiii–xxi)*. Garden City: Doubleday, 1970.

Burghardt, Walter J., SJ. *Preaching: The Art and the Craft*. Mahwah, NJ: Paulist Press, 1987.

Calvin, John. *Institutes of the Christian Religion* (Final edition, 1559). Translation of 1845 by Henry Beveridge. Grand Rapids, MI: Wm. B. Eerdmans Publishing Co., 1989; reprinted, 1997.

Campbell, Charles L. *The Word before the Powers: An Ethic of Preaching*. Louisville: Westminster: John Knox Press, 2002.

Carr, John. "Preaching and Catholic Social Teaching." In *A Handbook for Catholic Preaching*. Edited by Edward Foley, 275–86. Collegeville, MN: Liturgical Press, 2015.

Chang, Patrick S. *From Sin to Amazing Grace*. New York: Seabury Books, 2012.

Committee on Priestly Formation. *Fulfilled in Your Hearing: The Homily in the Sunday Assembly*. Washington DC: United States Conference of Catholic Bishops, 1982.

Cone, James H. *The Cross and the Lynching Tree*. Maryknoll, NY: Orbis Books, 2013.

Congar, Yves M-J. *Called to Life*. Slough, UK: St. Paul Publications, 1985.

Congar, Yves M-J. *I Believe in the Holy Spirit*. Translated by David Smith. New York: Seabury, 1983.

Congar, Yves M-J., "Pneumatologie dogmatique," In *Initiation à la pratique de la théologie*. Edited by Bernard Lauret and Francois Refoulé, Paris: Cerf, 1982.

Congar, Yves M-J. *Spirit of God: Short Writings on the Holy Spirit*. Edited by Mark E. Ginter, Susan Mader Brown, and Joseph G. Mueller. Washington DC: Catholic University of America Press, 2018.

Congar, Yves M-J. *The Word and the Spirit*. Translated by David Smith. London: Geoffrey Chapman, 1984.

Copeland, M. Shawn. "Marking the Body of Jesus, the Body of Christ." In *The Strength of Her Witness: Jesus Christ in the Global Voices of Women*. Edited by Elizabeth A. Johnson, 270–83. Maryknoll, NY: Orbis Books, 2016.

Copeland, M. Shawn. "The Cross of Christ and Discipleship." In *Thinking of Christ: Proclamation, Explanation, Meaning*. Edited by Tatha Wiley, 177–92. Maryknoll, NY: Orbis Books, 2003.

Copeland, M. Shawn. "'Wading though Many Sorrows': Toward a Theology of Suffering in Womanist Perspective." In *A Troubling in My Soul: Womanist Perspectives on Evil and Suffering*. The Bishop Henry Mcneal Turner Studies in North American Black Religion, Vol. 8. Edited by Emilie Maureen Townes, 109–29. Maryknoll, NY: Orbis Books, 1993.

Craddock, Fred B. *Preaching*. Nashville: Abington Press, 1985.

Crawford, Elaine. "Womanist Christology: Where have we come from and where are we going." *Review and Expository* 95:3 (1998): 367–82.

Daniélou, Jean. *The Bible and the Liturgy*. Notre Dame, IN: University of Notre Dame Press, 1956.

Department of Justice, Peace & Human Development. *Seven Themes of Catholic Social Teaching*. Publication No. 5-315. Washington DC: United States Conference of Catholic Bishops, 2005.

DeRomestin, H. *Saint Ambrose: Select Works and Letters*. A Select Library of Nicene and Post-Nicene Fathers of the Christian

Church, Second Series, Vol. 10. Grand Rapids, MI: Wm. B. Eerdmans Publishing Co., 1978.

Eiesland, Nancy L. *The Disabled God: Toward a Liberatory Theology of Disability*. Nashville: Abington Press, 1994.

Eiesland, Nancy L. "Encountering the Disabled God." *The Other Side* (September/October 2002): 10–15.

Evangelical Lutheran Church in America. *The Church in Society: A Lutheran Perspective*. Chicago: Evangelical Lutheran Church in America, 1991.

Evangelical Lutheran Church in America. "A Declaration of Inter-Religious Commitment: A Policy Statement of the Evangelical Lutheran Church in America." Chicago: Evangelical Lutheran Church in America, 2019.

Evangelical Lutheran Church in America. *Constitution for Synods*, †S8.12.a., b.

Evangelical Lutheran Church in America. *Evangelical Lutheran Worship*. Minneapolis: Augsburg Fortress, 2006.

Evangelical Lutheran Church in America. *Evangelical Lutheran Worship: Leaders Desk Edition*. Minneapolis: Augsburg Fortress, 2006.

Evangelical Lutheran Church in America. *Evangelical Lutheran Worship: Occasional Services for the Assembly*. Minneapolis: Augsburg Fortress, 2009.

Evangelical Lutheran Church in America. *Principles for Worship*. Renewing Worship, Vol. 2. Minneapolis: Augsburg Fortress, 2002.

Evangelical Lutheran Church in America. *The Use of the Means of Grace: A Statement on the Practice of Word and Sacrament*. Minneapolis: Augsburg Fortress, 1997.

Groppe, Elizabeth Theresa. "The Contribution of Yves Congar's Theology of the Holy Spirit." *Theological Studies* 62 (2001): 457–78.

Gutiérrez, Gustavo. *The God of Life*. Translated by Matthew J. O'Connell. Maryknoll, NY: Orbis Books, 1991.

Gutiérrez, Gustavo. *The Power of the Poor in History: Selected Writings*. Translated by Robert R. Barr. Maryknoll, NY: Orbis Books, 1983.

Gutiérrez, Gustavo. *A Theology of Liberation: History, Politics, and Salvation*. Maryknoll, NY: Orbis Books, 1988.

Heifetz, Richard A., and Marty Linsky. *Leadership on the Line: Staying Alive through the Dangers of Leading*. Boston: Harvard School of Business Press, 2002.

Hilkert, Mary Catherine, OP. "Introduction, Words of Spirit and Life: Preaching, Theology, Spirituality." Unpublished Manuscript. February 22, 2019. Cited with permission.

Hilkert, Mary Catherine, OP. *Naming Grace: Preaching and the Sacramental Imagination*. New York: Continuum, 1997.

Hilkert, Mary Catherine, OP. "Naming Grace: A Theology of Proclamation." *Worship* 60 (1986): 434–48.

Hilkert, Mary Catherine, OP. "Preaching from the Book of Nature." *Worship* 76, no. 4 (July 2002): 290–313.

Hopkins, Dwight N., and Edward P. Antonio. *The Cambridge Companion to Black Theology*. Cambridge: Cambridge University Press, 2012.

Irenaeus of Lyons. *Against Heresies. The Ante-Nicene Fathers*. Vol. 1, *The Apostolic Fathers with Justin Martyr and Irenaeus*. Edited by Alexander Roberts and James Donaldson, 315–567. Buffalo, NY: Christian Literature Publishing, 1885.

Johnson, Elizabeth A. "Jesus and Salvation," *Proceedings of the Catholic Theological Society of America* 49 (1994): 1–18.

Johnson, Elizabeth A. *She Who Is: The Mystery of God in Feminist Theological Discourse*. New York: Crossroads, 1992.

Justin Martyr. *First Apology. The Ante-Nicene Fathers.* Vol. 1, *The Apostolic Fathers with Justin Martyr and Irenaeus.* Edited by Alexander Roberts and James Donaldson, 159–87. Buffalo, NY: Christian Literature Publishing, 1885.

Kolb, Robert, and Timothy J. Wengert, eds. *The Book of Concord.* Minneapolis: Fortress Press, 2000.

Kreider, Alan. *The Change of Conversion and the Origin of Christendom.* Harrisburg: Trinity Press International, 1999.

Kreider, Alan. *The Patient Ferment of the Early Church: The Improbable Rise of Christianity in the Roman Empire.* Ada, MI: Baker Academic, 2016.

Krieg, Robert A., and Brandon R. Peterson. "Models of the Savior: Toward Ecumenical Mosaics," Unpublished Manuscript. August 2022.

Kusserow, Kurt F. "What is the rest that Jesus promises?" Letter to Craig A. Satterlee. March 9, 2021.

Long, Thomas G. *The Witness of Preaching.* Louisville: Westminster John Knox Press, 1989.

Luther, Martin. "A Brief Introduction to What to Look for and Expect in the Gospels (1521)," *Luther's Works, American Edition,* Vol. 35. Translated by E. Theodore Bachmann. Edited by E. Theodore Bachmann and Helmut Lehmann, 117–23. Minneapolis: Fortress Press, 1960.

Luther, Martin, "Concerning the Ministry (1523)." In *Luther's Works, American Edition,* Vol. 40. Translated by Conrad Bergendoff, 3–44. Minneapolis: Fortress Press, 1958.

Luther, Martin, "Preface to the Old Testament (1545)," In *Luther's Works, American Edition,* Vol. 35. Translated by Charles M. Jacob, revised by E. Theodore Bachmann, 235–51. Minneapolis: Fortress Press, 1960.

Luther, Martin, "The Small Catechism (1529)," In *Book of Concord.* Edited by Robert Kolb and Timothy J. Wengert. Minneapolis: Fortress Press, 2000.

Luz, Ulrich. *Matthew 8–20*. Translated by James E. Crouch, Hermeneia. Minneapolis: Fortress Press, 2001.

McDonnell, Killian, OSB. "A Trinitarian Theology of the Holy Spirit?" *Theological Studies* 46, no. 2 (May 1985): 191–227.

Melloh, John Allyn, SM. "Homily Preparation: A Structural Approach." *Liturgical Ministry* 1 (Winter 1992): 21–26.

Monson, Glenn L. *Afflicting the Comfortable, Comforting the Afflicted: A Guide to Law and Gospel Preaching*. Eugene, OR: Wipf & Stock, 2015.

Mulligan, Mary Alice, and Ronald J. Allen. *Make the Word Come Alive: Lessons from Laity*. St. Louis: Chalice Press, 2005.

Nissiotis, Nikos A. "Pneumatological Christology as a Presupposition of Ecclesiology." In *Oecumenica: An Annual Symposium of Ecumenical Research*, 235–52. Minneapolis: Augsburg Fortress, 1967.

Olson, Timothy V. "What is the rest that Jesus promises?" Email sent to Craig A. Satterlee. March 11, 2021.

Pickett, Raymond A. "Re: Exegetical help?" Email sent to Craig A. Satterlee. March 2, 2021.

Pilch, John J. *The Cultural World of Jesus: Sunday by Sunday, Cycle A*. Collegeville, MN: The Liturgical Press, 1995.

Pope Francis. *Evangelii Gaudium: The Joy of the Gospel*. Washington, DC: United States Conference of Catholic Bishops, 2013.

Powell, Mark Allan. *God with Us: A Pastoral Theology of Matthew's Gospel*. Minneapolis: Fortress Press, 1995.

Ryan, Robin. *Jesus and Salvation: Soundings in the Christian Tradition and Contemporary Theology*. Concord, MA: Michael Glazier, 2015.

Satterlee, Craig Alan. *Ambrose of Milan's Method of Mystagogical Preaching*. Collegeville, MN: Liturgical Press, 2002.

Satterlee, Craig A., and Ruth, Lester *Creative Preaching on the Sacraments*. Nashville: Discipleship Resources, 2001.

Satterlee, Craig Alan. "That Intimate Link–Ecumenical Contribution of *Fulfilled in Your Hearing.*" In *We Preach Christ Crucified*, edited by Michael E. Connors, 124–38. Collegeville, MN: Liturgical Press, 2013.

Satterlee, Craig A. *When God Speaks through Change: Preaching in Times of Congregational Transition.* Lanham, MD: Rowman and Littlefield, 2005.

Satterlee, Craig A. *When God Speaks through Worship: Stories Congregations Live By.* Lanham, MD: Rowman and Littlefield, 2009.

Satterlee, Craig A. *When God Speaks through You: How Faith Convictions Shape Preaching and Mission.* Lanham, MD: Rowman and Littlefield, 2007.

Stuempfle, Hermon G. Jr. *Preaching Law and Gospel.* Minneapolis: Fortress Press, 1978.

Taylor, Barbara Brown. *The Preaching Life.* Lanham, MD: Rowman and Littlefield, 1993.

Taylor, Walter F. Jr. "Response to Craig Satterlee on Matthew 11:28–30." Email Exegetical Note. March 6, 2021.

Terrell, Joanne Marie. *Power in the Blood?: The Cross in the African American Experience.* The Bishop Henry McNeal Turner/Sojourner Truth Series in Black Religion, Vol. 15. Maryknoll, NY: Orbis Books, 1998.

TeSelle, Eugene. *Augustine the Theologian.* New York: Herder and Herder, 1970.

Waters, Kelsei. "Solidarity and Suffering: Liberation Christology from Black and Womanist Perspectives." *Obscula* 12 1 (2019): 78–107.

West, Fritz. *Scripture and Memory: The Ecumenical Hermeneutic of the Three-Year Lectionary.* Collegeville, MN: Liturgical Press, 1997.

Williams, Delores S. *Sisters in the Wilderness; The Challenge of Womanist God-Talk.* Maryknoll, NY: Orbis Books, 2013.

Willimon, William H. "The Preacher as an Extension of the Preaching Moment." In *Preaching on the Brink: The Future of Homiletics*, edited by Martha J. Simmons, 164–72. Nashville: Abingdon Press, 1997.

Wilson, Paul Scott. *The Four Pages of the Sermon: A Guide to Biblical Preaching*. Nashville: Abingdon Press, 1999.